Cambridge English
Advanced

Practice
Tests

Plus 2 with Key

Nick Kenny

Jacky Newbrook

TEACHING NOT JUST TESTING

Pearson Education Limited
Edinburgh Gate
Harlow
Essex CM20 2JE
England
and Associated Companies throughout the world.

www.pearsonelt.com

© Pearson Education Limited 2011

The right of Nick Kenny and Jacky Newbrook to be identified as authors of this Work has been asserted by them in accordance with the Copyright, Designs and Patents Act 1988.

All rights reserved; no part of this publication may be reproduced, stored in a retrieval system, or transmitted in any form, or by any means, electronic, mechanical, photocopying, recording, or otherwise without the prior written permission of the Publishers.

First published 2011
Third impression 2013

ISBN: 978-1-4082-6787-5
Students' book with key and Multi-ROM and Audio CD pack

Set in 10.5pt Arial Regular
Printed in China
SWTC/03

Photocopying: The Publisher grants permission for the photocopying of those pages marked 'photocopiable' according to the following conditions. Individual purchasers may make copies for use by their staff and students, but this permission does not extend to additional institutions or branches. Under no circumstances may any part of this book be photocopied for resale.

Acknowledgements

The authors would like to thank the Picture Researcher Alison Prior.

We are grateful to the following for permission to reproduce copyright material:

Extract on page 6 adapted from Home free: a clan, a van and no plan, *Daily Telegraph (Weekend)*, 02/01/2010, W12 (Thompson, S.), copyright © Telegraph Media Group Limited 2010; Extract on page 7 from *Hard Time*, Penguin (Paretsky, S. 2000) p. 78, with permission from David Grossman Literary Agency Ltd; Extract on page 8 adapted from Watch out Daniel Craig, *Sunday Telegraph (Life)*, 19/10/2008, L21 (Benady, A.), copyright © Telegraph Media Group Limited 2008; Extract on page 10 adapted from How the internet is making us stupid, *Daily Telegraph*, 28/08/2010, p. 27 (Carr, N.), copyright © Telegraph Media Group Limited 2010; Extract on page 13 adapted from The way we worked, *Sunday Telegraph (Seven)*, 22/08/2010, pp. 12-14 (Lyle, P.), copyright © Telegraph Media Group Limited 2010; Extract on page 19 adapted from Fragile l'île mystérieuse risks being trampled away, *The Guardian*, 12/08/2010, p. 14 (Tearse, G.), Copyright Guardian News & Media Ltd. 2010; Interview on page 30 adapted from Digging for the Truth: Driven by Archaeology Mystery, An Interview with Josh Bernstein by K. Kris Hirst, About.com Guide, © Copyright 2010. All rights reserved by New York Times Syndication Sales Corp. This material may not be copied, published, broadcast or redistributed in any manner; Extract on page 35 adapted from Can't help singing in an American accent? It's only natural, *Daily Telegraph*, 03/08/2010, p. 12 (Alleyne, R.), copyright © Telegraph Media Group Limited 2010; Extract on page 36 adapted from Setting free the musical youth of Africa, *Sunday Telegraph*, 20/12/2009, p. 36 (Jardine, C.), copyright © Telegraph Media Group Limited 2009; Extract on page 37 from Fluttering down to Mexico, *Sunday Telegraph (Travel)*, 15/08/2010, T9 (Evans, S.), copyright © Telegraph Media Group Limited 2010; Extract on page 39 adapted from How a non-policy on holidays can be the break you need, *Sunday Telegraph (Business)*, 15/08/2010, B9 (Pink, D. H.), copyright © Telegraph Media Group Limited 2010; Extract on page 42 adapted from Seeing through the fakes, *Daily Telegraph*, 29/06/2010, p. 25 (Dorment, R.), copyright © Telegraph Media Group Limited 2010; Extract on page 48 adapted from Net Assets, *Eastern Daily Press Norfolk Magazine*, pp. 150-51 (Wedge, N.), August 2010, with permission from EDP Norfolk Magazine; Extract on page 49 adapted from Meat on the menu: bones with cut marks show stone tools in use 3.4m years ago, *The Guardian*, 12/08/2010, p. 6 (Sample, I.), Copyright Guardian News & Media Ltd. 2010; Extract on page 50 adapted from On the right track, *Eastern Daily Press Norfolk Magazine*, pp. 21-23 (Cassells, S.), March 2010, with permission from EDP Norfolk Magazine; Interview on page 56 adapted from What do you mean, you don't buy clothes?, *The Times*, 21/10/2003, p. 11 (Davies, E.), http://women.timesonline.co.uk/tol/life_and_style/women/fashion/article862454.ece, © Emily Davies, NI Syndication Limited, 21 October 2003; Interview on page 58 adapted from Slave labour gave us our big break *Evening Standard*, 20/06/2005, p. 5 (Williams, A.), esjobs, with permission from Solo Syndication; Interview on page 59 adapted from A CurtainUp Interview, Set Designer Derek McLane by Elyse Sommer, *CurtainUp.com* © Copyright Elyse Sommer, Curtainup.com, online since 1997 with theater features, news and reviews; Extract on page 63 adapted from If you go down to the woods, *Sunday Telegraph (Life)*, 12/10/2008, L21 (Beardsall, J.), copyright © Telegraph Media Group Limited 2008; Extract on page 64 adapted from Should you butter your frog, *Sunday Telegraph (Life)*, 12/07/2009, L18-19 (Gurdon, M.), copyright © Telegraph Media Group Limited 2009; Extract on page 65 adapted from Are we all born to boogie?, *Daily Telegraph*, 16/08/2010, p. 20 (Cumming, E.), copyright © Telegraph Media Group Limited 2010; Extract on page 66 adapted from Across Britain it's secateurs at dawn, *Sunday Telegraph*, 15/08/2010, p. 16 (Langley, W.), copyright © Telegraph Media Group Limited 2010; Extract on page 68 from *The Glass Room*, Penguin Ireland 2006 (Holmquist, K. 2006) pp. 14-16, Copyright © Kathryn Holmquist, 2006, reproduced by permission of Penguin Books Ltd; Extract on page 71 adapted from On the trail of Kit Man, *Sunday Telegraph*, 14/02/2010, p. 20 (Langley, W.), copyright © Telegraph Media Group Limited 2010; Extract on page 74 adapted from Caving, *The Guardian Guide to Adventure*, 01/09/2007, p. 34, Copyright Guardian News & Media Ltd. 2007; Extract on page 75 adapted from Why are sunglasses cool?, *Intelligent Life Magazine*, Vol. 3, Issue 4, Summer 2010, p. 66, © The Economist Newspaper Limited, London (1.7.10); Interview on page 81 adapted from Cambridge People: Interview with Adam Bridgland, *Explorer Magazine*, p. 77 (2009), Archant Herts and Cambs; Interview on page 84 adapted from Kathy Ireland: Fashion Model to Inspirational Role Model by Randy Duermyer, *About.com Guide*, © Copyright 2010. All rights reserved by New York Times Syndication Sales Corp. This material may not be copied, published, broadcast or redistributed in any manner; Extract on page 87 adapted from Vacuum cleaners - they just sweep me off my feet, *Sunday Telegraph*, 21/02/2010, p. 17 (Langley, W.), copyright © Telegraph Media Group Limited 2010; Extract on page 88 adapted from Stairway to heaven - or hell, *Daily Telegraph (Weekend)*, 13/02/2010, W5 (Roe, N.), copyright © Telegraph Media Group Limited 2010; Extract on page 89 adapted from Pet Croc swaps swamp for a cosy bungalow in the wilds of Kent, *Sunday Telegraph*, 17/01/2010, p. 9 (Copping, J.), copyright © Telegraph Media Group Limited 2010; Extract on page 90 adapted from Rise of publishing's natural phenomenon, *Daily Telegraph (Weekend)*, 17/10/2009, W17 (Marren, P.), copyright © Telegraph Media Group Limited 2009; Extract on page 92 adapted from The impossible moment of delight, *Daily Telegraph*, 06/08/2010, p. 25 (Hensher, P.), copyright © Telegraph Media Group Limited 2010; Extract on page 95 adapted from The intern's tale, *Sunday Telegraph Stella magazine*, 19/08/2010, pp. 30-35 (Barnes, S.), copyright © Telegraph Media Group Limited 2010; Extract on page 99 adapted from Cheating? Fine by me, *Intelligent Life Magazine*, Vol. 3, Issue 4, Summer, p. 47 (Standage, T. 2010), © The Economist Newspaper Limited, London (1.7.10); Interview on page 108 adapted from interview with Carlos Avila conducted for *In Motion Magazine* by Fred Salas in Los Angeles, December 23, 1999, http://www.inmotionmagazine.com/cavila.html, reprinted with permission from Fred Salas; Extract on page 111 from English language's lost and found, *Daily Telegraph*, 17/08/2010, p. 21 (Davidson, M.), copyright © Telegraph Media Group Limited 2010; Extract on page 112 adapted from Stone Age Lucy changes history, *Daily Telegraph*, 12/08/2010, p. 7 (Alleyne, R.), copyright © Telegraph Media Group Limited 2010; Extract on page 113 from *Black Wind* by Clive Cussler and Dirk Cussler, copyright © 2004 by Sandecker, RLLLP. Used by permission of G. P. Putnam's Sons, a division of Penguin Group (USA) Inc., Black Wind (Michael Joseph 2004, Penguin Books 2005). Copyright © Sandecker RLLLP, 2004, reproduced by permission of Penguin Books Ltd., extract taken from *Reader's Digest Select Editions* condensed version reproduced with permission from The Reader's Digest Association, Inc; Extract on page 114 adapted from Is Kieron Britain's most exciting painter?, *Daily Telegraph*, 04/08/2010, p. 21 (Stanford, P.), copyright © Telegraph Media Group Limited 2010; Extract on page 116 adapted from Say hello to your new management guru, *Sunday Telegraph (Business)*, 01/08/2010, B8 (Peacock, L.), copyright © Telegraph Media Group Limited 2010; Extract on page 119 adapted from The unstoppable spirit of inquiry, *Daily Telegraph*, 09/02/2010, p. 27 (Rees, M.), copyright © Telegraph Media Group Limited 2010; Interview on page 129 adapted from 60 second interview: Joanne Harris, *Metro*, p. 10 (Williams, A.), 8/4/2010, with permission from Solo Syndication; Interview on page 129 adapted from Hanging a work of art, *Metro*, p. 10 (Walsh, A.), 8/4/2010, with permission from Solo Syndication; Interview on page 132 adapted from *Daily News:* August 13/09 10:23 am - Interview: Daniel Martin - From Rower to Cyclist, *Canadian Cyclist*, http://www.canadiancyclist.com/dailynews.php?id=17281, with permission from Amy Smolens; Extract on page 135 adapted from Flying cups and saucers, *Daily Telegraph*, 05/08/2010, p. 17 (Thompson, D.), copyright © Telegraph Media Group Limited 2010; Extract on page 136 adapted from A people carrier with class, *Daily Telegraph (Travel)*, 10/05/2010, T15 (Ferguson, A.), copyright © Telegraph Media Group Limited 2010; Extract on page 137 adapted from The 36,000-mile helicopter flight, *Daily Telegraph (Weekend)*, 04/11/2006, W5 (Roe, N.), copyright © Telegraph Media Group Limited 2006; Extract on page 138 adapted from The birth of Coronation Street, *Daily Telegraph (Review)*, 11/09/2010, R29 (Little, D.), copyright © Telegraph Media Group Limited 2010; Extract on page 140 adapted from Cooking shouldn't be child's play, *Daily Telegraph*, 22/09/2010, p. 27 (Prince, R.), copyright © Telegraph Media Group Limited 2010; Extract on page 143 adapted from Top 15 Activities, *Daily Telegraph* supplement - Norway's Northern Lights, 18/09/2010, pp. 8-10 (Derrick, S.), with permission from Visit Norway, www.visitnorway.co.uk; Extract on page 146 adapted from Mr Expresso taught the world how to drink coffee, *Financial Times Weekend*, 20/03/2010, p. 11 (Boland, V.), © The Financial Times Ltd; Extract on page 147 adapted from Drift diving, *The Guardian Guide to Adventure*, 01/09/2007, p. 28, Copyright Guardian News & Media Ltd. 2007; Interview on page 156 adapted from Dead Interesting, *Latest Homes Sussex*, December, pp. 12-14 (Kay, A. 2007), Latest Homes Ltd; Extract on page 159 adapted from Clever and ugly: all life is found here, *Daily Telegraph*, 03/08/2010, p. 25 (Kean, S.), copyright © Telegraph Media Group Limited 2010; Extract on page 160 adapted from Age of discovery in science 'is over', *Daily Telegraph*, 24/09/2010, p. 14 (Blake, H.), copyright © Telegraph Media Group Limited 2010; Extract on page 161 adapted from Bears, banks and cavorting fruit bats win prizes, *Daily Telegraph*, 01/10/2010, p. 4 (Allyene, R.), copyright © Telegraph Media Group Limited 2010; Extract on page 162 adapted from Sky's the limit for a new high society, *Daily Telegraph (Weekend)*, 11/09/2010, W14 (Middleton, C.), copyright © Telegraph Media Group Limited 2010; Extract on page 164 from *Waiting for an Angel*, Hamish Hamilton 2002, 2003 (Habila, H. 2002) pp. 61-64, Copyright © Helon Habila, 2002, reproduced by permission of Penguin Books Ltd; Extract on page 167 adapted from What lies beneath, *Daily Telegraph*, 04/08/2010, p. 17 (Ecott, T.), copyright © Telegraph Media Group Limited 2010; Extract on page 170 adapted from Wind, Wave and Tidal Energy, *Independent, Supplement*, 20/10/2009, p. 1 (McCaffery, M.), Copyright The Independent 20 October 2009; Extract on page 171 adapted from You Take the Hire Road, *Financial Times Magazine*, 13/14 October, p. 16 (Tomkins, R. 2007), © The Financial Times Ltd; Extract on page 172 adapted from Towards a theory of finite niceness, *Financial Times Weekend*, 20/03/2010, p. 13 (Engel, M.), © The Financial Times Ltd; Interview on page 180 adapted from Interview with Lauren Burress, Amazing Young Kayaker by Brittany, Student Editor-in-Chief, http://www.amazing-kids.org/c9, with permission from *Amazing Kids!*, and adapted from Ben Oakley - Interview - UK National Team - Kayaking, http://www.exelement.co.uk/blog/2010/03/ben-oakley-interview-uk-national-team-ka, with kind permission from Extreme Element - Experience Day Gift Vouchers & Bookings.

In some instances we have been unable to trace the owners of copyright material, and we would appreciate any information that would enable us to do so.

The publisher would like to thank the following for their kind permission to reproduce their photographs:

(Key: b-bottom; c-centre; l-left; r-right; t-top)

Alamy Images: AKP Photos 220bc, Ashley Cooper 219r, Bill Bachmann 214tr, Claudia Veja 220br, David J Green 215tl, David Lyons 216b, David Pearson 205c, David R Frazier Photo Library Inc 211tl, 220bl, David R Frazier Photo Library Inc 211tl, 220bl, Dinodia Photos 205cr, Fashionshows 220cl, Graficart.net 216tr, I Love Images 220cr, Iain Masterton 213r, Image Source 204c, 208cr, 209l, 217cl, 220r, Image Source 204c, 208cr, 209l, 217cl, 220r, Image Source 204c, 208cr, 209l, 217cl, 220r, Image Source 204c, 208cr, 209l, 217cl, 220r, James Nesterwitz 206, Janine Wiedel 201br, Jeff Morgan 214bl, Jeremy Sutton-Hibbert 203tl, John Keates 217tr, Jon Arnold Images Ltd 214tc, Larry Malvin 205cl, MBI 212bl, 214br, 218tl, MBI 212bl, 214br, 218tl, MBI 212bl, 214br, 218tl, Mike Booth 200b, Milla Kontkanen 217br, Peter Horee 202cr, Peter Titmuss 202r, Photo Alto 210tr, Pierre Arsenault 208cl, Radius Images 206r, Redsnapper 200tl, Scott Hartop 201tr, 202tc, Scott Hartop 201tr, 202tc, Stuart Forster 215r, Tetra Images 219c, Thomas Imo 210tl, Transportimage Picture Library 207l, Travelib Sulawesi 214r; Corbis: Kelly-Mooney Photography 201l, Simon Plant 217c; Getty Images: 202bc, 209tr, 202bc, 209tr, AFP 208tl, Andrew Hetherington 213c, Bounce 208br, DAJ 212tl, Don Farrell 209br, Emanuele Biggi 211bc, Grant Faint 214bc, Image Bank 207tr, 217tl, 218tr, Image Bank 207tr, 217tl, 218tr, Image Bank 207tr, 217tl, 218tr, Jamie Grill 204r, Larry Melvin 205l, Lee Strickland 218, Marc Debnam 204l, Mark A Leman 217bl, Nick Clements 200bl, Pixland 211tr, Tom Grill 212r, Tyler Edwards 206tl; Kobal Collection Ltd: Lucas Film Ltd / Paramount 211cl; Photostage Ltd: Donald Cooper 220; Rex Features: 213l, Alex Segre 207br, George Sweeney 210b, Image Source 219l, Richard Jones 205r; Shutterstock.com: 217cr; Thinkstock: 208bl, Bananastock 202l, 215bl, Bananastock 202l, 215bl, Christopher Robbins 211tc, Comstock 202cl, 203tr, 203b, 216tl, Comstock 202cl, 203tr, 203b, 216tl, Comstock 202cl, 203tr, 203b, 216tl, Comstock 202cl, 203tr, 203b, 216tl, Creatas 202c, Digital Vision 208bc, 211br, Digital Vision 208bc, 211br, Jack Hollingsworth 211bl, Jupiter Images 205bl, 208r, Photodisc 214tl.

All other images © Pearson Education

Every effort has been made to trace the copyright holders and we apologise in advance for any unintentional omissions. We would be pleased to insert the appropriate acknowledgement in any subsequent edition of this publication.

Contents

Exam Overview

The **Certificate in Advanced English** (CAE) is an examination at Cambridge/ALTE level 4, set at C1 level on the Common European Framework of Reference scale. CAE offers a high-level qualification to people wanting to use their English for professional or study purposes. There are five papers, each representing 20 percent of the total marks.

Paper 1 Reading   1 hour 15 minutes
Paper 2 Writing   1 hour 30 minutes
Paper 3 Use of English   1 hour
Paper 4 Listening   40 minutes
Paper 5 Speaking   15 minutes

The examination questions are task-based and simulate real-life tasks. Rubrics (instructions) are important and should be read carefully. They set the context and give important information about the tasks. For Papers 1, 3 and 4 there is a separate answer sheet for recording answers.

Paper	Formats	Task focus
Reading four parts 34 questions	**Part 1:** three themed tests with multiple-choice questions **Part 2:** one long text with a gapped paragraphs task (choosing which paragraphs fit into gaps in a base text) **Part 3:** one long text with multiple-choice questions **Part 4:** one long text divided into sections, or a series of short texts, with a multiple-matching task	**Part 1:** reading different types of text for different purposes **Part 2:** reading to understand text structure **Part 3:** reading for detailed understanding of a text **Part 4:** reading to locate relevant ideas and information in a text or texts
Writing **Part 1:** one compulsory task **Part 2:** one task from a choice of five (question 5 refers to a set text and has a choice of two tasks)	**Part 1:** input texts provide the context and content for a text of a given type of 180–220 words **Part 2:** instructions provide information about text type, target reader and purpose of a text of 220–260 words	**Part 1:** producing a piece of effective writing in context by evaluating, expressing opinions, hypothesising, persuading, etc. **Part 2:** writing for a specific reader using appropriate layout and register
Use of English five parts 50 questions	**Part 1:** short text with a multiple-choice cloze **Part 2:** short text with an open cloze task **Part 3:** short text with a word formation cloze task **Part 4:** gapped sentences **Part 5:** keyword transformations	**Part 1:** use of vocabulary and relationships between words **Part 2:** sentence structure and accurate use of grammar **Part 3:** use of the correct form of a given word in context **Part 4:** use of appropriate vocabulary **Part 5:** use of grammatical and lexical structures
Listening four parts 30 questions	**Part 1:** three short unrelated extracts with two multiple-choice questions on each **Part 2:** long text with a sentence-completion task **Part 3:** long text with multiple-choice questions **Part 4:** series of five monologues on a theme with a multiple-matching task	**Part 1:** understanding gist, feeling, attitude, opinion, speaker purpose, etc. **Part 2:** locating and recording specific information **Part 3:** understanding attitude and opinion **Part 4:** understanding gist, attitude, main points, etc.
Speaking four parts	**Part 1:** general conversation **Part 2:** individual long turn based on visual prompts **Part 3:** two-way conversation between candidates based on visual and written stimuli **Part 4:** discussion on topics related to Part 3	**Part 1:** general interactional and social language **Part 2:** comparing and speculating **Part 3:** giving and eliciting opinions, negotiating, turn-taking, etc. **Part 4:** expressing and justifying opinions and ideas

Guidance

About the paper

The Reading paper lasts for one hour and fifteen minutes. It contains four parts, and has a total of thirty-four questions.

The texts are of varying lengths, with a range of text type and style of writing, for example extracts from newspapers, magazines, websites and novels, as well as other short texts.

Part 1

In Part 1, you have to read three texts on a theme. The texts are taken from different sources so there is a range of style and genre. You have to answer two four-option, multiple-choice questions on each text.

Part 2

In Part 2, there is one long text from which six paragraphs have been removed. These are placed in jumbled order after the text along with an extra paragraph that does not fit into any of the gaps. You have to use your knowledge of grammar, vocabulary, referencing and text structure in order to reconstruct the text.

Part 3

In Part 3, there is one long text to read. You have to answer seven four-option, multiple-choice questions, which follow the order of the text.

Part 4

In Part 4, there is either one long text that has been divided into sections, or a series of short texts on the same topic. There are also fifteen prompts which report information and ideas from the text(s). You have to match each prompt to the correct text or section of text.

How to do the paper

Part 1

- The three extracts in Part 1 are on the same theme, but each extract is separate and has its own questions. Work on each text and its questions separately.
- For each question, read through the text carefully. Don't worry if you don't understand every word.
- Look at each question or question stem and find the piece of text that it relates to. Underline any keywords and ideas in the text. Try to find the answer without looking at the options.
- Now look at the options (A–D) and choose the one which best matches your answer.
- Check that the other options are clearly wrong. If you're still unsure, see which of the options can be ruled out, and why.

Part 2

- Read the base text first, ignoring the gaps, to get a general understanding of what it's about and how it's organised.
- Next, carefully read the text around each gap and think about what type of information might be missing.
- Read paragraphs A–G. Check for topic and language links with the base text. Highlight words that relate to people, places, events and any time references. This will help you follow the development of the argument or narrative.
- Choose the best option to fit each gap. Make sure that all the pronouns and vocabulary references are clear.
- Once you've finished, re-read the completed text to be sure that it makes sense with the answers in the gaps.

Part 3

- Read the text quickly to get a general understanding of what it's about and how it's organised.
- Read through the questions or question stems without looking at the options (A–D), and underline keywords in the question stem.
- The questions follow the order of the text. Find the piece of text where a question is answered and read it carefully, underlining keywords and phrases.
- Try to answer the question. Then read the three options (A–D) and choose the one that is closest to your own answer. Look for the same meaning expressed in different ways.
- Check that the other options are all clearly wrong. If you're still unsure, see which of the options can be ruled out, and why.

Part 4

- In Part 4, you don't need to read the whole text or texts first. The text is long and contains information that you don't need to answer the questions.
- Read the prompts (20–34) first, underlining keywords and ideas.
- Read through the text(s) quickly and find information or ideas that are relevant to each question.
- For each question, when you find the relevant piece of text, read it very carefully to make sure it completely matches the meaning of the prompt.
- The ideas in each prompt are likely to occur in more than one section of the text, but only one text exactly matches the idea. You need to read all these sections carefully.

You are going to read three extracts which are all concerned in some way with families. For questions **1–6**, choose the answer (**A**, **B**, **C** or **D**) which you think fits best according to the text.

In the exam, mark your answers **on the separate answer sheet**.

The family with a van and no plan

For those of us who share a deep bond with our sofas, dishwashers and other home comforts, giving them all up for a life on the road in an old van might seem unimaginable. But for the Thibaulte family from north Devon, saying goodbye to their home was the drastic measure they needed. Running a busy seaside café and coping with the demands of their two small children, Ffynne and Orin, had left parents Janine and Yann exhausted. Their dream of family life had turned into a nightmare. Buckling under the pressure of it all, they knew something had to change.

Then they found a converted van for sale online. They'd seen it before, but hadn't been brave enough to bid for it. Now here it was again – fate was talking to them and this time they were listening. 'It was then we realised there was no turning back. We'd always travelled before we had children, so we bought the van and decided to head for France, where Yann is from, and explore.' They began to dismantle the trappings of their life – letting their house and giving up the café.

The family eats, sleeps and travels together in the van. There is no agenda or planned route. They started off in Brittany because of Yann's family connection, but have otherwise been led by their noses, usually letting the children choose where they would like to go and what they would like to do. 'We literally look at the map and someone will say "let's go there" and so we go,' says Janine.

1   What does the writer say about the family's decision to go travelling?

   A   It was made after a great deal of careful planning.
   B   It was a reaction to a feeling of great disappointment.
   C   It was something the parents felt they might regret.
   D   It was harder to make than they had expected.

2   Which of the following points does the writer make in the text?

   A   Many people would like to do what the Thibaultes are doing.
   B   What the family is doing might attract criticism from some people.
   C   The reader might not wish to do what the Thibaultes are doing.
   D   It is always exciting to travel without a planned route.

Tip Strip

Question 1: Look for the phrase 'They knew something had to change.' What caused them to think that?
Question 3: Look at the paragraph that begins with 'Mina's mother' to find the answer to this question.
Question 5: Look for the part of the text that talks about affection and conflict to find the answer.
Question 6: You have to read the whole text and decide which answer best describes it all.

EXTRACT FROM A NOVEL

'My mom doesn't speak English,' Mina warned me as she took me inside.

'Neither did mine.' I followed her up the narrow stairs, where the smell of old grease and mould vividly brought back the tenements of my own childhood. 'We spoke Italian together.'

'My mom only speaks Arabic. So you'll have to talk to me unless you know Arabic.' As we climbed the stairs, she took a fringed scarf out of her jeans pocket and tied it around her curls.

Mina's mother – Mrs Attar to me – received me in a living room that I also knew from my childhood. I used to sit in places like this when my mother took me with her on social calls in the neighbourhood: overstuffed furniture encased in plastic, a large television draped in a piece of weaving from the Old Country, a thicket of family photos on top.

Mrs Attar was a plump, worried woman who kept her daughter planted firmly next to her. Even so, she insisted on offering me hospitality, in this case a cup of thick sweet tea. Hers might be a seat of poverty, but her manners sure beat those in Oak Brook.

I drank the tea gratefully: the heat outside became overwhelming in the overstuffed room. After thanking her for the tea, and admiring the weaving on the television, I broached my subject. I hoped Mina would do an accurate job with the translation.

3 When arriving at Mina's mother's home, the narrator realised that

   A she had been there before.
   B Mina was unhappy about accompanying her.
   C she had a lot in common with Mina.
   D Mrs Attar was similar to her own mother.

4 When the narrator met Mrs Attar,

   A she suspected that Mrs Attar's English was quite good.
   B she was struck by how polite Mrs Attar was.
   C she began to feel more comfortable after a while.
   D she was surprised by some of the objects in the room.

Happy and healthy? Thank your sister

A recent study of families with more than one child concluded that 'siblings matter even more than parents do in terms of promoting being kind and generous to others'. The researchers reported that parents justifiably worry about the apparently constant fighting between very young siblings because hostility of this kind is connected to bad behaviour outside the family context. However, the fights give young children a chance to learn how to make up with people after a disagreement and how to regain control of their emotions and these are skills that come in handy as they grow up. If parents encourage affection between young siblings, this will make life easier for them when they reach adolescence, because the affection of siblings acts as 'a big protective factor' then. When it comes to delinquent behaviour outside the home, 'an absence of affection seems to be a bigger problem than high levels of conflict'.

And having a sister is especially good for you in this regard, the researchers concluded. Someone with a sister is less likely to suffer from feeling lonely, unloved or guilty, and feelings of self-consciousness and fear are also less prevalent among people with sisters. The study found that all siblings have positive effects on each other, however old they are and whatever their differences in age. However, sisters have the most positive influence because they are more caring and better at discussing problems.

5 What did the researchers conclude about arguments between siblings?

   A They are less important than positive feelings between them.
   B They tend to decrease after children reach adolescence.
   C They rarely have an impact on behaviour outside the family.
   D They are something that parents can have little influence on.

6 What is the main topic of the text?

   A contradictions in the research findings
   B differences between sisters and parents
   C how hard it is to generalise about siblings
   D how siblings can be helpful to each other

You are going to read a magazine article about a training session with a stuntman – someone who performs the dangerous and exciting actions in films. Six paragraphs have been removed from the article. Choose from the paragraphs **A–G** the one which fits each gap (**7–12**). There is one extra paragraph which you do not need to use.

In the exam, mark your answers **on the separate answer sheet**.

Learning to be an action hero

Alex Benady has a lesson in fitness from a film stuntman.

'Now see if you can touch your toes,' says Steve Truglia. As a former Army physical training instructor, he is used to dealing with less than sharp trainees. But how hard can that be? Fifteen seconds of blind confusion ensue before I finally locate my feet. The truth is I can't reach much past my knees and the effort of doing even that seems to be rupturing my kidneys.

| 7 | |

These days, Steve is one of Britain's top stuntmen. You might have seen him in various well-known action movies. Although I have no real desire to enter rooms through the ceiling or drive into walls at high speed like him, I wouldn't mind looking a bit more like an action hero, so Steve is showing me exactly how he stays 'stunt fit'. 'It's a very particular, very extreme kind of fitness,' he explains, 'consisting of stamina, flexibility, strength and core stability, balance and coordination.'

| 8 | |

Right now, we are working on spatial awareness, a subset of coordination which he says is key to being a stuntman. 'It's easy to get disorientated when you are upside down. But if you have a high fall and you don't know exactly where your body is, you won't be able to land safely. If you are lucky, you'll just end up with some serious injuries.' From where I'm hanging, that sounds like a pretty positive outcome. Yet it had all started so well.

| 9 | |

He usually does this at the end of the session. 'On set, you can guarantee that if you have a big dangerous stunt, you won't do it until the end of the day, when you are completely exhausted. So I design my training regime to reflect that.' At first, this part of the session consists of standard strength-building exercises: dips – pushing yourself up and down on the arms of a high chair, for triceps and chest; some bench presses, again for chest; lower back exercises; and curls to build up biceps. Then Steve introduces me to the chinning bar, which involves movements for building strength in your back and arms.

| 10 | |

We move on to balance and coordination, starting by walking along three-inch-wide bars. Not easy, but do-able. 'Now turn round,' says Steve. Not easy and not do-able. I fall off. Now he shows me how to jump on to the bar. Guess what? I can't do that either. Then he points to a two-inch-wide bar at about waist height.

| 11 | |

Now it's outside for some elementary falls. He shows me how to slap the ground when you land, to earth your kinetic energy. He throws me over his shoulder and I arc gracefully through the air, landing painlessly. But when it's my turn, I don't so much throw him as trip him up and he smashes into the ground at my feet, well short of the crash mat. Sorry, Steve.

| 12 | |

At least I'll never suffer from an anatomical anomaly – which is what happens when your thighs are so massive, the other parts of your anatomy look rather small by comparison.

Tip Strip

Question 7: Look for a word in the options that means 'weak'.

Question 9: The text before the gap says 'Yet it had all started so well.' Look for an option that talks about the beginning of something.

Question 11: The base text is talking about a bar. Find this word in the options.

A 'We'll just warm up first,' says Steve as we enter the Muscleworks Gym in East London. Five minutes on the recumbent cycle and I'm thinking this stunt lark is a piece of cake. Then we start some strength work, vital for hanging off helicopters, leaping off walls, etc.

B It's clear that I have some work to do before I am ready to amaze the world with my dripping physique and daredevil stunts. But I have taken one comforting piece of knowledge from my experience.

C Instead, we work on what he calls our 'cores'. 'All powerful movements originate from the centre of the body out, and never from the limbs alone,' he says. So we'll be building up the deep stabilising muscles in our trunks, the part of the body from the waist to the neck.

D He reckons anyone can get there with a couple of gym sessions and a couple of runs a week. 'The key is variety: do as many different types of exercise as possible. Even 20 minutes a day will do.'

E Much to my surprise, I can actually do a few. Then he says innocently: 'Just raise your legs so they are at 90 degrees to your body.' Pain, pain, pain. 'Now open and close your legs in a scissor motion.' I manage to do that once.

F You may think that this sounds a bit feeble. But I was dangling upside down at the time, suspended from a bar by a pair of gravity boots.

G With feet firmly together, he leaps on, balances himself, leaps off, on, off. For good measure he circuits the gym, leaping from one to another, using his thighs to generate the power to leap and the power to stop himself from falling when he lands. Despite his heavy build, he has the feet of a ballerina.

You are going to read an article about the effects of digital media on people's minds. For questions **13–19**, choose the answer (**A**, **B**, **C** or **D**) which you think fits best according to the text.

In the exam, mark your answers **on the separate answer sheet**.

Is the internet making us stupid?

In an article in *Science*, Patricia Greenfield, a developmental psychologist who runs UCLA's Children's Digital Media Center, reviewed dozens of studies on how different media technologies influence our cognitive abilities. Some of the studies indicated that certain computer tasks, like playing video games, increase the speed at which people can shift their focus among icons and other images on screens. Other studies, however, found that such rapid shifts in focus, even if performed adeptly, result in less rigorous and 'more automatic' thinking.

In one experiment at an American university, half a class of students was allowed to use internet-connected laptops during a lecture, while the other half had to keep their computers shut. Those who browsed the web performed much worse on a subsequent test of how well they retained the lecture's content. Earlier experiments revealed that as the number of links in an online document goes up, reading comprehension falls, and as more types of information are placed on a screen, we remember less of what we see.

Greenfield concluded that 'every medium develops some cognitive skills at the expense of others'. Our growing use of screen-based media, she said, has strengthened visual-spatial intelligence, which can strengthen the ability to do jobs that involve keeping track of lots of rapidly changing signals, like piloting a plane or monitoring a patient during surgery. However, that has been accompanied by 'new weaknesses in higher-order cognitive processes', including 'abstract vocabulary, mindfulness, reflection, inductive problem-solving, critical thinking and imagination'. We're becoming, in a word, shallower.

Studies of our behaviour online support this conclusion. German researchers found that web browsers usually spend less than ten seconds looking at a page. Even people doing academic research online tend to 'bounce' rapidly between documents, rarely reading more than a page or two, according to a University College London study. Such mental juggling takes a big toll. In a recent experiment at Stanford University, researchers gave various cognitive tests to 49 people who do a lot of media multitasking and 52 people who multitask much less frequently. The heavy multitaskers performed poorly on all the tests. They were more easily distracted, had less control over their attention, and were much less able to distinguish important information from trivia. The researchers were surprised by the results. They expected the intensive multitaskers to have gained some

mental advantages. That wasn't the case, though. In fact, the multitaskers weren't even good at multitasking. 'Everything distracts them,' said Clifford Nass, one of the researchers.

It would be one thing if the ill effects went away as soon as we turned off our computers and mobiles, but they don't. The cellular structure of the human brain, scientists have discovered, adapts readily to the tools we use to find, store and share information. By changing our habits of mind, each new technology strengthens certain neural pathways and weakens others. The alterations shape the way we think even when we're not using the technology. The pioneering neuroscientist Michael Merzenich believes our brains are being 'massively remodelled' by our ever-intensifying use of the web and related media. In 2009, he said that he was profoundly worried about the cognitive consequences of the constant distractions and interruptions the internet bombards us with. The long-term effect on the quality of our intellectual lives, he said, could be 'deadly'.

Not all distractions are bad. As most of us know, if we concentrate too intensively on a tough problem, we can get stuck in a mental rut. However, if we let the problem sit unattended for a time, we often return to it with a fresh perspective and a burst of creativity. Research by Dutch psychologist Ap Dijksterhuis indicates that such breaks in our attention give our unconscious mind time to grapple with a problem, bringing to bear information and cognitive processes unavailable to conscious deliberation. We usually make better decisions, his experiments reveal, if we shift our attention away from a mental challenge for a time.

But Dijksterhuis's work also shows that our unconscious thought processes don't engage with a problem until we've clearly and consciously defined what the problem is. If we don't have a particular goal in mind, he writes, 'unconscious thought does not occur'. The constant distractedness that the Net encourages is very different from the kind of temporary, purposeful diversion of our mind that refreshes our thinking. The cacophony of stimuli short-circuits both conscious and unconscious thought, preventing our minds from thinking either deeply or creatively. Our brains turn into simple signal-processing units, shepherding information into consciousness and then back again. What we seem to be sacrificing in our surfing and searching is our capacity to engage in the quieter, attentive modes of thought that underpin contemplation, reflection and introspection.

Tip Strip

Question 13: Look for what Patricia's work actually involved.

Question 17: You need to read the whole paragraph to get this answer.

Question 18: Look before the name in the text to see what point his research supports.

13 What do we learn about Patricia Greenfield's research in the first paragraph?

   A It focused on problems resulting from use of media technologies.

   B It did not produce consistent patterns in connection with computer use.

   C It involved collating the results of work done by other people.

   D It highlighted differences between people when using computers.

14 Two of the experiments mentioned in the second paragraph concerned

   A the amount of attention people pay to what they see on computers.

   B the connection between computer use and memory.

   C the use and non-use of computers for studying.

   D changes that happen if people's computer use increases.

15 One of Greenfield's conclusions was that

   A certain claims about the advantages of computer use are false.

   B computer use has reduced a large number of mental abilities.

   C people do not care about the effects of computer use on their minds.

   D too much emphasis has been placed on the benefits of computer use.

16 One of the pieces of research mentioned in the fourth paragraph indicated that

   A some people are better at multitasking than others.

   B 'mental juggling' increases the mental abilities of only a few people.

   C beliefs about the effectiveness of multitasking are false.

   D people read online material less carefully than other material.

17 What is the writer's purpose in the fifth paragraph?

   A to advise on how to avoid the bad effects of new media technology

   B to present opposing views on the consequences of use of new media technology

   C to warn about the damage done by use of new media technology

   D to summarise the findings of the previously-mentioned research

18 The writer mentions Ap Dijksterhuis's research in order to make the point that

   A not all research supports beliefs about the dangers of computer use.

   B the mind functions in ways that computers cannot.

   C problem-solving can involve very complex mental processes.

   D uninterrupted concentration on something is not always a good thing.

19 The writer's main point in the final paragraph is that

   A constant computer use makes people incapable of complex thought processes.

   B the stimulation provided by computer use causes people to become confused.

   C it is natural for some people to want to avoid thinking deeply about problems.

   D both conscious and unconscious thought are affected by computer use.

Tip Strip

Question 23: Look for all the years and dates in the texts. Which one is linked to 'a significant event'?

Question 26: Look for bad aspects of the jobs that have changed over the years. Which text talks about improvements?

Question 29: Look at the end of all the texts. At the end of which text do you find information about the type of people doing it?

Question 34: The question talks about Britain. Look for a reference to 'elsewhere'.

You are going to read a magazine article about jobs in Britain that used to be common but are uncommon now. For questions **20–34**, choose from the sections of the article (**A–D**). The jobs may be chosen more than once.

In the exam, mark your answers **on the separate answer sheet**.

In connection with which of the jobs are the following mentioned?

how hard it can be to find someone who does this job | 20 | |

a time when demand for this kind of work was at its height | 21 | |

people noticing examples of what people doing this job produced | 22 | |

a significant event involving people doing this job | 23 | |

the kind of people who need this kind of expertise | 24 | |

a comment on how little interest there is now in this kind of work | 25 | |

improvements that were made for people doing this job | 26 | |

a prediction that proved to be accurate | 27 | |

what people doing the job today use in order to do it | 28 | |

the kind of people still doing this job | 29 | |

the impact of the cost of materials on demand for this kind of work | 30 | |

a positive result of not many people doing this job anymore | 31 | |

something that people doing the job now find surprising | 32 | |

an attempt to teach the skills involved in this kind of work | 33 | |

the reason why this job is no longer common in Britain but exists elsewhere | 34 | |

THE WAY WE WORKED

Britain's disappearing jobs, and the people keeping them alive.

A Advertising signwriter

A couple of years into his career, Wayne Tanswell told his father he was in a dying trade. Having left school in 1980, to train in sign-painting, he then watched as high streets moved to plastic shop-front lettering. 'But my dad said: "Wait and stick at it; these things will come back. The more technology comes into it, the more you'll be seen as a specialist." He had a lot of foresight.'

Technology has helped Tanswell. Now that his trade has become such a rare one, he is summoned far from his home, with work ranging from period numerals by the doors of London houses to shop fronts in villages with strict planning restrictions.

Sam Roberts curates an online archive, blog and burgeoning maps of hand-painted wall ads. These signs, painted onto brickwork, once kept sign-painters in demand. Their work remains, faded but unmistakable, in many cities. 'Mention them to people and they'll look quizzical,' Roberts says, 'but next time they see you, they'll have started to spot them.'

B Typewriter repairer

Though a few thousand new electric models are still sold in Britain each year, the typewriter is not what it once was. Search online for a once-indispensable brand of correction fluid and the first page of hits will be for something completely different. Search your high street for a typewriter repairman and your chances of a result at all are ribbon-thin.

There are still a handful of typewriter repair businesses operating in Britain, mostly on the South Coast. They not only serve septuagenarian retirees and technophobes (and diehard novelists who shun PCs), but are also approached by people weaned on digital keyboards who see typewriters as relics of a distant past.

In 1986, George Blackman set up an equipment and typewriter repair shop. He trained on the old manual machines and Blackman's employees still find themselves working on those beautiful, formidably heavy old machines. 'It amazes us the price the old manual machines sell for on the internet,' one explains, and their new buyers want them spruced up when they've splashed out. They get the old machines gleaming and operational by raiding the vast collection of spare parts they've accumulated over the years (and you can't buy them any more).

C Matchgirl

There's a light that never goes out, even if it burns less brightly than it once did. Female match-makers have long been a celebrated part of British labour history. In 1888, thousands of matchgirls at the Bryant and May factory in London famously went on strike to protest over conditions. Over subsequent decades, the long hours, tiny pay packets and exposure to toxic chemicals were addressed before the industry largely relocated its production to other countries where labour was cheaper.

Today, there are still female match-makers in Britain – in Bristol, at the country's last match factory, Octavius Hunt. The company long ago diversified into other products but still makes matches. Its commercial director, Kerry Healey, says that the majority of staff are still female. 'Matches are a small part of our business, but an important one. Depending on the size of orders, we have between two and 12 people working in the department, of which two are men – so it's still mainly female.'

D Lacquerer

Since the first pieces of Oriental lacquer work arrived on the Continent in the seventeenth century, European craftsmen have attempted to replicate the incredible effects of this time-consuming process. By the time the craze for buying newly-available arts and crafts from Japan was at its height in the second half of the nineteenth century, wealthy Britons and Americans spent huge sums on lacquered objects *d'art*. They fell out of favour towards the turn of the twentieth century and by the 1920s, chemical shortcuts had been developed to replace the Japanese approach of applying, sanding and polishing numerous layers of paint. And shiny, affordable substitutes, like shellac, began to eat away its aura. Import restrictions and the make-do-and-mend spirit of the Second World War saw lacquering revived – one magazine reprinted several slabs of an eighteenth-century manual on the subject as a how-to guide.

Today, there are only a handful of traditional lacquerers. Pedro da Costa Felgueiras, who runs the London Lacquer Studios, has been the capital's go-to guy for authentic lacquer work and period pigments for over a decade. In a world where even 'most paints are just plastic and dye', he's called in to provide historically accurate colours for walls and furniture from the Seventeenth to the Nineteenth century and to lacquer new things the old way, with 30 or 40 coats of paint, each being left to dry and then being polished before the next. 'I remember a friend once telling me to be careful with my recipes as someone might steal and use them,' he recalls. 'My answer was: even if I show them how to do it, no one wants to.'

Guidance

About the paper

There are two parts to the paper. In each part, you have to complete one task. You have 1 hour 30 minutes to complete the paper.

Part 1

Part 1 is compulsory. You have to manipulate given information from the input text or texts, and write around 180–220 words.

The focus of assessment is how well you achieve the task. You must cover all the points required with enough detail to fulfil the task. The target reader must be able to understand and respond to your answer.

It is not necessary for you to be too imaginative and invent a lot of extra detail in this answer, as this might mean that you include things that are irrelevant, don't cover the required points and have a negative effect on the reader.

Part 2

Part 2 has five questions, from which you must choose only one question to answer. You should write 220–260 words.

The questions may ask you to write an article, a competition entry, a contribution to a longer piece, an essay, an information sheet, a letter, a proposal, a report or a review.

In this part, you can use your imagination and be inventive.

How to do the paper

General points

- Spend at least 10 minutes thinking about and planning your writing. Your answer should be well-organised with clear linking of ideas between sentences and paragraphs. In the exam, you won't have enough time to write a rough answer and a final, neat copy. If you plan properly, this will not be necessary.

- Make sure your writing is legible. If necessary, leave a line between paragraphs so that it is clear where one paragraph ends and the next begins.

- Everything you write should have a beginning, a middle and an end. Remember to use an appropriate style and layout for the type of text, and the person you are writing to.

- Make sure you use a range of language, which includes vocabulary and structures. At this level, your language should not be too simple.

- Check that your answer is neither too long nor too short. If you write too much, you may include irrelevant information, which could have a negative effect on the target reader. If your answer is too short, you may not cover all the required points.

- Leave enough time to check your answer. Check grammar and spelling (you can use British or American spelling, but try not to mix them up) and that you have included all the points necessary to answer the question. Make sure you have included enough detail on each point, check that you have included all the language functions required in the task, and that you have used a range of appropriate language.

Part 1

- Read the instructions carefully. This will clarify what you have to do and who your target reader is.

- Make sure you understand everything you are asked to do, for example, outline the situation, make recommendations and give reasons.

- You must use information from the input texts; you will need to read these carefully. Process and combine the information before you start to plan your answer.

- Don't copy long phrases or sentences from the texts as they will probably be in the wrong register for your answer. You should use the ideas from the texts but express them in your own words, making sure that they are appropriate for the type of text you are writing.

Part 2

- Read through all the questions in Part 2. Before you choose which one to answer, think about what the tasks involve, so that you are confident about including everything required in the task. Always check the context, reason for writing and the target reader. Each task has a given target reader and a purpose which will determine what register and kind of language is appropriate.

- Think about what kind of writing you are best at. If you are good with more formal language and expressing your ideas concisely, you might consider writing a report, proposal, information sheet or contribution to a longer piece. If you are good at writing in an interesting way, you might choose an article or competition entry. If you have studied the set text in class, you should consider answering this question.

  Consider whether you have enough ideas for the topic of each task – don't just choose a task because you like the text type.

- Question 5 is always on the set text. Don't answer this question if you have not studied the book!

Part 1

You **must** answer this question. Write your answer in **180–220** words in an appropriate style. In the exam, write your answer **on the separate answer sheet provided**.

Tip Strip
Question 1:
- Your proposal is for the College Principal, so it should be written in a semi-formal or formal style.
- You need to give the Principal the required information as clearly as possible, so headings are appropriate.
- Bullet points are useful for making recommendations, but you must show a range of language in the rest of your answer.
- Don't use words or phrases from the forum as they are too informal. Read the forum entries carefully, make a note of the ideas then use your own words.
- In this task, you have to consider the comments about previous events and the Principal's concerns about them, and make recommendations based on these. You can expand on the key areas mentioned in the notes.
- Provide extra details as appropriate, but don't be too imaginative or give too much detail about one point in case you forget to include all the required points.
- Check what language functions you should use. In this task, you have to outline what happened previously, make recommendations and justify them.
- Remember that this is a serious proposal and the Principal needs information that he can act on.

1   Your college is planning to hold a careers day for students who are about to complete their courses, giving them information about jobs and advice on possible training courses. The Principal has asked you to write a proposal setting out what should happen on the day and how it should be organised, with reasons to support your ideas.

Read the information from the website forum which students wrote after a previous event, and the email from the Principal, on which you have noted some ideas. Then, **using the information appropriately**, write your proposal for the Principal.

Need practical stuff – 'question and answer' panels with business people?

More info on vocational courses – especially unusual jobs. Nothing to inspire us!

Same old ideas from college advisors. Didn't stay long!

Started too early – had lectures so could only go to the afternoon session.

No networking opportunities – need contacts, not just information

---

In your proposal, please take into account the points raised in last year's forum – I'm particularly concerned that students don't feel we're giving them what they need – we must make the day interesting, relevant and practical. Could you consider ways of doing this?

— external speakers

— hands-on workshops?
— practice interviews?

— timing? 2 days?

Write your **proposal**. You should use your own words as far as possible.

Tip Strip

Question 2:

- This is a college prospectus, a formal booklet, so you should use formal or semi-formal language. Headings may be useful for conveying the information clearly.

- Make sure that you use all the required language functions – you have to outline the social and sporting activities available, give advice on how to make friends and suggest interesting and useful activities to take up.

Question 3:

- Choose the film you want to nominate, making sure that you have enough ideas about it to write a complete answer.

- Your aim in this task is to win the competition, so think of interesting ways of expressing your ideas so that you engage the readers.

- Finish with a final good reason why your film should be included in the set, and try to make this memorable and interesting.

Question 4:

- Read the instructions carefully so that you identify the job, what skills are required and any other relevant information you might want to include. In this task, the job is working in a busy office, and the person needs to be well organised, work well with others and have good communication skills.

- You may write the reference in the form of a letter, but it should be written in a formal or semi-formal style.

- You should decide whether you want to recommend the person, giving your reasons clearly.

Write an answer to one of the questions **2–5** in this part. Write your answer in **220–260** words. In the exam, write your answer **on the seperate answer sheet provided**, and put the question number in the box at the top of the page.

2 You have been asked to write a contribution to a college prospectus giving advice for new students about the kind of social and sporting activities that are on offer in the college. Your contribution should include advice on the best ways of making new friends, and recommendations for useful and interesting activities to take up.

Write your **contribution to the college prospectus**.

3 You see the following advertisement in a film magazine:

Best Film Ever Competition

We are planning to produce a limited edition set of DVDs of the ten best films of all time, and would like your suggestions for films to include in the set. Write to us describing your chosen film, outlining the plot and explaining why the film should be included in the set of DVDs. The best entries will win a DVD player.

Write your **competition entry**.

4 A friend has applied for a job in the office of an English Language College that teaches students from all over the world, and you have been asked to provide a reference. The advertisement has asked for applicants who are good with people and have good communication skills. Applicants should also be well organised and be team players.

In your reference, you should include information about your friend's relevant work experience and personal qualities, and your reasons for recommending them for the job.

Write your **reference**.

5 Answer one of the following two questions based on a book you have read. In the exam you will have to write about one of two specific titles. Write the letter **(a)** or **(b)** as well as the number 5 on your answer sheet.

(a) Your local book club has asked its members to recommend novels for club members to read and discuss. Write a report about a novel which you would like to recommend, briefly outlining the plot, describing any particularly good features of the novel and explaining why you recommend it for the book club.

Write your **report**.

(b) Your class has had a discussion about scenes in novels that are very dramatic. Your teacher has asked you to write an essay describing two dramatic scenes from a novel you know, describing what happens in these scenes and explaining what you think makes them dramatic.

Write your **essay**.

Guidance

About the paper

The paper lasts one hour. It contains five parts with a total of fifty questions.

Part 1

In Part 1, you read a short text and complete a multiple-choice cloze task. Twelve words or phrases have been removed from the text. For each gap, you have to choose from four options the word or phrase which fits best.

Part 2

In Part 2, you read a short text and complete an open cloze. Fifteen words have been removed from the text. You have to complete the gaps.

Part 3

In Part 3, you read a short text and complete a word formation task. Ten words have been removed from the text. You are given the base form of each missing word and you have to create the correct form of the base word to fit the gap.

Part 4

In Part 4, you read three unrelated sentences, and complete a gapped sentence task. The same word in the same form has been removed from all three sentences. You have to find the common missing word.

Part 5

In Part 5, you read eight pairs of sentences and complete a key-word transformation task. The pairs of sentences have the same meaning, but are expressed in different ways. Three to six words have been removed from the second sentence, and one of these words, the key word, is given as a prompt. You have to complete the second sentence, using the key word.

How to do the paper

Part 1

- Read the text, ignoring the gaps, to get a general understanding.
- Only one of the options (A–D) fits the gap.
- Check the words before and after the gap, e.g. some words can only be followed by one preposition.
- Some questions focus on linking words and require an understanding of the whole passage.
- If you are not sure which word to choose, eliminate the options you know are wrong.
- When you have finished, read your completed text again and check that it makes sense.

Part 2

- Read the text, ignoring the gaps, to get a general understanding.
- Think about the missing words. Each gap only needs one word, usually a grammatical word, e.g. pronoun, linker or preposition, rather than topic vocabulary.
- Carefully read the text around each gap and think about what type of word is missing, e.g. dependent preposition or part of a fixed expression.
- When you have finished, read your completed text again and check that it makes sense.

Part 3

- Read the text, ignoring the gaps, to get a general understanding.
- Decide which type of word is needed in each gap, e.g. noun, adjective, adverb. Look at the whole sentence, not just at the line including the gap.
- Look at the word in capitals on the right of the gap. You may need to add a prefix or suffix, or make other changes. More than one change may be required.
- Check to see if nouns should be singular or plural.
- When you have finished, read your completed text again and check that it makes sense.

Part 4

- Read all three sentences.
- Choose the easiest sentence to understand and think of all the words that could fit there. Can any of them fit the other two sentences?
- The missing word will be familiar, but in each gap, the word will have a slightly different meaning, or create a new meaning when combined with the other words around it.
- The word you are looking for must appear in all three sentences in exactly the same form, e.g. if it is a verb, it will always be in the same form – infinitive, past or past participle.

Part 5

- Look at the key word. What type of word is it? What usually follows it, e.g. an infinitive, a preposition, or could it be part of a phrasal verb?
- Think about the other words that need to change in the new word order, e.g. an adjective may become a noun or vice versa.
- Your answer may include words or expressions not used in the first sentence, but these must express exactly the same idea.
- Remember that contracted words count as two words, e.g. won't = will not.

Tip Strip

Question 3: These words all have a similar meaning, but which one is used to refer to a precise location.

Question 5: These are all linking phrases, but only one of them tells you that another surprising thing will follow.

Question 9: Only one of these verbs is usually used together with the noun 'opportunity'.

Question 11: Which of these words can be followed by the preposition 'from'?

Question 12: Which of these verbs is commonly used together with the noun 'party'?

For questions **1–12**, read the text below and decide which answer (**A**, **B**, **C** or **D**) best fits each gap. There is an example at the beginning (**0**).

In the exam, mark your answers **on the separate answer sheet**.

Example:

0 **A** hit   **B** knocked   **C** banged   **D** beat

0	A	B	C	D
	▬	▭	▭	▭

The Mysterious Isle

In the early morning of 23 January, 2009, the most powerful storm for a decade **(0)** .... western France. With wind speeds in **(1)** .... of 120 miles per hour, it flattened forests, **(2)** .... down power lines and caused massive destruction to buildings and roads. But it also left behind an extraordinary creation. Seven miles out to sea at the **(3)** .... where the Atlantic Ocean meets the estuary of the River Gironde, a small island had **(4)** .... out of the water. Locals soon gave it the name The Mysterious Isle. What was so remarkable, **(5)** .... its sudden apparition, was the fact that the island **(6)** .... intact in what is often quite a hostile sea environment. It could well become a permanent **(7)** ....

Scientists **(8)** .... realised that the island's appearance **(9)** .... a unique opportunity to study the creation and development of a new ecosystem. Within months, it had been colonised by seabirds, insects and vegetation. Unfortunately, however, they were not alone in **(10)** .... the island attractive. It became increasingly difficult to **(11)** .... the site from human visitors. In its first year, day trippers came in powered dinghies, a parachute club used it as a landing strip, and a rave party was even **(12)** .... there one night.

1	A	surplus	B	advance	C	excess	D	put
2	A	fetched	B	brought	C	carried	D	sent
3	A	scene	B	mark	C	stage	D	point
4	A	risen	B	grown	C	lifted	D	surfaced
5	A	in spite of	B	instead of	C	apart from	D	on account of
6	A	prolonged	B	remained	C	resided	D	persevered
7	A	item	B	issue	C	matter	D	feature
8	A	quickly	B	briskly	C	hastily	D	speedily
9	A	delivered	B	awarded	C	proposed	D	offered
10	A	regarding	B	finding	C	seeking	D	deciding
11	A	prevent	B	preserve	C	protect	D	prohibit
12	A	held	B	made	C	done	D	given

Part 2

Tip Strip

Question 14: Which linking word is needed here?

Question 15: Which preposition is used with the verb *to* 'invest'?

Question 17: Which word completes the common expression that tells you that another point is going to be made?

Question 18: You need a possessive pronoun here.

Question 25: Which preposition do you need to create a phrasal verb meaning 'requires'?

For questions **13–27**, read the text below and think of the word which best fits each gap. There is an example at the beginning (**0**).

In the exam, you have to write your answers **IN CAPITAL LETTERS on the separate answer sheet**.

Example: | 0 | | O | F | | | | | | | | | | | | | | | | | | | |

Choosing Binoculars

For independent travellers, a good pair of binoculars often represents an essential piece **(0)** .... kit. Unless you're planning to do a **(13)** .... deal of bird-watching or other specialist activities, **(14)** ...., there's no need to invest **(15)** .... a full-size pair. Compact binoculars are fine when **(16)** .... comes to general all-purpose viewing in good light. What's **(17)** ...., they are certainly easier to carry round.

Everyone has **(18)** .... own idea of what makes a comfortable pair of binoculars. When you're considering **(19)** .... of the many brands and models on the market you should choose, don't base your decision **(20)** .... price alone. A better idea **(21)** .... to pop down to your local photographic store and **(22)** .... those that fall within your price range a test run.

(23) .... you might like the look of a particular pair, you may not find the handling and viewing position comfortable. Spend some time holding them to your eyes and finding the right position to get the best field of view. But don't expect to be **(24)** .... to look through and get an instant image. Some models call **(25)** .... a certain degree of practice to find the best viewing position.

Finally, **(26)** .... sure the binoculars come with a decent case and a comfortable neck strap. These details can make **(27)** .... the difference when you're out in the field.

Tip Strip

Question 28: You need to add a prefix to create the opposite meaning of this word.

Question 30: Add another word to 'let' to form a compound word which completes a common collocation with 'retail'. Your answer needs to be plural.

Question 34: Add a suffix to turn this verb into a noun.

Question 36: What adjective can you make from this verb? It means 'that functions'.

Question 37: Add a suffix to make a noun. Which letter from the verb is dropped?

For questions **28–37**, read the text below. Use the word given in Capitals at the end of some of the lines to form a word that fits in the gap **in the same line**. There is an example at the beginning (**0**).

In the exam, you have to write your answers **IN CAPITAL LETTERS on the separate answer sheet**.

Example: | 0 | D | A | I | L | Y | | | | | | | | | | | | | |

The Inventor of the Bar Code

Although you may never have heard of Joe Woodland,

you almost certainly use his invention on a **(0)** ....   **DAY**

basis. For Joe was the man who came up with the idea of

the bar code – that little box containing parallel lines of **(28)** ....   **REGULAR**

width and **(29)** .... that you find on the packaging   **LONG**

of most products that are offered for sale at retail **(30)** ....   **LET**

world wide. Joe Woodland actually invented the bar code

way back in 1949, when the manager of a supermarket in

Philadelphia asked him to design an electronic **(31)** ....   **CHECK**

system which would be both simple and effective. The

purpose of the bar code is to store **(32)** .... information   **CODED**

about the product, which **(33)** .... speeds up the   **POTENTIAL**

process of recording sales and restocking the shelves.

Joe's **(34)** .... came from Morse code and he formed   **INSPIRE**

his first barcode in the sand on the beach one day. The idea

was way ahead of its time however, and didn't find any

immediate practical **(35)** .... Convinced that the system   **APPLY**

was **(36)** .... with further development, however,   **WORK**

Woodland didn't give up. It was the **(37)** .... of laser   **ARRIVE**

gun technology decades later which allowed Joe's invention

to come into everyday use.

Tip Strip

Question 38: Look at the third sentence. Which phrasal verb means 'gained control'? The word you need collocates with 'seriously' in the first sentence and 'courage' in the second.

Question 40: Look at the third sentence. Only one specific word is used in this context, whereas in the first two sentences various words could be used.

Question 41: You need a verb in each gap, but which tense is it in?

Question 42: Look at the second sentence. The missing word completes a common fixed expression. The word collocates with 'fat' in the first sentence and with 'opinion' in the second.

For questions **38–42**, think of one word only which can be used appropriately in all three sentences. Here is an example (**0**).

Example:

0 I was on the .... of booking my holiday when my boss said I might have to change the dates.

As the meeting drew to a close, the chairperson moved on to the final .... on the agenda.

Theo couldn't see the .... of getting to the airport too early, as the check-in desk only opened one hour before the flight departed.

Example: | 0 | P | O | I | N | T | | | | | | | | | | | | | | |

In the exam, write **only** the missing word **IN CAPITAL LETTERS on the separate answer sheet**.

---

38 Although she enjoyed going out with friends, Harriet always .... her college work very seriously.

John remembers that it .... quite a lot of courage to sing in public for the first time.

When the new manager .... over the football club, not everybody liked him.

39 Sandra .... got used to her new job at the fashion magazine.

If you eat too ...., you may find that you get a stomach ache.

You can get to the town centre quite .... by bike, as there is a dedicated cycle track.

40 The detective said he hadn't ruled out a .... between the two burglaries in the village.

A new high-speed rail .... will connect the Olympic Stadium with the city centre.

Graeme found the name of the hotel by following a .... on the tourist board website.

41 The battery in my laptop needs .... before I leave for London.

The museum is not .... local residents an entrance fee if they visit on weekdays.

The police say they won't be .... the man because he hasn't committed a criminal offence.

42 When you're trying to lose weight, it's a good idea to avoid foods with a .... fat content.

So many people drive into the town centre these days, it's .... time a car park was built.

It seems that everyone has a .... opinion of our new colleague, but I'm not convinced he's right for the job.

Part 5

Tip Strip

Question 43: You need a phrase that talks about time. It also has a definite article.

Question 44: The key word is an adjective. Which verb usually comes before it?

Question 45: The key word comes first in the gap, and needs to be followed by an adjective and noun combination. Change two words from the input sentence to make this expression. You also need to add an article.

Question 47: Find the adjective in the input sentence. Use the noun of this word in the new phrase.

Question 49: Which tense of the verb *to be* will follow 'it'?

Question 50: You need a phrasal verb that uses the verb 'run'.

For questions **43–50**, complete the second sentence so that it has a similar meaning to the first sentence, using the word given. **Do not change the word given.** You must use between **three** and **six** words, including the word given. Here is an example (**0**).

Example:

0 'Chloe would only eat a pizza if she could have a mushroom topping'.

ON

Chloe .... a mushroom topping when she ate a pizza.

The gap can be filled with the words 'insisted on having', so you write:

Example:	**0**	INSISTED ON HAVING

In the exam, write **only** the missing words **IN CAPITAL LETTERS on the separate answer sheet**.

---

43 We were late arriving at the cinema and so missed the start of the film.

BY

The film had .... we arrived at the cinema.

44 Simon found the recipe book very hard to follow.

DIFFICULTY

Simon .... in following the recipe book.

45 The ice-skater performed faultlessly and received full marks.

GAVE

The ice-skater .... and received full marks.

46 I was just about to call you to see what time you were coming.

POINT

I .... you to see what time you were coming.

47 Harry was disappointed to hear the news that the match had been cancelled.

CAME

News of the cancellation of the match .... to Harry.

48 At this time of year, the area is often affected by violent storms.

FEELS

At this time of year, the area often .... violent storms.

49 The trees blown down in the storm were not cleared away for weeks.

BEFORE

It .... the trees blown down in the storm were cleared away.

50 There was very little paper left in the printer.

RUN

The printer had .... paper.

Guidance

About the paper

Paper 4 lasts about forty minutes and has four parts, with a total of thirty questions. There are texts of varying lengths and types, e.g. extracts from media broadcasts and announcements, as well as everyday conversations. You hear each recording twice. You have time to read the questions before you listen.

Part 1

In Part 1, you listen to three unrelated extracts of around one minute each. Each extract has two speakers. You have to answer two three-option multiple-choice questions on each extract.

Part 2

Part 2 involves one long monologue of around two to three minutes where the speaker is talking about a particular subject. A set of eight sentences reports the main points from the listening. A word or short phrase has been removed from each sentence. You have to listen and complete the gaps.

Part 3

In Part 3, there is one long interview or discussion of around four minutes. You have to listen and answer six four-option multiple-choice questions.

Part 4

In Part 4, you hear a series of five short monologues on a theme, of around thirty seconds each. You have to complete two tasks as you listen. Each task has eight options (A-H). As you listen, you match one option from Task 1 and one option from Task 2 to each speaker. You match the gist of what the speakers say to the ideas in the prompts, e.g. their occupation, opinions, etc.

How to do the paper

Part 1

- The three extracts are not linked in any way. All three are dialogues, but there will be a variety of text types and interaction patterns.
- Before you listen to each extract, look at the context sentence. Think about who the speaker is and about the context, e.g. is it a broadcast interview, an informal chat?
- Before you listen, think about which of the speakers you are listening for in each question and underline keywords in the question stem.
- Listen first to find the correct answer to the question posed in the stem.
- Listen again to match that answer to the correct option (A–C).

Part 2

- Before you listen, read the rubric and think about the context.
- You have 45 seconds to read through the sentences before you listen. Think about the type of information that is missing in each sentence.
- Most answers are concrete pieces of information, e.g. numbers and proper nouns.
- The sentences on the page follow the same order as the information in the listening text. Use the sentences to help you keep your place as you listen.
- The words you need to write are heard on the recording. There is no need to change the form of the word or find a paraphrase.
- Write no more than three words in each gap. Most answers will be single words or compound nouns.
- Check that your answer fits grammatically and makes sense in the complete sentence.

Part 3

- Before you listen, read the rubric and think about the context.
- You have one minute to read through the set of sentences before you listen.
- Underline the keywords in the question stems and options.
- The questions follow the order of the text. Listen out for discourse markers or interviewer's questions that introduce the topic of each question that you have to answer.
- Listen first to find the correct answer to the question posed in the question stem.
- Listen again to match that answer to the correct option (A–D).
- The words in the options will not be the same as those you hear in the recording.

Part 4

- There are five different speakers all talking about the same topic. You will hear all five of them and the listening extracts will be repeated.
- You have 45 seconds to read the two tasks before you listen. Read the options (A–H) in both tasks so that you are ready to choose one from each set for each speaker as you listen.
- The first time you listen, pay attention to the speaker's main idea. Mark the option closest to this idea.
- The second time you listen, check your answers. You may need to change some of them. Remember that in each task there are three options that you don't need to use.
- Don't worry if you don't understand every word. If you're not sure of an answer, then guess. You have probably understood more than you think.

Part 1

You will hear three different extracts. For questions **1–6**, choose the answer (**A**, **B** or **C**) which fits best according to what you hear. There are two questions for each extract.

In the exam, mark your answers **on the separate answer sheet**.

Tip Strip

Question 1: Listen for the phrase 'I get a buzz from that side of it'. What is he referring to when he says this?

Question 4: Listen to everything the woman says. In general, was it a positive experience or not? Which option matches this feeling?

Question 6: Listen for the phrase 'for what it's worth'. The answer comes just after it.

Extract One

You hear two people talking about their work as website designers.

1   How does the man feel about the work?

    A   He finds the creativity stimulating.

    B   He would like to use his academic training more.

    C   He gets most satisfaction from being part of a team.

2   What do they both think about the job?

    A   It's a difficult career to get started in.

    B   It's important to be able to work flexible hours.

    C   It's a poorly paid job for the amount of work involved.

Extract Two

You hear two cyclists talking about their sport.

3   The man thinks his success as a cyclist is due to

    A   his complete dedication.

    B   the age at which he started.

    C   a series of great role models.

4   When talking about cycling in a velodrome, the woman reveals her

    A   fear of dangerous sports.

    B   inability to follow instructions.

    C   willingness to accept a challenge.

You hear a man called Roy talking about bees on a phone-in programme.

5 Why has he phoned the programme?

    A to raise issues not previously discussed

    B to challenge the opinions of other contributors

    C to lend his support to a view that's been expressed.

6 When talking about gardens, he is

    A describing what he does in his own.

    B encouraging people to grow certain things.

    C suggesting that people keep bees themselves.

You will hear a student called Tim Farnham giving a class presentation about a seabird called the albatross. For questions **7–14**, complete the sentences.

In the exam, mark your answers **on the separate answer sheet**.

THE ALBATROSS

Tim thinks that the name 'albatross' comes originally from a word in

the ⬛ **7** language.

There are currently thought to be a total of ⬛ **8** species of albatross.

The fact that it relies on ⬛ **9** explains why the albatross isn't found in some areas.

By using a locking mechanism in its ⬛ **10** , the albatross can save energy when flying.

Tim explains that the albatross has a surprisingly good sense of ⬛ **11**

Tim was surprised to discover that ⬛ **12** attack albatross nests.

The albatross used to be hunted mostly for its ⬛ **13** as well as for food.

Tim gives the example of ⬛ **14** as plastic objects commonly eaten by albatrosses.

Tip Strip
Question 7: Be careful. Three languages are mentioned, but only one of them fits here.
Question 8: The words 'a total of' in the sentence tell you that you are listening for a number.
Question 9: Listen for the word 'found' when you listen. It's also in the sentence.
Question 11: What are the five senses? Which of them would you not expect a bird to use?
Question 14: Tim mentions three plastic objects, but which does he say is most common?

Tip Strip

Question 15: Listen for when Dan says 'that really pushed me to do it actually'. What is he referring to?

Question 18: Listen for the interviewer's question about critics. Dan's answer follows.

Question 19: Listen to the end of Dan's turn. His answer comes here. Go back and check why the other options are wrong.

Question 20: Listen to Dan's whole last turn. Does he think it was a good thing to include this scene or not?

You will hear an interview with the television presenter Dan Heckmond. For questions **15–20**, choose the answer (**A**, **B**, **C** or **D**) which fits best according to what you hear.

In the exam, mark your answers **on the separate answer sheet**.

15 Dan was particularly attracted to the idea of working on the programme because

  A it was a way of continuing his academic studies.
  B he agreed with the approach adopted by the team.
  C it involved working with experts in their subjects.
  D he welcomed the chance to visit interesting places.

16 How does Dan feel about the way topics are selected for the programme?

  A keen to ensure that his opinions are taken into account
  B worried that he hasn't time to focus on the issues
  C sorry to play rather a minor role in the process
  D content to leave the main decisions to others

17 Dan says that any topic accepted for the programme must

  A involve filming in a place with many picturesque views.
  B have at its heart a well-known mystery from the past.
  C give him the chance to engage in exciting activities.
  D require only a small amount of additional research.

18 When asked about those who criticise the series, Dan says that

  A they may misunderstand its aims.
  B they are unfair to judge it by its style.
  C they underestimate how much it can achieve.
  D they might learn something from its methods.

19 What does Dan suggest about the first programme in the new series?

  A It was lucky to reach a conclusion.
  B It will fulfil the viewer's limited expectations.
  C It should have addressed a much wider question.
  D It could make a valuable contribution to ongoing research.

20 How does Dan feel about including scenes where things go wrong?

  A certain that it will become a popular regular feature
  B unsure whether it's the best use of programme time
  C worried that it might show his colleagues in a bad light
  D hopeful that it will provide insights into everyday archaeology

Part 4

You will hear five short extracts in which people are talking about how they gave up office jobs to do other types of work.

In the exam, mark your answers **on the separate answer sheet**.

TASK ONE

For questions **21–25**, choose from the list (**A–H**) what made each speaker decide to give up office work.

A	poor motivation	Speaker 1	21
B	lack of exercise	Speaker 2	22
C	the regular hours	Speaker 3	23
D	limited contact with people	Speaker 4	24
E	overcrowded workplace	Speaker 5	25
F	dull colleagues		
G	few career prospects		
H	stressful deadlines		

TASK TWO

For questions **26–30**, choose from list (**A–H**) what each speaker likes best about their present job.

A	being my own boss	Speaker 1	26
B	feeling appreciated by clients	Speaker 2	27
C	being able to offer advice	Speaker 3	28
D	feeling respected for my skills	Speaker 4	29
E	being fully qualified	Speaker 5	30
F	feeling committed to the work		
G	being relatively well paid		
H	being able to help others		

Tip Strip

Speaker 1: Listen for the phrase 'The thing I couldn't stand'. What she says next explains why she decided to give up office work (Task One).

Speaker 2: Listen to what she says about clients – it helps with Task Two.

Speaker 3: What 'got him down' in his previous job? This tells you the Task One answer.

Speaker 4: When she says 'I love that feeling' about her present job, what is she referring to?

Speaker 5: Listen to the first part of what he says. What was his general feeling about his old job?

Guidance

About the paper

The Speaking test lasts for 15 minutes and there are four parts. You take the test with a partner. There are two examiners, although only one (the interlocutor) speaks to you.

Part 1

Part 1 takes about three minutes. First the interlocutor asks each of you direct questions asking for personal information. Then the interlocutor asks you and your partner questions in turn on general topics such as your interests, daily routines and likes and dislikes.

Part 2

Part 2 lasts around three to four minutes, during which you each speak on your own for about a minute. You are given three photographs. You compare two of the pictures and say something more about them. You are also asked a short question about your partner's photographs after they have finished speaking.

Part 3

Part 3 lasts around four minutes. You discuss a given task with your partner for around three minutes. This involves talking about several pictures which are on a given theme or topic, and reaching a decision.

Part 4

Part 4 takes around four minutes. The interlocutor leads a general discussion that broadens the topic of the Part 3 task by discussing more abstract questions on related issues.

How to do the paper

Part 1

- For the questions on personal information, you only need to give short answers; don't prepare long speeches about who you are and where you are from, but try to say something more than yes or no.
- Think of the rest of Part 1, where you are asked about general topics, as similar to meeting someone in a social situation. You should provide enough detail to give interesting answers, without monopolising the time.

Part 2

- Listen to the interlocutor's instructions carefully. The task is also written on the paper with the photographs so you won't forget what you have to do.
- You can ask the interlocutor to repeat the task if you have to, but only do this if it is really necessary as you will lose time from your minute.
- Compare the pictures and then move on to the second part of the task. Don't describe the pictures; describing them won't allow you to show a range of language at the right level.
- Listen to what your partner says about their pictures as the interlocutor will ask you a short question about them. In your answer, you should give some detail, but be careful not to say too much as you only have a short time for this.

Part 3

- Listen to the task carefully so that you understand exactly what to do. The task is written on the paper with the pictures to remind you. You can ask the interlocutor to repeat the task if you are not sure, or check what you have to do with your partner.

- Discuss each visual in turn. The pictures represent issues or aspects of the task, so you should not describe what you can see in them – try to discuss the issue or aspect that they represent.
- Make sure that you say everything you can think of about each visual before you move on to the next.
- Remember to ask your partner for their views, as well as giving your own opinion. Really listen to what your partner says so that you can respond to their ideas and suggestions appropriately.
- Don't try to reach a decision too soon, or you won't speak for three minutes.
- It is not important to reach a decision in the time – you should concentrate on using a range of language in your discussion about the pictures and the task. There is no 'right' decision.

Part 4

- The interlocutor may ask questions for you both to discuss, or they may ask you each a question in turn. You can contribute to your partner's question, as long as you do this appropriately.
- The questions in this part are more abstract, and you should give longer answers than you did in Part 1. Try to develop your ideas, and give your opinions in an interesting and coherent way.
- You can disagree with what your partner says! There are no 'right' answers to the questions.

Part 2:

Learning a new skill:

- Candidate A, you could say: *it's incredibly satisfying to be independent / it gives life-long pleasure / recipes can be hard to understand / it's probably hard not to be nervous / you'd really need to be well-prepared.*
- Candidate B, don't say too much, but give details, e.g. *I think … would get most satisfaction because …*

Entertaining others:

- Candidate B, you could say: *they're probably hoping people will give them money / busking / it looks like a school entertainment / families must feel proud / no one watches entertainment at a sports event, which must be frustrating.*
- Candidate A, you could say: *I think …. needs most practice because …*

Part 3:

- Don't describe the visuals. Decide what they illustrate, e.g. gym = healthy life v/s sedentary, office life.
- Focus your discussion on why these things are important and how important they might be in the future.
- You could say: *education is vital in the current economic climate / we need to make sure there's a planet for our grandchildren / relaxation will become increasingly important.*

Part 4:

Consider the abstract issues behind the questions. For example, you could talk about:

- *too much focus on earning money, not enough time to spend with friends / family*
- *media creates expectations, young people think they can succeed easily*

PART 1

The interlocutor will ask you a few questions about yourself and on everyday topics such as work and study, travel, entertainment, daily life and routines. For example:

- What would your ideal job be? Why?
- If you could travel to any country in the world, where would it be? Why?
- What is your favourite way to relax?

PART 2

Learning a new skill

Turn to pictures 1–3 on page 200, which show people learning a new skill.

Candidate A, compare two of the pictures and say what you think the people might be enjoying about learning this new skill, and how easy it might be for them to master it.

Candidate B, who do you think would get the most satisfaction from learning the new skill?

Entertaining others

Turn to pictures 1–3 on page 201, which show people entertaining others in different places.

Candidate B, compare two of the pictures and say why the people might be entertaining others in these different places, and how memorable it might be for the people watching.

Candidate A, who do you think would need the most practice?

PART 3

Turn to the pictures on page 202, which show some things that have become important in many people's lives.

Talk to each other about why these things have become important to some people in today's world. Then decide which two things will continue to be important to people in the future.

PART 4

Answer these questions:

- Do you think that people have the right priorities in life nowadays? Why/Why not?
- Some people say that certain jobs are overvalued and overpaid. What's your opinion?
- What part does the media play in people's expectations of life nowadays?
- Do you think that people's expectations of what is achievable are too high nowadays? Why/Why not?
- Do you think that life is easier now than it was in our grandparents' day? Why/Why not?
- Some people say that it's only possible to be happy if you have a lot of money. What's your opinion?

Guidance

Testing focus

Part 1

Although they all have the same multiple-choice format, the questions in Part 1 have a range of testing focuses.

Some questions will test a detailed understanding of parts of the text, or the use of particular vocabulary or expressions. Other questions may test your understanding of the text as a whole, or of the writer's intended message. For example, you may be asked to identify the writer's attitude or purpose in all or part of a text.

Questions targeting the whole of a text will usually come second in the pair of questions about that extract.

Part 2

Part 2 tests your ability to see the links between the different parts of a text and use these to put jumbled text in the correct order. This will mean looking for the links the writer makes between paragraphs in order to tell the story, or develop the argument coherently. These links can be of different types and, often, more than one type of link will help you answer the question. Look for:

- vocabulary links between the paragraphs, especially where an idea from one paragraph is developed in the following one. Don't expect to see the same word used, however. You should look for different words with a similar meaning.

- grammatical links between the paragraphs, especially the use of pronouns and other words that summarise or refer to things already mentioned.

- logical links of topic and focus. Look for where people, places or ideas are first introduced in the base text. If these are referred to in an option, then that paragraph must fit later in the text.

You are looking for links that work, but also looking for links that don't work. For example, if a paragraph in the options seems to fit a gap logically and contains the right sort of ideas and vocabulary, you need to check whether there are any pronouns, e.g. 'his', 'these', etc., or other references in the option that don't have a point of reference in the preceding text.

Part 3

Part 3 tests your detailed understanding of the meaning of the text, as well as general language and reading skills. Most questions relate to specific pieces of text. The last question in a set targets the text as a whole.

There is a range of testing focuses in Part 3 questions. For example, some questions will focus on a phrase or sentence in the text, whilst others will ask you to interpret the meaning of a whole paragraph.

Look for clues in the question stems to help you find the targeted piece of text. For example, 'In the third paragraph,' is a clear indication of the piece of text you need to read; but it also tells you not to consider information and ideas from elsewhere in the text when choosing your answer.

Part 4

In Part 4, you are being tested on your ability to locate relevant parts of the text, or texts, and match them to the ideas in the prompt questions. Two types of reading skill are involved.

Firstly, the ability to read through a text, understand the organisation and locate the parts relevant to a particular prompt. This involves reading quickly to get a general idea of the text, without worrying about the meaning of every word or the exact point being made by the writer.

Secondly, the skill of careful reading to understand the precise meaning in both the prompt question and in the relevant part of the base text. The prompt question will report ideas from the text, but will not use the same vocabulary and ideas to do this.

Preparation

- Do as many practice tests as possible so that you fully understand what is expected of you, and you feel confident going into the exam.

- Remember that the CAE exam aims to test real life skills. The reading that you do outside the classroom will help you become a more fluent reader.

- Read one of the set texts. Not only will this help you with comprehending longer texts at the CAE level, but you may be able to write about it in Paper 2.

- To help with Part 1, read (online or elsewhere) texts which express people's attitudes and opinions, such as interviews with famous people, and concentrate on understanding how the people feel.

- Look at English-language news articles and note down the phrases used to link the paragraphs. This will help you with Part 2 in particular.

- Practise reading texts quickly all the way through to understand the gist. You could read online articles and summarise the main ideas or opinions in them.

Part 1

You are going to read three extracts which are all concerned in some way with music. For questions **1–6**, choose the answer (**A**, **B**, **C** or **D**) which you think fits best according to the text.

In the exam, mark your answers **on the separate answer sheet**.

Tip Strip

Question 1: Be careful. Option B includes the word 'Americans', but it is not the right answer. Look for a phrasal verb in one of the numbered lines of text that will give you the answer.

Question 4: Look at the references to how long Dan has been at the school for the answer to this question.

Question 5: Be careful. Option A includes the same word as the question stem, but it is not the right answer. Look in the last paragraph for the correct answer.

Singing in an American accent

It is natural to sing with an American accent – not just a way to break into the US charts, a study has suggested. Since the 1960s, some of the biggest names in British music have been accused of faking their style to become stars in the United States. But the study found that people lapse naturally into a US *line 4* twang, because it is easier to sing that way and feels more natural.

According to researcher Andy Gibson, it is easier to sing with an American voice and is so commonplace that it should be called the 'pop music accent' instead. Mr Gibson, of the Auckland University of Technology, made the claim after tests he carried out on singers in New Zealand. He found that despite speaking with distinct Kiwi accents, they automatically sang the same words like true Americans. Singing in a local accent would sound peculiar, and the *line 11* American tendency to round off words made it easier to sing them.

Mr Gibson said, 'There were huge differences between the song and the spoken pronunciation of the same words. Studies in the past have suggested that non-American singers wilfully put on American accents but my research *line 15* suggests the opposite – that an American-influenced accent is the default when singing pop music'.

Mr Gibson believes his findings also explain why many people end up sounding like American singers when they sing their favourite songs in private. 'The American-influenced accent is automatic in the context of singing pop music, and it is used by people from all around the world,' he said. 'It actually requires effort to do something different.'

1 Which phrase from the text describes a common view of non-Americans singing with American accents?

  A lapse naturally (line 4)
  B like true Americans (line 11)
  C sound peculiar (line 11)
  D wilfully put on (line 15)

2 Which of the following is emphasised in the text as a whole?

  A It is hard not to sing pop music with an American accent.
  B People feel they should sing pop music with an American accent.
  C Singing pop music is different from singing other kinds of song.
  D The most well-known pop singers sing with an American accent.

The musical youth of Africa

The Starehe Boys Choir is singing Jambo Bwana, a Swahili classic with a simple tune and lyrics to match. So far, so jolly, with a dozen young men enthusiastically belting it out while dancing. Then, over the top of the other voices soars one so remarkable that it brings shivers to the spine. Up and up goes the descant, improvising wildly.

This is the voice of Dan Abissi, a 17-year-old pupil who had almost zero knowledge of music until he joined the school in Nairobi, Kenya, two years ago. All he knew was that he loved it. 'He wanted to come to Starehe school because we have a marching band,' says Barney Everett, a volunteer music teacher at the school. For two years, Mr Everett has been watching amazed as Dan has produced wonderful music – and not only with his voice. The piano in the music room is a terrible instrument, tinny and missing a number of notes. It takes considerable force to get it to yield a sound. Yet, in just two years, Dan is ready to take the Grade 8 exam and plays long pieces by Chopin and Liszt from memory. He has also reached a similar standard on the trumpet, trombone, violin and saxophone – none of which he had touched before he arrived at the school. Poor children in Kenya don't have access to such instruments, let alone tuition.

3 Which phrase in the first paragraph describes the writer's feeling?

   A so jolly

   B belting it out

   C shivers to the spine

   D improvising wildly

4 What is emphasised about Dan Abissi in the second paragraph?

   A how easy he has been to teach

   B how much he enjoys music

   C the effort he has made to improve

   D the speed of his musical progress

Music at work hits the wrong note

For many years, it has been believed that background music at work has all kinds of benefits, such as increasing productivity and motivation. Companies, acting on this principle, have provided music at work in the belief that it alleviates boredom, reduces stress and enhances creativity. Research has indicated that background music improves the mood of people at work and increases their brain power. However, a recent study has found that this is not necessarily true.

Researchers from the University of Wales carried out a series of simple memory tests on a group of volunteers. They did the tests while listening to a variety of background music. They also did them while listening to recordings of a sequence of random numbers being read out and recordings of the same number being repeated. They did best when listening to the same number being repeated and their scores were lowest when different kinds of music were played.

The researchers concluded that when workers are doing a 'serial recall' task, listening to music does not improve their performance, but affects it adversely. This is the case whether they are listening to music they like or music they don't enjoy. Any varied sound in the background acts as a distraction from the task at hand.

5 What do we learn about the research that was carried out?

   A It produced results that surprised the researchers.

   B It asked volunteers for their opinions on music at work.

   C It focused on how well people did one particular kind of task.

   D It included doing tasks with no background sounds at all.

6 What is the main point made in the text?

   A Music may have no impact on how well people do their work.

   B Commonly held beliefs about music at work are completely wrong.

   C Some people benefit from music at work more than others.

   D Music may cause people to do their jobs less well.

You are going to read a newspaper article about butterflies. Six paragraphs have been removed from the article. Choose from the paragraphs **A–G** the one which fits each gap (**7–12**). There is one extra paragraph which you do not need to use.

In the exam, mark your answers **on the separate answer sheet**.

Fluttering down to Mexico

Sara Evans is enchanted by the millions of butterflies that migrate to the Sierra Madra mountains for the winter.

As golden light filters through the trees, slumbering butterflies begin to wake. Amber wings unfold and lift delicate bodies into the warm Mexican air. Gentle as wood smoke rising, butterfly after butterfly leaves the safety of oaks and fir trees, until the air fills with millions of them.

7

They are just some of the nearly 250 million or so Monarch butterflies that overwinter here in the Sierra Madra mountains, in the highlands of central Mexico. Every November, this particular patch of mountainside forest in Mexico State, 130 miles north of Mexico City, becomes a temporary retreat for Monarchs escaping the colder faraway climes of Eastern Canada and the US. Their journey here is nothing short of fabulous.

8

Our journey here has been less epic. On horseback, it has taken half an hour or so to reach the butterflies. At 12,000 ft, their roosting site lines a steep, tree-filled gully. We pause by the side of it to get a closer view. There are butterflies everywhere. From trunk bottom to the highest branch, the trees are coated in them. Boughs bend under their weight and sway softly in the breeze. The purple petals of wild lupins turn orange as butterflies smother them in search of nectar. Around pools on the ground, huge clusters of thirsty Monarchs make a fluttering carpet of wings as they drink.

9

The Aztecs once believed that Monarchs were the souls of warrior ancestors migrating through the forests on their way to the land of the dead. For centuries, local people have welcomed the arrival of the butterflies in early winter, holding special celebrations in their honour.

10

En route, generations of Monarchs mate, hatch and die. The ones that reach the US and Canada are fourth generation – the great grandchildren of those that left Mexico. These fourth-generation Monarchs then fly back to Mexico in one go, somehow finding their way here and tripling their lifespan as they do so. How and why this happens remains a mystery. What is known, though, is that this unique migration is not invincible. While the Monarch butterfly itself is not endangered (populations thrive elsewhere around the world), this migration route is.

11

This is why this pocket of forest was given UNESCO World Heritage Site status in 2008. Logging is banned here and the butterflies are officially protected. Comprised of more than 58,000 hectares, the Reserve – known as the Monarch Butterfly Biosphere Reserve – is divided into five main areas, four of which are open to the public.

12

Stretching out their evergreen branches to the millions of butterflies that flutter around them, these trees are butterfly guardians, keeping the Monarchs warm and safe until they fly north on the start of one of the Earth's most complex and beautiful migrations – a journey that continues to mystify scientists and bewitch those of us fortunate enough to witness it.

Tip Strip

Option A: What does 'this' refer to in 'much of this' at the beginning of this option? Check the base text for possible references.

Option D: Look for what 'these creatures' and 'this mass of insects' could refer to in the base text.

Option G: Look for a description of a journey in the base text.

A Much of this is down to deforestation. Quite simply, as trees tumble, so does the number of Monarchs. Without the warmth and protection of the trees, butterflies that have flown thousands of miles to avoid the ravages of northern winters find themselves folding cold wings, like icy shrouds, over their tiny bodies. They freeze to death overnight.

B It is also possible to walk or hike up to see the butterflies. Paths are well-defined, but the hour-long journey can be arduous and is at altitude, so a reasonable level of fitness is required. The best time to visit is in February, when the butterflies are at their most active.

C Fed and watered, they sky dance. Tangerine bright, they fly through the gully riding the thermals, flitting between branches and sunbeams. Moving through dappled sunlight in their millions, the Monarchs cast a nectar-fuelled spell that turns the forest into a bedazzling butterfly kingdom.

D Moving closer to the sun, these creatures – a deep orange filigreed with bold black markings – look like vast stained-glass windows and block out the blue of the sky. As the butterflies dip and soar, the sound of this mass of insects in motion rumbles like a distant waterfall.

E I'm in the newest of these, El Capulin, which is the least visited and the least affected by illegal tree-cutting. The forest here thrives. Fir trees in their thousands stand tall and solid against a bright sky.

F But it was only in the 1970s that scientists discovered that it was to this remote mountainside that the Monarchs leaving North America were headed each autumn. Later research also revealed that the Monarchs arriving back in North America, in March, are not the ones that overwinter here.

G Fluttering, dipping and soaring for over 3,000 miles at around seven and a half miles an hour, the butterflies span a continent – passing over the Great Lakes, prairies, deserts, mountain ranges, cities and motorways to get to this place. Surviving storms and burning sunshine, these fragile creatures are the stars of one of the world's most dazzling migration spectacles.

You are going to read an article about a company and its employees. For questions **13–19**, choose the answer (**A**, **B**, **C** or **D**) which you think fits best according to the text.

In the exam, mark your answers **on the separate answer sheet**.

Take as much holiday time as you want

Most organisations treat vacations in the same reluctant way that parents dole out candy to their children. They dispense a certain number of days each year – but once we've reached our allotment, no more sweets for us. One US company, however, has quietly pioneered an alternative approach. Netflix Inc. is a streaming video and DVD-by-mail service that has amassed 15 million subscribers. At Netflix, the vacation policy is audaciously simple and simply audacious. Salaried employees can take as much time off as they'd like, whenever they want to take it. Nobody – not employees themselves, not managers – tracks vacation days. In other words, Netflix's holiday policy is to have no policy at all.

Back in the old days – 2004 – Netflix treated holidays the old-fashioned way: it allotted everyone 'n' days a year. You either used them up or you tried to get paid for the time you didn't consume. But eventually some employees recognised that this arrangement was at odds with how they really did their jobs. After all, they were responding to emails at weekends, they were solving problems online at home at night. And, every so often, they would take off an afternoon to ferry a child to the paediatrician or to check in on an ageing parent. Since Netflix weren't tracking how many hours people were logging each work day, these employees wondered, why should it track how many holidays people were taking each work year?

Fair point, said management. As the company explains in its *Reference Guide on our Freedom & Responsibility Culture*: 'We should focus on what people get done, not how many hours or days are worked. Just as we don't have a 9-to-5 day policy, we don't need a vacation policy'. So the company scrapped the formal plan. Today, Netflix's roughly 600 salaried employees can vacation any time they desire for as long as they want – provided that their managers know where they are and that their work is covered. This ultra-flexible, freedom-intensive approach to holiday time hasn't exactly hurt the company. Launched in 1999, Netflix is now a highly successful and growing enterprise.

Perhaps more importantly, this non-policy yields broader lessons about the modern workplace. For instance, more companies are realising that autonomy isn't the opposite of accountability – it's the pathway to it. 'Rules and policies, and regulations and stipulations are innovation killers. People do their best work when they're unencumbered,' says Steve Swasey, Netflix's Vice President for corporate communication. 'If you're spending a lot of time accounting for the time you're spending, that's time you're not innovating.'

The same goes for expenses. Employees typically don't need to get approval to spend money on entertainment, travel or gifts. Instead, the guidance is simpler: act in Netflix's best interest. It sounds delightfully adult. And it is – in every regard. People who don't produce are shown the door. 'Adequate performance,' the company says, 'gets a generous severance package.'

The idea is that freedom and responsibility, long considered incompatible, actually go together quite well. What's more, Netflix's holiday policy reveals the limits of relying on time in managing the modern workforce. In an era when people were turning screws on an assembly line or processing paper in an office, the connection between input and output was tight. The more time you spent on a task, the more you produced. But in much white-collar work today, where one good idea can mean orders of magnitude more valuable than a dozen mediocre ones, the link between the time you spend and the results you produce is murkier. Results are what matter. How you got here, or how long it took, is less relevant.

Finally, the Netflix technique demonstrates how the starting premises of workplace arrangements can shape behaviour. In his new book, *Cognitive Surplus: Creativity and Generosity in a Connected Age*, New York University scholar Clay Shirky argues that when we design systems that assume bad faith from the participants, and whose main purpose is to defend against that nasty behaviour, we often foster the very behaviour we're trying to deter. People will push and push the limits of the formal rules, search for every available loophole and look for ways to game the system when the defenders aren't watching. By contrast, a structure of rules that assumes good faith can actually encourage that behaviour.

Tip Strip

Question 14: Look in the second paragraph for the answer to this question. What does 'at odds with' mean?

Question 16: Look for Steve Swasey's name in the text. What is he quoted as saying?

Question 17: Find the word 'adult' in the text. Look at the text after this to find the answer to the question.

Question 19: Read the whole paragraph to answer this question. You are looking for the writer's opinion. Is he generally in favour of rules or against them?

13 In the first paragraph, the writer emphasises

    A how popular Netflix's holiday policy is.
    B how unusual the situation at Netflix is.
    C how important holidays are to employees.
    D how hard it can be to change a holiday policy.

14 Employees at Netflix pointed out that the company's holiday policy

    A gave them less time off than they deserved.
    B was fairer for some employees than for others.
    C was not logical in the circumstances.
    D did not reflect the way their jobs had changed.

15 The management of Netflix came to the conclusion that

    A a happy workforce was the key to future success and growth.
    B employees would be willing to do some work during their holidays.
    C they should introduce both flexible working hours and flexible holidays.
    D employees' achievements were the company's top priority.

16 Steve Swasey expresses the view that company policies often

    A prevent employees from being as effective as they could be.
    B result in employees being given the wrong roles.
    C cause confusion among employees because they are so complex.
    D assume that only certain employees can make decisions for themselves.

17 The writer says that one way in which the situation at Netflix is 'adult' is that

    A competition among employees is fierce.
    B managers' expectations of employees are very high.
    C expenses allowed for employees are kept to a minimum.
    D employees are given a lot of help to improve their performance.

18 In the writer's opinion, Netflix's approach addresses the modern issue of

    A employees wanting more responsibility than in the past.
    B wasted time being more damaging than in the past.
    C good ideas taking longer to produce than mediocre ones.
    D outcomes being more important than methods.

19 What is the main point in the final paragraph?

    A The more a company trusts its employees, the more effective they will be.
    B Netflix's attitude towards its employees would not work in every company.
    C It is understandable that many companies do not trust their employees.
    D Many employees like being given strict rules of behaviour.

Tip Strip

Question 27: Look for a word in the text that suggests 'investigative work'.

Question 31: Look for the names of occupations in the text.

Question 32: Look for words that mean 'upset' in the text.

Question 34: Look at the dates in the text. Which of them relates to the development of a particular ingredient?

You are going to read an article about an art exhibition that focuses on the subject of whether paintings are authentic or fake. For questions **20–34**, choose from the sections of the article (**A–F**). The sections may be chosen more than once.

In the exam, mark your answers **on the separate answer sheet**.

In which section of the article are the following mentioned?

how easy it is to suggest that a picture is not authentic | **20** |

the fact that keepers of pictures frequently examine paintings | **21** |

information that solved a mystery about a painting known to be authentic | **22** |

an incorrect idea about the attitude of people responsible for exhibiting pictures | **23** |

the fundamental issue surrounding research into a picture | **24** |

similarities in an artist's style in more than one place | **25** |

reasons why it is understandable that a certain mistake was made | **26** |

investigative work that showed that a picture was an unusual example of an artist's work | **27** |

the willingness of experts to accept that their beliefs are wrong | **28** |

the different categories of people involved in examining pictures | **29** |

evidence of changes made to a picture | **30** |

evidence from an expert outside the world of art | **31** |

an accusation that upset the writer personally | **32** |

a picture that would not be mistakenly considered authentic | **33** |

the early history of a particular ingredient | **34** |

Seeing through the fakes

A   *Close Examination* at the National Gallery looks at 40 problematic works from the Gallery's collection – including outright forgeries, misattributions, pastiches, copies, altered or over-restored paintings, and works whose authenticity has wrongly been doubted. The curators have taken on a huge subject – the range of possibilities museum professionals take into consideration when they investigate a picture's status and the variety of technical procedures conservation scientists use to establish authorship and date. The case histories they discuss have a single common denominator. In whatever direction and to whatever conclusion the combined disciplines of connoisseurship, science and art history may lead, the study of any work of art begins with a question: is the work by the artist to whom it is attributed?

B   A good example is an Italian painting on panel that the National Gallery acquired in 1923, as the work of an artist in the circle of the Italian fifteenth-century painter Melozzo da Forlì. Today, we find it incredible that anyone was ever fooled by a picture that looks like it was painted by a Surrealist follower of Salvador Dalí. But this is to forget how little was known about Melozzo 90 years ago, and how little could be done in the conservation lab to determine the date of pigments or wood panel. Even so, from the moment the picture was acquired, sceptics called its status into question. Nothing could be proved until 1960 when a costume historian pointed out the many anachronisms in the clothing. When technological advances enabled the gallery to test the pigments, they were found to be from the nineteenth century.

C   Scientific evidence can be invaluable but it has to be used with caution and in tandem with historical research. For example, Corot's ravishing sketch *The Roman Campagna, with the Claudian Aqueduct* has always been dated to about 1826, soon after the artist's arrival in Rome. However, the green pigment called viridian that Corot used throughout the picture only became available to artists in the 1830s. The landscape wasn't a fake and for stylistic reasons couldn't have been painted later than the mid-1820s. All became clear when art historians did further research and discovered that the firm that sold artists' supplies to Corot in Paris started making the newly developed colour available to selected customers in the 1820s, long before it came into widespread use.

D   The flipside of a fake, but capable of doing equal violence to an artist's reputation, occurs when an authentic work is mistakenly labelled a forgery. Back in 1996, I well remember how distressing it was to read an article in which the former director of the Metropolitan Museum of Art, Thomas Hoving, declared that Uccello's lovely little canvas of *St George and the Dragon* was forged. The gallery therefore X-rayed the picture and tested paint samples, before concluding that it was a rare survival of a work by Uccello dating from the early 1470s. Hoving was irresponsible not because he questioned the attribution of a much-loved work, but because he went public without first asking the gallery to carry out a thorough scientific analysis.

E   Anyone can label a picture a fake or a copy, but their opinions are worthless unless they can support them with tangible proof. One picture that's been smeared in this way is Raphael's *Madonna of the Pinks*. In this exhibition, we are shown infrared photographs that reveal the presence both of major corrections which a copyist would not need to make, and also of under drawing in a hand comparable to Raphael's when he sketched on paper. The pigments and painting technique exactly match those that the artist used in other works of about the same date.

F   For all its pleasures, the show also has an unspoken agenda. It is a riposte to the mistaken belief that museums have anything to gain by hiding the true status of the art they own. As the downgrading in this show of Courbet's *Self-Portrait* to the status of a posthumous copy of a picture in the Louvre shows, the opposite is the case: museums and galleries constantly question, revise, reattribute and re-date the works in their care. If they make a mistake, they acknowledge it. If a respected scholar re-attributes a painting, the picture is relabelled or taken off view. The press loves to publish stories and letters accusing museums of lurid cover-ups, usually originating from a very small number of amateurs who rarely know what they are talking about. But any curator or director will tell you that art museums have to deal in the truth, because if they lose credibility, they lose the reason for their existence.

Guidance

Testing focus

Part 1

The focus of assessment in Part 1 is on manipulating given information so that the target reader can respond appropriately. You must include all the points raised in the task; otherwise the target reader will not be fully informed. Marks are awarded for appropriate content, organisation, coherence and cohesion, range of language and the effect created on the target reader. You should use an appropriate register for the given task.

Part 2

The focus of assessment in Part 2 is on writing appropriately, coherently and answering the question. You should use an appropriate organisation and layout for the given task. Marks are awarded for suitable content, clear organisation and good coherence and cohesion (which might include using appropriate linking words). You should also use a range of language (vocabulary and structures) in the right register for the given task, and achieve the appropriate effect on the target reader.

Preparation

General points

- Practise writing tasks in the given time. There is no point in spending longer than 45 minutes when writing a practice task. In the exam, each task carries equal marks, so there is nothing to gain by spending too long on Part 1 and then not having enough time to complete Part 2.
- Practise writing only the required number of words. There is no point in writing answers that are too long as they may be irrelevant and take up too much time.
- Work with a partner so that you can help each other to spot recurring mistakes by editing each other's work. Keep a checklist of your own grammatical and spelling mistakes so that you know what to look out for.
- Get into the habit of reading the instructions carefully every time you answer a question, and always check your writing to make sure that you have included everything required.
- Check that you understand the appropriate format and register for every type of task found in the exam.
- Revise connectors so that you can use these appropriately in any task.
- Always read your answer through after you have written it to check that it is coherent and makes sense. Don't only check for grammatical mistakes.

Part 1

- Read all the input texts before you start to write, and don't lift words or phrases from the input as they may be in the wrong register.
- Do as much work as you can on different registers and ways of saying the same thing. Work on Paper 3 will also help you with this.
- Practise rewriting sentences using your own words.

Part 2

- Spend time thinking of issues and ideas for different topics so that you have ideas for the different tasks. You could build up a file with these ideas and refer to it when you practise writing a task or revise for the exam.
- Consider what your own strengths in writing are. Do you like writing lively and interesting answers, or more formal and informative answers? This will help you choose the best type of task in the exam.
- Consider reading one of the set texts. Reading is an excellent way of improving your writing, and it means that you could answer Question 5 if you wanted to.
- The questions in the exam may require you to use different language functions. Work on different ways of saying things such as giving advice, describing, explaining, and so on.

You **must** answer this question. Write your answer in **180–220** words in an appropriate style. In the exam, write your answer **on the separate answer sheet provided**.

Tip Strip

Question 1:

- Although this is an informal letter, you are giving serious information to a friend who has asked for your help.

- Read all the input and decide what Juan needs to know. You should answer his questions, using your notes as a guide.

- Don't use words or phrases from your diary in your answer, but use them as a starting point. You should read the diary carefully, write down the ideas and then use your own words in your letter.

- You have to decide whether Juan should apply for the job. Start with his priorities, match them up to your own experience and then explain whether you would recommend it or not.

- You can provide extra details but don't be too imaginative or give too much detail about one point, in case you forget to include all the required points.

- Use a range of vocabulary and language functions. In this task you have to explain why Juan's requirements are reasonable or not. Justify your ideas using your own experience and recommend a course of action.

1   Last year, you spent four months working for an international company that organises winter holidays. Your friend, Juan, has contacted you to ask whether he should apply for the same job this year.

Read the extract from Juan's letter and the notes from your diary. Then, **using the information appropriately**, write a letter to Juan saying whether you think he should apply for the job, giving reasons for your opinion.

> I love skiing and I'd like to try snowboarding too – without paying for it! I could earn money before going to university and I'd get to learn another language. It sounds pretty easy really.
>
> Should I go for it?
>
> Juan

December 15th: Busy day – clients needed to get equipment. Paid for my own ski pass!

December 20th: Snow conditions poor – lots of complaints. Organised other activities. Pretty stressed.

January 10th: Good snow but had to do paperwork. Clients of mixed nationalities, so using English.

March 29th: Skied all day – fantastic! Leaving tomorrow . . .

Write your **letter**. You do not need to include postal addresses. You should use your own words as far as possible.

Tip Strip

Question 2:

- This article should be interesting and engaging for the reader, so it should not be too formal in style. It should be clearly organised and paragraphed.
- Think of an engaging title to catch the reader's interest.
- Use techniques, such as rhetorical questions, to interest and engage readers.
- In this task, you must describe the event, explain what made it interesting or unusual and justify your reasons for enjoying it or not.

Question 3:

- This is an essay for your teacher, so you should use formal or semi-formal language.
- Decide whether you agree with the statement or not, then plan your argument in clear paragraphs.
- Discuss all three issues mentioned in the task – communication, relationships and working life.
- Make sure you introduce the topic clearly, and that your conclusion follows your argument logically.

Question 4:

- Your information sheet may have headings and bullet points to make it easy for students to pick out relevant information.
- In this task you must describe the club and its activities, explain the costs, evaluate the advantages of joining the club and outline future plans.
- Make sure that you show a range of language. As it is for college students, think of interesting and colourful language and structures to use.

Write an answer to one of the questions **2–5** in this part. Write your answer in **220–260** words. In the exam, write your answer **on the separate answer sheet provided**, and put the question number in the box at the top of the page.

---

2   You see the following announcement in an international magazine.

> Have you been to an interesting and unusual celebration recently? For example, an eighteenth birthday or a wedding that was a bit different? Write an article and tell us about it, explaining why it was interesting and unusual, and whether you enjoyed it. We will publish the most interesting articles in the next edition!

Write your **article**.

3   Following a class discussion on how technology has affected the way we live today, your teacher has asked you to write an essay discussing the statement 'We would all be better off without technology!'. You should consider how technology has affected communication, relationships and working life.

Write your **essay**.

4   You are organising a new sports club at your college, and want to produce an information sheet about the club in order to get people interested and attract members. In your information sheet, you need to tell people about the sporting activities they can do, the costs involved, the advantages of joining and any future plans the club may have.

Write your **information sheet**.

- In **Question 5a)** you have to write a review for a college magazine, so you can use a semi-formal style, but you should include personal opinions.
- The point of the review is to give the magazine readers enough information about the book so they understand the importance of the title and can decide whether they want to read it.
- Think carefully about the title of your book and reasons why it is good.
- Outline the story briefly, explain why it is a good title and whether you would recommend the book to others, giving your reasons.
- In **Question 5b)**, you must write an article for a magazine. The point of the article is to get your article published, so try to make it as interesting as possible.
- You should use different language functions – identify, describe and explain.
- Use techniques such as rhetorical questions and try to finish with an interesting punchline or conclusion.

5 Answer one of the following two questions based on a book you have read. In the exam you will have to write about one of two specific titles. Write the letter **(a)** or **(b)** as well as the number 5 on your answer sheet.

(a) A college magazine is running a series of book reviews featuring books which have particularly good titles. Write a review for the magazine about a book you have read which you think had a good title. You should briefly say what your book is about, explain why you think its title is particularly good and whether you would recommend it to other students at the college.

Write your **review**.

(b) You see an announcement in a magazine.

They changed the way we think!

We are making a list of the most influential characters in fiction.

Write an article telling us about a character in fiction who has changed your opinion about something. In your letter you should:

- identify who the character is

- describe what the character is like

- explain why the character changed your way of thinking

We will publish the best articles in the magazine.

Write your **article**.

Guidance

Testing focus

Part 1

In Part 1, there is a range of testing focuses. Most questions focus on your knowledge of vocabulary and how it is used. Questions may focus on:

- your knowledge of general vocabulary related to the topic of the text.
- the relationship between words, e.g. which preposition is used after a word, or whether it is followed by an infinitive or a gerund.
- your knowledge of fixed expressions and collocations, including phrasal verbs.
- your knowledge of linking words and phrases. This tests whether you have understood the meaning of the whole text.

Part 2

Part 2 mostly tests your knowledge of grammar and sentence structure. Questions can focus on:

- the relationship between words, e.g. which words go together to form a fixed expression or phrasal verb.
- sentence structure, e.g. asking you to insert the correct relative pronoun or a conjunction.
- other grammatical words, e.g. quantifiers, determiners, articles, etc.
- linking words and phrases to test whether you have understood the meaning of the whole text.

Part 3

Part 3 tests whether you can create the correct form of the word to fit in the sentence. Questions may focus on:

- your knowledge of prefixes and suffixes.

- your grammatical knowledge, e.g. which form of the word is needed to complete the meaning in the sentence.
- common expressions and collocations, e.g. which form of the word is used to form a common expression.
- your knowledge of compound words.

Part 4

In Part 4, you are tested on your knowledge of vocabulary. The tested words will all be familiar to you, though you may not be familiar with all three uses of the word.

- Questions may test your knowledge of lexical patterns, e.g. collocations, phrasal verbs.
- Questions require you to identify the correct form of the word to complete each sentence, e.g. whether nouns are singular or plural and which form verbs should appear in.

Part 5

Part 5 tests both your grammatical and lexical knowledge. Questions always have two testing points, e.g. a change to a word from the input sentence, plus a change to the word order to create a new sentence pattern.

- You are tested on your ability to express the same ideas using different grammatical forms and patterns, e.g. in a sentence that starts with a different word, or using a different part of speech.
- Questions may test your knowledge of fixed phrases and collocations by asking you to find the words that combine with those already in the target sentence.
- Your answer must be grammatically accurate.

Preparation

- Do as many practice tests as possible so that you fully understand what is expected of you and you feel confident going into the exam.
- Keep a vocabulary notebook in which you write down useful vocabulary you come across, arranged by topic.
- Try to learn words in chunks rather than in isolation. When you learn a new word, write down not only the word, but also the sentence it is used in.
- When you're doing practice tests, keep a note of items you get wrong and attempt them again two weeks later.

- Write a verb on one side of a card, and its dependent preposition on the other. Test yourself on them in your free time.
- Choose a text in English and underline all of the prepositions. Then go back through and decide which ones are part of set word patterns.
- Go through a reading text and write a list of all of the adjectives. Is there a noun in the same verb family? What about an adjective?

Part 1

For questions **1–12**, read the text below and decide which answer (**A**, **B**, **C** or **D**) best fits each gap. There is an example at the beginning (**0**).

In the exam, mark your answers **on the separate answer sheet**.

Example:

0 A turns   **B** swaps   **C** reforms   **D** switches

0	A	B	C	D
	—	☐	☐	☐

Tip Strip
Question 2: The word you are looking for creates a phrasal verb with 'up'. Which of the words suggests water?
Question 5: Which of the words creates an expression with 'afield' which means 'a long way away'?
Question 9: Only one of these words can be followed by the preposition 'with'.
Question 10: Only one of these words collocates with 'direct' to mean the customers' real opinions.
Question 12: Which of these words means 'look for' and doesn't need a preposition after it?

Seaside Artist

He was once a textile designer for a leading fashion house, but these days Andrew Ruffhead **(0)** .... seaside rubbish into art. Andrew is what is sometimes **(1)** .... a beachcomber. He goes out gathering rubbish on his local beach, where all sorts of interesting things are **(2)** .... up. He later uses these as the **(3)** .... materials for his artwork, mostly sculptures and collages in the shape of fish, like tuna, and crustaceans, **(4)** .... crabs and lobsters. Andrews's eye-catching work, which looks equally good in kitchens, bathrooms and gardens, has been a great success with seaside fans all over the globe, with his funky fish drifting as **(5)** .... afield as Greece and Cape Cod in New England.

(6) .... as Andrew can tell you which beach the materials from each sculpture came from, he is also **(7)** .... to know where his work will be hung. It is this interaction with the public that he particularly enjoys. Open to the public by **(8)** ...., his small informal studio also **(9)** .... him with an opportunity to get direct **(10)** .... from his customers. People often bring their own beach finds to the studio, although they are not always willing to **(11)** .... their treasures, preferring to **(12)** .... Andrew's advice about how to make them into works of art. It's advice that Andrew's happy to give.

1	**A** named	**B** known	**C** entitled	**D** called
2	**A** thrown	**B** washed	**C** dumped	**D** tossed
3	**A** natural	**B** crude	**C** plain	**D** raw
4	**A** such as	**B** for instance	**C** for example	**D** much as
5	**A** distant	**B** long	**C** far	**D** remote
6	**A** Indeed	**B** Quite	**C** Rather	**D** Just
7	**A** desire	**B** fond	**C** keen	**D** wish
8	**A** schedule	**B** appointment	**C** timetable	**D** booking
9	**A** provides	**B** gains	**C** gives	**D** produces
10	**A** review	**B** feedback	**C** opinion	**D** report
11	**A** let go	**B** part with	**C** give out	**D** leave off
12	**A** search	**B** enquire	**C** seek	**D** pursue

Part 2

Tip Strip

Question 13: Which verb is used together with the noun 'use'?

Question 14: Which word completes the comparison with 'earlier'?

Question 17: Which preposition usually follows 'similar'?

Question 19: Which word completes the fixed expression?

Question 21: A modal verb is needed here.

For questions **13–27**, read the text below and think of the word which best fits each gap. There is an example at the beginning (**0**).

In the exam, you have to write your answers **IN CAPITAL LETTERS on the separate answer sheet**.

Example: | 0 | L | E | D | | | | | | | | | | | | | | | | |

Early Stone Tools

A recent discovery has **(0)** .... scientists to revise their ideas about the ancestors of early humans. It seems they started to **(13)** .... use of stone tools nearly one million years earlier **(14)** .... had previously been thought. Archaeologists revised the date **(15)** .... spotting distinctive marks made by stone tools on animal bones dating **(16)** .... nearly three and a half million years. The remains, including a rib from a cow-like creature and a thigh bone from an animal similar in size **(17)** .... a goat, were recovered from an old river bed **(18)** .... was being excavated in Ethiopia.

The use of simple stone tools to remove meat from bones represents a crucial moment in human history. **(19)** .... a result of turning to meat for sustenance, the early humans developed larger brains, which **(20)** .... turn enabled them to make more sophisticated tools. The bones unearthed in Ethiopia **(21)** .... well represent the very beginning of that process.

(22) .... scientists are still hoping to discover is whether the stone tools were manufactured specifically to meet a need **(23)** .... whether they were natural stones that **(24)** .... chance had the right shape and the necessary sharp edges. Either **(25)** ...., it seems likely that the early humans carried the tools around with them **(26)** .... than relying on being able to find suitable ones **(27)** .... the need arose.

Tip Strip

Question 28: You need to add a suffix to this verb to make a noun.

Question 32: This word needs a prefix which means 'again'.

Question 33: You need to form an adverb here.

Question 35: Add another word before 'night' to create a compound adjective.

Question 37: Add a suffix to turn this verb into an adjective.

For questions **28–37**, read the text below. Use the word given in capitals at the end of some of the lines to form a word that fits in the gap **in the same line**. There is an example at the beginning (**0**).

In the exam, you have to write your answers **IN CAPITAL LETTERS on the separate answer sheet**.

Example: | 0 | A | P | P | E | A | L | I | N | G | | | | | | | | | |

Marathon Dreams

The idea of taking part in long-distance running races seems **(0)** ....   **APPEAL**

After all, who hasn't watched TV **(28)** .... of the London or   **COVER**

New York Marathon and been moved by the stories of everyday

people tackling that most epic of **(29)** .... races. From the   **ENDURE**

comfort of your armchair, your heart swells with **(30)** .... for   **ADMIRE**

the contenders as they cross the finish line, on the point of

(31) ...., yet exhilarated.   **EXHAUST**

Inspired, you vow to **(32)** .... your own previous fitness levels   **GAIN**

and do something similar. In fact, tomorrow you'll put on your

trainers and have a go at 20 minutes around the park.

But when tomorrow comes, the motivation is not quite so strong.

(33) ...., you give up because you find the wet weather rather   **POSSIBLE**

(34) ...., or you make the effort and ache terribly afterwards.   **COURAGE**

This happens when you try to do too much too soon. Fitness can't

be built up **(35)** ...., it has to be done gradually.   **NIGHT**

Taking part in a marathon is a serious undertaking and calls for

thorough training and a great level of **(36)** .... Indeed,   **COMMIT**

top runners say that it's **(37)** .... to begin with a trip to the doctor   **ADVISE**

to see if you are physically fit enough to embark on the training.

Tip Strip

Question 38: All three sentences are phrasal verbs with 'up', but in each one the meaning is slightly different. The first sentence has the most literal meaning.

Question 39: The second sentence contains a very common collocation.

Question 40: Do the second sentence first. It's a part of the body that is being used as a verb.

Question 42: In the second sentence, you need the precise term in the context of a magazine.

For questions **38–42**, think of only one word which can be used appropriately in all three sentences. Here is an example (**0**).

Example:

0   I was on the .... of booking my holiday when my boss said I might have to change the dates.

As the meeting drew to a close, the chairperson moved on to the final .... on the agenda.

Theo couldn't see the .... of getting to the airport too early, as the check-in desk only opened one hour before the flight departed.

Example: | 0 | P | O | I | N | T | | | | | | | | | | | | | | |

In the exam, write **only** the missing word **IN CAPITAL LETTERS on the separate answer sheet**.

---

38   Sam .... up his books and made his way towards the library exit. He'd done enough studying for one day.

The coach moved really slowly through the city streets, but .... up speed once it was on the motorway.

Jennie has .... up a bit of an American accent since she's been living in New York.

39   It's always best to write up your lecture notes immediately, when the facts are still .... in your mind.

Simona had a bit of a headache, so went outside to get some .... air.

When buying .... rather than frozen fish, always check the sell-by date on the label.

40   To get to the place where the rock festival's being held, ... north on the motorway and turn right at the second exit.

In football, you can .... the ball, but you can't touch it with your hand unless you're the goalkeeper.

Philip was invited to .... the team's next expedition into the rainforest.

41 The new airport terminal has been in .... for three months now.

The building's main .... will be to act as a meeting place for local teenagers.

What's the .... of asking for a pay rise if you know there's no chance of getting one?

42 I know you don't approve of the way I drive, but there's no need to make a big .... of it.

You can read about the competition in this week's .... of the magazine.

There's a rather delicate .... we need to discuss, concerning one of your classmates.

Tip Strip

Question 44: You need to create a passive sentence here.

Question 45: You need to introduce a new verb into this sentence.

Question 46: Which modal verb will you use after 'wish'?

Question 47: Which phrasal verb will match 'attend' in the input sentence?

Question 50: The second sentence is in direct speech. What tense comes after 'since'?

For questions **43–50**, complete the second sentence so that it has a similar meaning to the first sentence, using the word given. **Do not change the word given.** You must use between **three** and **six** words, including the word given. Here is an example (**0**).

Example:

0 Chloe would only eat a pizza if she could have a mushroom topping.

ON

Chloe .... a mushroom topping when she ate a pizza.

The gap can be filled with the words 'insisted on having', so you write:

Example:	**0**	INSISTED ON HAVING

In the exam, write **only** the missing words **IN CAPITAL LETTERS on the separate answer sheet**.

---

43 It's difficult to say why some cars are easier to drive than others.

MAKES

It's difficult to say .... easier to drive than others.

44 Many people have blamed the hot weather for the rise in petty crime.

WIDELY

The hot weather .... for the rise in petty crime.

45 The wind was so strong that we couldn't walk along the seafront.

STRENGTH

The .... meant it was impossible to walk along the seafront.

46 Sandra regrets not being able to visit her grandmother more often.

WISHES

Sandra .... visit her grandmother more often.

47 Everyone expects a lot of people to attend the rock band's farewell concert.

TURN

A huge crowd is .... the rock band's farewell concert.

48 I want to say that I'm not at all satisfied with the service at this hotel.

MY

I want to express .... with the service at this hotel.

49 Tomorrow's match is very likely to be cancelled.

CHANCES

. The .... cancelled are quite high.

50 Diana complained that she hadn't had a good cup of coffee for ages.

SINCE

'It .... a good cup of coffee,' Diana complained.

Guidance

Testing focus

Part 1

There is a range of testing focuses in Part 1 questions.

- Some questions focus on a detailed understanding of parts of the text, or on the use of particular vocabulary or expressions.

- Some questions test your understanding of the text as a whole, or of the speakers' attitudes, feelings or opinions. The second question in a pair usually targets the whole text.

Part 2

Part 2 tests your ability to locate, understand and record specific information from the listening text.

- This task does not test grammar, so you don't have to change the form of the words you hear. However, you should check the grammar of the sentence to check if the word you have heard is, for example, singular or plural.

- This task doesn't test extra information. If you write too much, you risk losing the mark by not creating a good sentence.

Part 3

Part 3 tests a detailed understanding of the speakers' feelings, attitudes and opinions. Each question relates to a specific section of text and there is a range of testing focus.

- Some questions will focus on a phrase or sentence in the text.

- Some questions ask you to interpret the meaning of a whole long turn from the main speaker.

Part 4

Part 4 is designed to test your understanding of what people say, as well as the ability to pick out keywords and phrases. Each of the two tasks has a separate focus and the testing focus in each task is separate. So getting the right answer for a speaker in Task One doesn't help you to get the right answer in Task Two.

Preparation

- Remember that the CAE exam aims to test real life skills, so any listening practice you do is likely to improve your general listening skills.

- When you're doing practice tests, pay attention to synonyms and paraphrasing in questions, and try to use these techniques yourself in speaking and writing. This will help you become familiar with how these devices work and help you to spot them in the exam.

- Practise using the sample answer sheets so that you will know how to fill them in on the day of the exam.

- Search online for an English language radio programme that interests you. Listen and try to note down the key ideas as you listen.

- Watch English language DVDs with the subtitles on. Concentrate on connecting what you hear with what you read in the subtitles. Watch the film (or sections of the film) again with the subtitles turned off. This time you'll already have an idea of what's being said, and can really focus on what you hear.

Part 1

You will hear three different extracts. For questions **1–6**, choose the answer (**A**, **B** or **C**) which fits best according to what you hear. There are two questions for each extract.

In the exam, write your answers **on the separate answer sheet**.

Extract One

You hear two students talking about shopping for clothes.

1   What do they agree about?

    A   It's better to buy inexpensive clothes.

    B   Shopping for clothes is to be avoided.

    C   People should respect your taste in clothes.

2   According to the man, many people see shopping as a way of

    A   achieving social status.

    B   making a comment on society.

    C   identifying with a particular social group.

Extract Two

You hear part of an interview with a musician called Max.

3   What does he say about his music in his teenage years?

    A   He wanted to keep it to himself.

    B   He felt quite self-confident about it.

    C   He was reluctant to ask for help with it.

4   What does he suggest about his recording contract?

    A   It didn't guarantee him ongoing success.

    B   It didn't mean he could give up other work.

    C   It didn't have very good terms and conditions.

You hear part of a discussion programme in which two dancers are talking about their careers.

5 The man was inspired to train as a dancer by

   A one reaction to a performance he gave.

   B some encouragement from his friends.

   C the athletic nature of the activity.

6 The woman admits that as a teenager, she

   A behaved unreasonably at times.

   B resented her parents' ambitions for her.

   C managed to keep certain feelings to herself.

Part 2

You will hear a radio reporter called Sally Nelson telling a group of teenagers about how work-experience schemes have helped her in her career. For questions **7–14**, complete the sentences.

In the exam, write your answers **on the separate answer sheet**.

RADIO REPORTER

At university, Sally did a degree in a subject called ▢ **7**

After graduating, Sally's first job was as a ▢ **8**

Sally uses the word ▢ **9** to describe how she felt on her first day at a radio station.

Sally was asked to join a ▢ **10** by the boss of the Brighton radio station.

Sally most enjoyed doing ▢ **11** on air during her time in Brighton.

One of Sally's colleagues in Brighton advised her to study

▢ **12** at evening classes.

At the national broadcasting company, Sally worked mostly on the

▢ **13** desk.

Sally identifies ▢ **14** as the main benefit of doing work experience.

Tip Strip

Question 7: Be careful. Three degree courses are mentioned. What was the exact name of the one Sally did?

Question 9: You are listening for an adjective that means 'rather frightened by everything around her'.

Question 10: Two schemes are mentioned. One is the name of what Sally did, the other is a comparison she makes with another scheme. Be sure to write the correct one.

Question 13: Be careful. Three desks are mentioned. Listen for the one Sally worked on most often.

Question 14: You are listening for an abstract noun that describes a quality.

Tip Strip

Question 15: Listen for the phrase 'it was pure chance'. The answer comes soon afterwards.

Question 17: Listen for the interviewer's question about 'starting work on a production' and listen to Neil's answer. What does he say is 'pretty vital'?

Question 19: Does Neil read reviews? How often? Why?

Question 20: Listen to the last thing Neil says. What does he prefer, films or plays? Why?

Part 3

You will hear an interview with a man called Neil Strellson, who works as a set designer in the theatre. For questions **15–20**, choose the answer (**A**, **B**, **C** or **D**) which fits best according to what you hear.

In the exam, write your answers **on the separate answer sheet**.

15 Neil first decided he wanted to work as a set designer when

    A he went to see plays with his parents.

    B he started studying drama at university.

    C he was asked to help out on a student production.

    D he gave up on his childhood dream of becoming an actor.

16 What does Neil say about working as an assistant set designer?

    A He did it because he was short of money.

    B He saw it as a way of making useful contacts.

    C He was too young to take full advantage of it at first.

    D He appreciated the chance to put theory into practice.

17 For Neil, the most important aspect of starting work on a new production is

    A establishing a working relationship with the director.

    B agreeing how many scenery changes are needed.

    C feeling an involvement with the play itself.

    D doing a set of preliminary sketches.

18 Why does Neil prefer working on several productions at once?

    A He finds that it stimulates his creativity.

    B He feels it gives him increased financial security.

    C It means he can avoid going to all of the opening nights.

    D It stops him getting too involved in the problems of any one show.

19 How does Neil feel about reviews?

    A It's better not to take them too seriously.

    B It helps to read a range of them regularly.

    C It's flattering if the set's singled out for praise.

    D It's annoying if the set isn't specifically mentioned.

20 What does Neil say about designing film sets?

    A He finds it less challenging than the theatre.

    B He'd like the chance to work on a really good film.

    C He hasn't really worked out how to approach it yet.

    D He isn't sure whether he has the skills to do it effectively.

Part 4

You will hear five short extracts in which people are talking about a four-day hiking trip to a remote historical site in the mountains.

In the exam, mark your answers **on the separate answer sheet.**

TASK ONE

For questions **21–25**, choose from the list (**A–H**) the reason each speaker gives for going on the trip.

While you listen you must complete both tasks.

A to fulfil a long-held ambition	
B to keep someone company	Speaker 1 [ ] [21]
C to set a personal challenge	Speaker 2 [ ] [22]
D to celebrate something	Speaker 3 [ ] [23]
E to prove someone wrong	Speaker 4 [ ] [24]
F to complete a set of experiences	Speaker 5 [ ] [25]
G to follow someone's example	
H to meet like-minded people	

TASK TWO

For questions **26–30**, choose from list (**A–H**) the aspect of the trip each speaker found most memorable.

A the impressive architecture	
B the view from the site	Speaker 1 [ ] [26]
C the support of companions	Speaker 2 [ ] [27]
D the historical notes	Speaker 3 [ ] [28]
E the route taken	Speaker 4 [ ] [29]
F the overnight accommodation	Speaker 5 [ ] [30]
G the food provided	
H the attitude of the guide	

Tip Strip

Speaker 1: Listen to what he says about his wife. It helps with Task One.

Speaker 2: When she says 'what made it for me', what is she referring to? This helps with Task Two.

Speaker 3: When he says 'I went along for her sake', what does he mean?

Speaker 4: Listen to the beginning of what she says. It helps with Task Two.

Speaker 5: When he says 'I'll never forget' ..., what is he referring to?

Guidance

Testing focus

General points

- The examiner marks in different categories – grammatical and lexical resource, discourse management, pronunciation, and interactive communication, and will be marking on all aspects of the assessment criteria throughout the test.
- The interlocutor gives a global mark at the end of the test.
- It is important to remember that you are not being assessed on your actual ideas, just on the language you use to express them. Don't worry if you feel you have nothing important to say – it is the language that counts!

Part 1

- The focus is on general interactional language and social interaction. Try to be relaxed and answer the questions in an interesting way.

Part 2

- The focus is on organising a longer unit of discourse and you have to compare the pictures, express opinions and speculate about them.

Part 3

- The focus is on keeping an interaction going by exchanging ideas, giving and justifying opinions, agreeing and disagreeing, suggesting, speculating, evaluating and reaching a decision through negotiation with your partner. This means that you should develop the discussion as much as possible and use a range of language.

Part 4

- The focus is on giving and justifying opinions and agreeing and disagreeing with your partner's ideas. Although you may be asked individual questions, you can develop your partner's ideas.

Revision tips

Part 1

- Although you should not prepare speeches, practise talking about general topics in small groups or with your partner.
- Prepare questions for your partner on given topics, and take it in turns to ask and answer the questions.
- Practise this part for three minutes so that you feel how long your answers should be.
- Practise using different tenses in your answers, e.g. if you are asked what you like doing in the evenings, you could say that you used to play tennis, but now you prefer to watch films.

Part 2

- Practise comparing pictures from newspapers or magazines. Focus on comparing, not describing, and think about different ways of making comparisons.
- When you practise exam tasks, work with a partner and try to find three things to say when comparing pictures and three things about the rest of the task. This technique will help you to organise your talk.
- Practise organising your talk by linking ideas using connectors, e.g. *whereas, conversely*. Build up a list of these connectors so that you can use them confidently.
- Practise by yourself by looking at pictures and thinking of interesting things to say about them. You could practise by writing down keywords and using them to organise your talk in a logical way.

Part 3

- Practise doing exam tasks in three minutes. Although you should not worry about the time as the interlocutor will stop you after three minutes, you should make sure that you don't stop before the three minutes are over.

- Make sure that you practise listening to your partner so that you can respond appropriately to what they say.
- Think about different ways of asking your partner for their opinion, and of agreeing and disagreeing, e.g. *that's interesting, but not exactly what I think*.
- It is important for you to initiate ideas as well as responding to what your partner says, so practise ways of doing that, e.g. *What do you think about …*
- Practise using conversation 'fillers' to give yourself time to think, if you need to.
- Keep a list of language functions such as interrupting politely, moving a discussion on and reacting to what your partner says.

Part 4

- Discuss issues in the news so that you have ideas on different topics. You can also get ideas from the CAE reading and listening texts that you study in class. Keep a note of any good ideas so that you can read them again before the exam in case that topic comes up.
- Remember that you can disagree with your partner and that this is often very productive! Practise with a partner by making statements for your partner to agree or disagree with.
- Remember that the examiners can only mark what they hear. Try to contribute to general discussions in class as much as possible so that you get used to expressing your opinions.

PART 1

The interlocutor will ask you a few questions about yourself and on everyday topics such as work and study, travel, entertainment, daily life and routines. For example:

- Do you think it would be a good idea to work in another country for a short time? Why/Why not?
- What is your favourite kind of music to listen to?
- Are you an organised kind of person? Why/Why not?

PART 2

Playing games

Turn to pictures 1–3 on page 203, which show people playing games.

Candidate A, compare two of the pictures and say how people might benefit from playing games like these, and how the players might be feeling.

Candidate B, who do you think is benefiting most from playing the game?

Taking a break

Turn to pictures 1–3 on page 204, which show people taking a break in different ways.

Candidate B, compare two of the pictures and say why the people might need to relax and how relaxing these situations might actually be.

Candidate A, who seems to be finding it most difficult to relax?

PART 3

Turn to the pictures on page 205, which show some things that give people satisfaction.

First, talk together about what satisfaction people get from having things like these. Then decide which two things would provide the most satisfaction in the long term.

PART 4

Answer these questions:

- How important is it to follow trends in fashion? Why?
- Do you think it's better to make your own entertainment or be entertained? Why?
- Do you think that people's priorities change as they get older? Why/Why not?
- Some people say that having money is not the most important thing. What's your opinion?
- Is it possible to be too rich? Why/Why not?
- What kind of responsibilities do you think rich people have?

Part 1

You are going to read three extracts which are all concerned in some way with courses. For questions **1–6**, choose the answer (**A**, **B**, **C** or **D**) which you think fits best according to the text.

In the exam, mark your answers **on the separate answer sheet**.

If you go down to the woods …

I am tracking animals with Alan English, who runs inspirational courses in the Forest of Dean – days so strangely gripping that as soon as I get home, I will be out in woods at dusk trying to recall everything he taught me. With my back against a trunk to break up my silhouette, I will sit tight and wait. I will hope to bump into a roe deer and when I do, I will follow it until the light fails. Just how thrilling will that be?

For three years, Alan's company has been teaching others how to recognise the signs left when an animal moves through the woods, rubs against a tree, grazes on a plant or takes a breather in the grass. At first, the small groups he leads on four-hour walks through these ancient woods see only trees. He urges me to slow down and we sit for 40 minutes in a glade and wait to see if a roe, fallow or muntjae deer will emerge; or perhaps a fox, badger or wild boar … but up pops a rabbit.

Alan waits until it scampers off before examining the fresh prints in the U-shaped track pattern. 'You learn a lot from this,' he says. There is more to a footprint than meets the eye. 'Look here,' he observes as we find deer tracks a few minutes later. 'A fresh print has a shine and hasn't absorbed water, which would make it wider, and it has no leaf litter in it.' From a footprint, you can tell the sex of an animal and which way it has been looking by how it shifts its weight. You can also tell if it knows you are following it, how fast it's moving and, if you are really good, if it has a full belly.

---

1   The writer suggests in the text that the course

   A   was more exciting than he had expected.
   B   has improved skills he already had.
   C   has had a major effect on him.
   D   was something he had always wanted to do.

2   The group that the writer was a member of

   A   had to wait longer than normal to see an animal.
   B   observed both an animal and its tracks.
   C   saw footprints that were not fresh.
   D   learnt that a certain animal had recently eaten.

Could you build your own wall?

The students at Malcolm Machin's month-long (four weekday evenings) basic bricklaying course have many reasons for attending. Mike Long, who gladly swapped a banking career to start his own gardening business, is on the course for practical reasons. 'I wanted to learn this so I can do hard landscaping, it's a skill that I need.' Atika Lee came so that she could build a small L-shaped wall. 'I love doing things for myself,' she says. 'By doing this, I thought I could save some money and learn something new,' she says, explaining that her spirit of adventure had led her to learn about painting and domestic wiring.

'I think they're surprised at how well they do and how quickly,' says Malcolm. 'This is a short course so we lay some bricks on the first evening. The biggest thing I have to highlight is that they're all individuals. They can get despondent if they think they're falling behind, but that's irrelevant. When you're doing a job for yourself, it doesn't matter how long it takes.'

There's gentle banter between everyone as they work, but a lot of communication is what might be described as 'brickie speak,' with references to 'frogs' and 'muck'. It's a vocabulary that Darren Moody, a plasterer by trade, might be already fairly familiar with. His brick corner goes up quickly and looks straight, neat and regular (in a whisper, Malcolm tells me that it's not surprising given his background) but it's interesting that everyone else is close behind.

You start to appreciate the craft, thought and skill involved in a job laypeople might otherwise see as repetitive and, as the amateur brickies mark each other's work, it's apparent that they've got more from the experience than knocking up some walls.

3   What does the writer learn from watching and talking to people?

   A   The students make mistakes if they try to work too quickly.
   B   Sometimes students show each other how to do the work well.
   C   Some students have unrealistic expectations of the course.
   D   Sometimes students feel that they are doing badly on the course.

4   What do we learn about the students doing the course in the text as a whole?

   A   They all make rapid progress at learning the skill of bricklaying.
   B   Some of them are not expecting to become good at bricklaying.
   C   They are all learning other skills as well as bricklaying.
   D   Some of them get confused about the technical terms used.

Street dancing

Up and down a tiny maze of corridors, none of them wider than two people, swarm what feels like thousands of small, lithe, dancey folk. Half are sodden with sweat, limping from practice studios. The other half are limbering up, shifting from foot to foot, waiting for their own turn to sweat. The temperature is about 50 degrees, and the humidity about 90 percent. The smell is otherworldly – perspiration mixed with ambition.

I was at the Pineapple Dance Studios to see how 'Hip Hop Street Dance', one of its most popular courses, might improve my fitness. Having seen the rather average moves on display up and down modern British nightclubs, I wasn't too worried. All that bopping and strutting and sliding to rap music: how hard could it be? It wasn't as if I was taking up kickboxing or the triathlon.

'It's a good cardiovascular workout,' my instructor had said as I booked my beginners class by phone. 'It's great for the legs, and it's also good for the upper arms because street dance uses a lot of arm work. It's also low-impact – a few people develop knee or ankle problems after a long time because of the stress on them, or in their shoulders from all the body-popping, but not many people get hurt.' This didn't sound too bad, and I was further enthused by her report that 'to be honest, I'd say that you need to do it at least three times a week to see any improvement in fitness'.

5 The writer's description of the place is intended to show

   A how uncomfortable he feels there.
   B his excitement at what he sees there.
   C how much he differs from the other people there.
   D what the lessons there involve.

6 The writer's attitude to the course is that

   A it is likely to be more interesting than other fitness courses.
   B he is unlikely to find it very challenging.
   C he will not need to do classes as often as the instructor suggests.
   D it is sure to result in some injuries for him.

You are going to read an article about a competition in Britain in which the winners are the towns and cities considered the most attractive, particularly with regard to flowers and plants. Six paragraphs have been removed from the article. Choose from the paragraphs **A–G** the one which fits each gap (**7–12**). There is one extra paragraph which you do not need to use.

In the exam, mark your answers **on the separate answer sheet**.

The 'Britain in Bloom' competition

Every year, more than 1,000 towns and villages across Britain are in fierce competition to reap the benefit of the Britain in Bloom awards. William Langley reports.

Another town, another riot of begonias, hollyhocks and lupins. Cruising down streets thick with hanging baskets, planted tubs and flower-filled horse troughs, Jim Buttress, the Head Judge of the annual Britain in Bloom competition, needs no reminding that his verdict can make or break the place where you live. A nod from Jim can raise house prices, attract businesses, bring in tourists and secure council grants. Towns will do a lot to please him.

7

From barely noticed beginnings nearly half a century ago, Britain in Bloom has become a cultural phenomenon, stoking passions and rivalries that are changing the way the country looks and, as a consequence, refashioning our sense of what makes a place appear attractive. More than 1,000 towns, villages and cities now enter and the event has grown into the most fiercely contested of its kind in the world. Last week, the judging entered its tense final stages and Jim was weighing up the contenders for the biggest prize of all, the Champion of Champions trophy. In the early days, according to Jim, winning depended more or less on how many flowers you could plant and how much colour you could create.

8

The competition's influence extends far beyond the committees that enter it. Extravagant manifestations of floweriness have become a part of the country's visual texture. Traffic roundabouts have been turned into giant bouquets; ornamental gardens are springing up in industrial wastelands. Hanging baskets were relatively rare in Britain until the competition began. Now it's hard to find a high street in the country that isn't awash with them.

9

The competition's defenders consider such criticisms over the top or, at least, out of date. Since 2001, it has been run by the Royal Horticultural Society, with the aim of supporting 'environmentally sustainable, socially responsible, community-based' programmes. The old tricks of concealing urban grime beneath forests of fuchsias or creating rustic pastiches in built-up suburbs no longer work.

10

However badly these developments go down with the traditionalist element, the competition has become too important for many communities to ignore. A spokesman in Stockton-on-Tees, which won the Champion City award three years ago, says: 'Say you're a business trying to recruit staff and your town's won Britain in Bloom. It's very helpful in image terms. It makes people feel happier about living here.'

11

With so much at stake, the competitive tempo of Britain in Bloom has risen to a point that has started to cause alarm. Tales of dirty tricks abound. Recently, the village of Cayton, winner of several prizes, awoke to find that a mystery attacker had destroyed its prized flower beds. Jealous local rivals were rumoured to be responsible, though nothing has been proved. Some years earlier, in one village a water bowser used for irrigation was spiked with toxic chemicals.

12

Last week found Jim on his final tour before the results are announced in a month's time. 'It's been great,' he says. 'You see a lot of things when you do this job, and what I've seen most of is pride.'

A This is because, over the past decade, the judging criteria have been subtly changed. They now take into account 'conservation and biodiversity', 'recycling and limiting demand on natural resources' and 'community awareness and understanding'.

B It's not always like that, however, says Jim. 'I arrived somewhere on the train once, and there were flowers planted all around the station. It looked fantastic. When I got in the taxi, the driver said: "I don't know where all these flowers came from, they weren't here yesterday."'

C 'Some of this is exaggerated,' says Jim. 'There are rivalries, but there's a good spirit too. The competition brings out the best in communities. Go to places where there's poverty, vandalism, drugs, and you will see people working together, trying to make their surroundings look better.'

D Sometimes too much. One hired a stretch limousine to ferry him around in luxury. 'The thing had blacked-out windows,' he huffs. 'I couldn't see a thing.'

E Not everyone is thrilled, though. In a celebrated attack some years ago, the eminent historian and gardener Roy String accused Britain in Bloom of burying the country beneath an avalanche of flowers, which, he claimed, was destroying the character of otherwise perfectly attractive communities.

F Aberdeen, long wreathed in a reputation for charmlessness, has invested a great deal of money in reviving its image through the competition. Four years ago, it was awarded a gold award and a citation that described it as 'providing an outstanding combination of floral displays, wonderful trees, and numerous lovely parks'. Once known as the Granite City, the tourist-hungry city now styles itself the 'City of Roses'.

G 'But it's much more sophisticated, much more competitive now,' he says. 'People are in this thing to win it. There's a lot at stake. That sign on the way into town that says "Britain in Bloom Winner" is a real asset.'

Part 3

You are going to read an extract from a novel. For questions **13–19**, choose the answer (**A**, **B**, **C** or **D**) which you think fits best according to the text.

In the exam, mark your answers **on the separate answer sheet**.

Louisa Maguire, wedding and portrait photographer, gave her clients images of themselves as they wanted to be seen – confident and happy, with the polish of an expensive American advertising campaign. She had arrived from New York in 1993, just as Ireland was beginning to transform itself from a country of staunch Catholic conservatives into a society dominated by the neo-liberal *nouveaux riches*. In Celtic Tiger Ireland, people were no longer suspicious of success, and instead of emigrating to get rich, they were living the American Dream at home. And who better to document it than an American photographer?

Although Louisa had once harboured higher aspirations, she didn't mind doing weddings and portraits of bonny babies. After all, that was how Dutch painters had made their livings centuries before, churning out portraits that reflected their clients' prosperity. Louisa Maguire, photographer, had introduced Dubliners to high-quality black-and-white portraits in life-size formats shot with her beloved Hasselblad, which they hung on their walls like works of art. She was expensive, but that was part of her appeal.

Weddings were the other mainstay of her business. She shot them in documentary style, always telling the story of the day in a way that showed the fairytale, but she also caught the uniqueness of every occasion. Digital cameras were far easier to use than the analogue cameras she preferred, but the old-fashioned method had a timelessness and depth that digital couldn't match. And there were few things she enjoyed more than spending hours in the darkroom, fine-tuning a thousand shades of grey until she got a picture exactly right. Black and white was more evocative than colour, which stripped people of the dark sides that made them interesting …

Louisa drove into Dalkey Village and pulled up in front of her studio. Her assistant, Paul, was waiting for her. 'Hey, what's up? You're late,' he said, as he loaded Louisa's middle-aged Volvo Estate with equipment, then stretched himself out in the passenger seat. She would tell him eventually, but not yet. For now, Louisa wanted to drive without having to think. Sensing her mood, Paul put music on the CD player, sat back and closed his eyes. She found her way to the M50, then gunned the engine as she headed west, determined to make up time. Speeding along the highway that circled the city, she felt regret at the paving of Ireland; they were passing high-tech factories, warehouses and shopping malls, which made the outskirts of Dublin look like any European suburb.

'You ever visit the cairns?' Louisa asked Paul.

'The what?'

'The Bronze Age tombs in Meath. They're five thousand years old. There's one you can actually go inside, if you borrow the key from the people in the Big House. I'll never forget crawling down there. It was like going back to the very beginning. I had an eerie feeling that I'd been there before.'

'You Americans and your history. I thought you hated all that sentimental diddle-eye-doe aul' Oirlan' nonsense.'

'I do. I'm not talking about Oirlan'. I mean the real place underneath all that sentimental nonsense.'

'If I can't see it, I'm not interested. We're photographers, Lou. Surface is what we do.'

'I know it.' Too well, she realised.

They left the M50 and headed north on the N23 into countryside that was like a green quilt with grey stitching made stone by stone with muscle and sweat. The earth beneath held buried treasure – bronze goblets, gold torques, wisps of fabric and even human bodies preserved in the peat-rich soil. This was the Ireland she loved, although she usually kept her thoughts to herself. She didn't want anyone to suppose she was just another daft American looking for her roots.

13 What do we learn about Louisa Maguire in the first paragraph?

    A She moved to Ireland because of social changes there.
    B Being American helped her to get photographic work in Ireland.
    C The attitudes of Irish people confused her when she arrived there.
    D She had more success in Ireland than in America.

14 Louisa's attitude to doing weddings and portraits was that

    A the money she could make from that kind of work was its main advantage.
    B the responses of clients often made that kind of work rewarding.
    C she was only likely to do that kind of work temporarily.
    D she was not ashamed of doing that kind of work.

15 In the third paragraph, what is implied about Louisa's work for weddings?

    A She sometimes had to persuade clients that her methods were right for them.
    B She preferred photographing weddings to doing portraits.
    C She showed aspects of the occasion that clients had not been aware of.
    D She used analogue cameras for photographing weddings.

16 When Louisa met Paul at her studio and they got into the car,

    A he did something that annoyed her.
    B her mood changed.
    C she decided to delay answering the question he asked her.
    D he misunderstood how she was feeling.

17 When Lousia mentioned the cairns to Paul,

    A he said that her attitude to the place was typical of Americans.
    B he indicated that he had had a different experience at the place.
    C he said that he was not at all surprised by her feelings about the place.
    D he suggested that he did not regard it as a place worth visiting.

18 During their conversation, Louisa agreed with Paul that

    A his attitude to his work was more limited than hers.
    B she had a tendency to be too sentimental.
    C her attitude to aul' Oirlan' was a foolish one.
    D only what was visible mattered to them in their work.

19 In the final paragraph, we learn that Louisa

    A often recommended this particular area to other Americans.
    B was keen not to be regarded by Irish people as a typical American.
    C no longer had the same feelings about Ireland as when she had first arrived.
    D normally explored the countryside of Ireland on her own.

Part 4

You are going to read a magazine article about the use of gadgets by people doing outdoor activities. For questions **20–34**, choose from the sections of the article (**A–D**). The jobs may be chosen more than once.

In the exam, mark your answers **on the separate answer sheet**.

In which section of the article are the following mentioned?

why people were willing to suffer outdoors in the past	**20**
the need to understand certain terminology	**21**
a belief about what the reason for doing outdoor activities should be	**22**
a feeling of reassurance provided by a certain gadget	**23**
how many people have taken up outdoor activities because of gadgets	**24**
a criticism of the motivation of people who get a lot of gadgets for outdoor activities	**25**
the noise made by certain gadgets	**26** **27**
a belief that gadgets may prove not to be useful	**28**
evidence that people in general lack a particular ability when outdoors	**29**
a belief that someone with gadgets would not be a good companion in certain circumstances	**30**
the lack of certain abilities among people who use gadgets	**31** **32**
the high level of demand for gadgets connected with outdoor activities	**33**
an advantage of outdoor gadgets in addition to the benefits for users	**34**

On the trail of Kit Man

Gadgets that bring home comforts to the great outdoors have given rise to a new breed of outdoor adventurer. But purists are unconvinced.

A

Up there, in the clear fresh air, it isn't just the stars that are glowing. You can climb a mountain and find at the top of it a bleeping nightmare of hi-tech gadgetry and hardship-avoidance devices. Worried about getting lost? Relax with a handheld GPS unit, featuring 3D and aerial display, plus built-in compass and barometric altimeter. Even the sacred covenant between outdoor types and wet socks has come unravelled with the development of 'hydrophobic' fabrics which repel all moisture. At next month's Outdoors Show in Birmingham, all this kit and more will be on display for an audience which seemingly can't get enough of it. 'When we ask people what they come to the show for, they list two things,' says the event's sales manager, Mike Simmonds. 'One is the inspiration to get outdoors in the first place, and the other is to see the new gear, the gadgets, the breakthroughs. That's what they love.' The event, the showcase of Britain's booming adventure business shows everything the tech-savvy adventurer could wish for, from solar-heated sleeping bags to remote-controlled lanterns.

B

The rise of Kit Man, as the gizmo-fixated menace of the 21st-century mountains has been christened, reflects both changing social trends and the dizzying speed of scientific advance. Modern hikers have moved on from the Spartan routines of 50 years ago, when discomfort, bad food and danger were seen as part of the authentic outdoor experience. They also have more money and a conditioned attachment to life's luxuries. However, basic pioneering disciplines – map-reading, camp-laying, First Aid – have declined, to be shakily replaced by the virtual skills offered by technology. With so much gear now available, Kit Man and his kind stand accused by the old-schoolers of being interested only in reaching the summits of gadgetry.

C

'I think these people are completely missing the point,' huffs author and TV presenter Guy Grieve, who spent a year living alone in the Alaskan wilderness. 'The whole idea of going into the wild is to get away from the things that tie you in knots at home. I'd prefer to take as little as possible – a tent, a rifle, and a few pots and pans. All this technology,

I mean, it might look fantastic on paper, but when there's a real problem, it's almost certainly going to let you down. What will see you through is the old stuff, the maps and the bits of rope. There are times when you need that kind of dependability. Who'd want to be stranded out in the wild with a gadget freak?' Travel and adventure writer Clive Tully agrees. 'Be suspicious of anything that claims to make your life easier,' he warns. 'My experience is that people who depend on technology are woefully ill-prepared in other ways. You still need to be able to read a map and do the basic stuff.'

D

None of which is enough to keep Kit Man from his toys. The mountains and hills are alive with the sound of ringing mobiles, beeping biometric pressure metres, clicking ultra-violet radiation sensors and the whirring of the current ultimate in gadget chic – a micro-helicopter which can be controlled from an iPod to send back live pictures of the route ahead. Thus tooled up, Kit Man must consider what he is to wear. And as any visit to a contemporary outdoor store shows, this involves not only acquiring new clobber, but new jargon. When he asks about a pair of pants, he will learn about Moisture Vapour Transfer Rate, Hydrostatic Heat Resistance and Wickability. He'll be told that the vest he's interested in is fitted with a polytetrafluroethylene membrane, and that the boots which caught his eye have a built-in air-conditioning system with advanced longitudinal flex and heel-to-toe shock absorbers.

E

It is tempting to scoff at Kit Man, but not everyone sides with the romantics. Many in the adventure business say gadgets have encouraged thousands who would otherwise not have ventured into the great outdoors. Evidence from the American market also suggests that technology has had a positive environmental impact, and increased safety standards. Then there's research from Germany's Institute for Biological Cybernetics, which suggests that, left to their own devices, humans are doomed to wander round in circles. 'We cannot trust our own senses,' says its director Dr Jan Souman. 'The déjà vu that you feel when you are lost in the woods is real. The brain will bring you back to where you started.'

Part 1

You **must** answer this question. Write your answer in **180–220** words in an appropriate style. In the exam, write your answer **on the separate answer sheet provided**.

1   Last month you went to observe a one-day training session for new employees at your place of work in order to write a short report on it for your manager.

Read the email from your manager and the notes you made during the session. Then, **using the information appropriately**, write the report for your manager, describing what happened during the session and making recommendations for improving it.

Dear Jan,

I'm concerned that the induction session for new employees is not as good as it might be. I'd like you to attend the next one and let me know what you think about it, and how it could be improved.

Thanks,

Mike

Too much information given – not enough chance to ask questions.

Good presentation on structure of company.

Some didn't understand the flexible working hours system.

Not enough on benefits like cafeteria, gym membership, etc.

Too long! Six separate parts!

Write your **report**. You should use your own words as far as possible.

Part 2

Write an answer to one of the questions **2–5** in this part. Write your answer in **220–260** words. In the exam, write your answer **on the separate answer sheet provided**, and put the question number in the box at the top of the page.

---

2   You have received a letter from an English friend who wants to come and live in your town and learn your language. Your friend wants to know which kind of accommodation is available locally and what possibilities there will be to do sport in your area. He/she also wants to know how easy it will be to find a part-time job that will help him/her practise your language. Reply to your friend, giving the information he/she needs.

Write your **letter**.

3   You see this announcement on a media website.

Best TV series ever!

We want to find out what people think is the best TV series they've ever seen. Help us compile a list of the top ten! Submit a review of your own favourite TV series, explaining why it appeals to you and giving reasons why it should be included in our top ten list.

Write your **review**.

4   Your school wants to improve the facilities it provides for language students without spending too much money, and has asked students to submit proposals. In your proposal, you should explain what the current facilities for language students are and make recommendations for improvements to them, giving reasons to support your proposal.

Write your **proposal**.

5   Answer one of the following two questions based on a book you have read. In the exam, you will have to write about one of two specific titles. Write the letter **(a)** or **(b)** as well as the number 5 on your answer sheet.

(a) You have read the following announcement in a magazine.

> Do novels always make good films? Send us an article about your favourite novel, outlining the plot and saying whether it would make a good film or not. We will publish the best articles in the magazine.

Write your **article**.

(b) Your class has had a discussion on memorable characters in fiction. Your teacher has asked you to write an essay describing a memorable character in fiction, saying what the character is like and why you find him/her memorable. You should support your ideas with examples from the book.

Write your **essay**.

Part 1

For questions **1–12**, read the text below and decide which answer (**A**, **B**, **C** or **D**) best fits each gap. There is an example at the beginning (**0**).

In the exam, mark your answers **on the separate answer sheet**.

Example:

0 **A** takes   **B** fetches   **C** carries   **D** brings

0	A	B	C	D

Caving

Caving is an adventure sport that, quite literally, **(0)** .... you to another world. But it's also quite a well **(1)** .... secret, enjoyed by a relatively small group of devoted enthusiasts. Caving **(2)** .... for a range of skills because it involves climbing, squeezing and squirming your way into openings in the Earth's rocks to discover the many fascinating, sometimes very large and beautiful, caverns that **(3)** .... under the surface.

(4) .... its rather dangerous image, largely **(5)** .... thanks to rather sensationalist television programmes, the sport has an excellent safety **(6)** ...., so long as you go with a qualified instructor or caving club. Wearing a helmet and waterproof clothing, you're privy to a hidden world of stalagmites and stalactites, although you may have to **(7)** .... through torrential underground rivers and negotiate thunderous waterfalls in order to **(8)** .... the most impressive spots.

The challenge of entering the unknown in the **(9)** .... dark can be, let's **(10)** .... it, pretty terrifying, so it's as well to choose your location carefully. And there's also a conservation **(11)** .... behind the sport too, because caves are a very **(12)** .... environment that is easily damaged. All cavers are encouraged to 'take nothing but photographs and leave nothing but footprints'.

1	**A** cared	**B** held	**C** kept	**D** minded
2	**A** demands	**B** calls	**C** asks	**D** requires
3	**A** stay	**B** sit	**C** rest	**D** lie
4	**A** Despite	**B** Moreover	**C** Nonetheless	**D** Albeit
5	**A** accepted	**B** acquired	**C** assumed	**D** admitted
6	**A** report	**B** history	**C** standard	**D** record
7	**A** amble	**B** wade	**C** stroll	**D** hike
8	**A** manage	**B** arrive	**C** achieve	**D** reach
9	**A** pitch	**B** utter	**C** full	**D** pure
10	**A** own	**B** face	**C** confront	**D** grant
11	**A** opinion	**B** message	**C** view	**D** notion
12	**A** flimsy	**B** feeble	**C** fragile	**D** frail

Part 2

For questions **13–27**, read the text below and think of the word which best fits each gap. There is an example at the beginning (**0**).

In the exam, write your answers **IN CAPITAL LETTERS on the separate answer sheet**.

Example:

0	W	E	L	L																

Why are Sunglasses Cool?

When you go shopping for sunglasses, you soon realise that as (**0**) .... as being overpriced, they are heavily associated (**13**) .... images of celebrity. Sunglasses are cool, and it is a cool (**14**) .... seems set to endure. Have you ever wondered (**15**) .... this should be?

The roots of sunglasses are anything (**16**) .... glamorous, however. Amber-tinted spectacles first appeared in the nineteenth century and were a medical remedy for people (**17**) .... eyes were oversensitive to light. The first mass-produced versions, made by Sam Foster (**18**) .... Foster Grant fame, were sold in the 1920s in US seaside resorts. (**19**) .... this point, however, they remained functional objects, and were (**20**) .... to acquire the cool image they now enjoy.

This (**21**) .... about thanks to the US air force. In the 1930s, airmen started to wear anti-glare glasses which were (**22**) .... 'aviators'. In the early days of flight, these men were regarded (**23**) .... heroes. Down on the ground, actors keen to cash (**24**) .... on a little of that glory realised that sunglasses represented a short cut to intrigue. (**25**) .... audiences couldn't see an actor's eyes, then they couldn't read his or her thoughts. (**26**) .... human, audiences wanted to know more. So it (**27**) .... that the link between the fascination of celebrity and a pair of sunglasses was forged.

Part 3

For questions **28–37**, read the text below. Use the word given in capitals at the end of some of the lines to form a word that fits in the gap **in the same line**. There is an example at the beginning (**0**).

In the exam, write your answers **IN CAPITAL LETTERS on the separate answer sheet**.

Example: | 0 | P | U | B | L | I | C | A | T | I | O | N | | | | | |

Customer Reviews

The **(0)** .... in paperback of Matthew Quick's debut novel   **PUBLISH**

represented something of a milestone. The promotional material that

(28) .... the launch featured glowing, five-star reviews such as   **COMPANY**

'charming and well-written, **(29)** .... the best book I've read   **ARGUE**

this year'. Nothing so unusual in that, you might think. Except that

these notices came not from the pens of **(30)** .... critics on   **PROFESSION**

national newspapers, but from actual readers who had bought

the book on the internet, and enjoyed it enough to post a positive

review on the site. Presumably, no **(31)** .... incentive or other   **FINANCE**

consideration coloured the view of these readers, whose opinions

appear in an **(32)** .... form, as can be seen from the various   **EDIT**

spelling and grammatical mistakes they often contain.

It could be argued, of course, that the **(33)** .... of an informed   **ANALYSE**

literary critic may well be more **(34)** .... than the thoughts of   **RELY**

one casual reader. But along with the actual words penned by the

amateur reviewers, the site records the star rating awarded

to each title by all readers providing **(35)** .... The book receives   **FEED**

a cumulative star rating based on the average number of

stars awarded, and constant **(36)** .... are made as further reviews   **ADJUST**

come in. The more people like the book, the higher the star rating.

Maybe that kind of **(37)** .... speaks for itself.   **RECOMMEND**

Part 4

For questions **38–42**, think of one word only which can be used appropriately in all three sentences. Here is an example (**0**).

Example:

0 I was on the .... of booking my holiday when my boss said I might have to change the dates.

As the meeting drew to a close, the chairperson moved on to the final .... on the agenda.

Theo couldn't see the .... of getting to the airport too early, as the check-in desk only opened one hour before the flight departed.

Example: | **0** | P | O | I | N | T | | | | | | | | | | | | | |

In the exam, write **only** the missing word **IN CAPITAL LETTERS on the separate answer sheet**.

---

38 By the morning, the concrete in the new path had set ...., and you could clearly see Paul's footprint!

Alicia pushed herself .... in training in order to qualify for the national championships.

It was raining quite .... by the time they came out of the cinema.

39 From the expression on Miranda's face, I .... that something had gone wrong with our plan.

During our stay in the mountains, we .... wild berries each morning to eat for breakfast.

A small crowd had .... outside the hotel where the rock group was staying overnight.

40 All the best theatres are in the .... of the city and are easily reached by public transport.

Although the project was tough, we took .... from the positive feedback we received from our tutor.

Sean was disappointed to find that the leather jacket that he'd set his .... on had been sold.

41 It's only .... that you miss your family when you first go to college in a new city.

Some people have a .... ability to understand the behaviour of animals.

Helen has a very .... manner and makes everyone feel at ease.

42 Simon had put a great .... of effort into the firm's marketing campaign.

Gina was very proud to have appeared on television, but Dave thought it was no big .... really.

When you're buying electronic goods, you often get the best .... by shopping around on the internet.

Part 5

For questions **43–50**, complete the second sentence so that it has a similar meaning to the first sentence, using the word given. **Do not change the word given.** You must use between **three** and **six** words, including the word given. Here is an example (**0**).

Example:

0   Chloe would only eat a pizza if she could have a mushroom topping.

ON

Chloe .... a mushroom topping when she ate a pizza.

The gap can be filled with the words 'insisted on having', so you write:

Example: | **0** | | INSISTED ON HAVING |

In the exam, write **only** the missing words **IN CAPITAL LETTERS on the separate answer sheet**.

___

43   A lack of work in his home area forced Frank to move to the capital.

CHOICE

Frank .... move to the capital because of the lack of work in his home area.

44   'The race is going to start in a minute,' said Rod.

ABOUT

Rod said that .... start.

45   Thanks to the success of the concert, the singer was offered a recording contract.

LED

The success of the concert .... offered a recording contract.

46   As soon as Alex finished his homework, he went out on his bike.

HAD

No .... than he went out on his bike.

47 I find it boring to watch television every evening.

SPEND

I get .... every evening watching television.

48 Sarah's father thinks she should come home earlier in the evening.

APPROVE

Sarah's father .... staying out so late in the evening.

49 Gary received an income from some investments he had inherited.

PROVIDED

Some investments which Gary had inherited ....
an income.

50 Not many people predicted the result of the race.

MANAGED

Only .... the result of the race.

Part 1

You will hear three different extracts. For questions **1–6**, choose the answer (**A**, **B** or **C**) which fits best according to what you hear. There are two questions for each extract.

In the exam, write your answers **on the separate answer sheet**.

Extract One

You hear part of a discussion programme in which two artists are talking about their work.

1 What do they agree about inspiration?

    A An artist must know where it comes from.

    B Non-artists are unlikely to understand it.

    C Not all artists are willing to talk about it.

2 In his latest work, the man is exploring whether

    A holiday brochures are actually works of art.

    B the visual material in holiday brochures is effective.

    C we are misled by the image projected in holiday brochures.

Extract Two

You hear two club DJs talking about their work.

3 What did the man dislike about his previous job as a radio DJ?

    A He lacked the necessary background knowledge.

    B He didn't have one of the key skills required.

    C He often disagreed with the management.

4 What do they agree about being a club DJ?

    A It's difficult to make enough money to live well.

    B It's best not to play music you don't like personally.

    C You have to be responsive to the needs of the audience.

You hear part of an interview with the owner of a new cake shop.

5 What does she say about cake-making?

    A It's always been her dream to do it professionally.

    B It appealed to her because it calls for a range of skills.

    C It was something she learnt to do as part of her first job.

6 How does she feel about her new business?

    A confident in her own judgement

    B relieved that she followed expert advice

    C concerned that its early success will not last

Part 2

You will hear a man called Paul Osborne giving a careers talk about his work as a computer game designer. For questions **7–14**, complete the sentences.

In the exam, write your answers **on the separate answer sheet**.

COMPUTER GAME DESIGNER

Paul says that people often think that he's a game [**7**] rather than a designer.

As part of his degree, Paul did a course in [**8**] which has proved the most useful in his career.

In his first job, Paul was designing [**9**] most of the time.

Paul worked on what are known as [**10**] in his first job.

Paul mentions a game with the name [**11**] as the one he's enjoyed working on most.

Paul uses the word [**12**] to describe what multi-players in a game can create for themselves.

Paul says that achieving the correct [**13**] is the biggest challenge when designing a game.

Paul feels that [**14**] is the most important personal quality that a game designer needs.

Part 3

You will hear an interview with a successful businesswoman called Faye Brandon. For questions **15–20**, choose the answer (**A**, **B**, **C** or **D**) which fits best according to what you hear.

In the exam, write your answers **on the separate answer sheet**.

---

15 Looking back, how does Faye feel about her previous career as a model?

    A   She regrets not being more successful at it.

    B   She admits that it was not the right thing for her.

    C   She denies that she only did it as a way of making money.

    D   She insists that she only intended to do it in the short-term.

16 What does Faye suggest about the sock collection she designed?

    A   It was the wrong product for a new business.

    B   Persistence was needed to convince shops to sell it.

    C   She wishes she hadn't listened to those who criticised it.

    D   Using a backpack to carry it around created a bad impression.

17 Faye thinks that to be successful a new business needs above all to

    A   avoid being distracted by negative feedback.

    B   ensure that delivery times are always met.

    C   agree to fulfil all its customers' requests.

    D   make a careful choice of retail partners.

18 What does Faye suggest about the 'home testing' of her products?

    A   It's not popular with all her employees.

    B   It's the only way of ensuring product quality.

    C   It can have a negative affect on children's behaviour.

    D   It can put unreasonable demands on some of them.

19 Faye is keen to point out that her company's website

    A   isn't oriented towards sales.

    B   benefits from being a team effort.

    C   is mostly devoted to product information.

    D   has established customers as its main target.

20 What advice does Faye have for working mothers?

    A   Don't give up in the face of problems.

    B   Learn from all the mistakes you make.

    C   Concentrate on the things you're best at.

    D   Try to do equally well in everything you do.

Part 4

You will hear five short extracts in which college students are talking about being a member of a club.

In the exam, write your answers **on the separate answer sheet.**

TASK ONE

For questions **21–25**, choose from the list (**A–H**) what made each speaker decide to join the club.

A the advice of a friend	
B seeing an advertisement	Speaker 1 [ ] 21
C wanting to meet people	Speaker 2 [ ] 22
D a desire to try something new	Speaker 3 [ ] 23
E hoping to learn a skill	Speaker 4 [ ] 24
F a need for exercise	Speaker 5 [ ] 25
G wishing to please someone else	
H going along with a group decision	

TASK TWO

For questions **26–30**, choose from list (**A–H**) the main disadvantage of being a club member which each speaker mentions.

A the cost	
B the regular commitment	Speaker 1 [ ] 26
C the attitude of other members	Speaker 2 [ ] 27
D the location	Speaker 3 [ ] 28
E the way it's organised	Speaker 4 [ ] 29
F the level of challenge	Speaker 5 [ ] 30
G the timing of sessions	
H the lack of feedback on progress	

PART 1

The interlocutor will ask you a few questions about yourself and on everyday topics such as work and study, travel, entertainment, daily life and routines. For example:

- Where would you recommend tourists to visit in your country? Why?
- Do you think you spend more or less time watching television now than you did in the past? Why?
- Do you think that it's good to have a daily routine? Why/Why not?

PART 2

Experiencing emotions

Turn to pictures 1–3 on page 206, which show people's emotions in different situations.

Candidate A, compare two of the pictures and say why the people might be feeling emotional, and how long the feeling might last.

Candidate B, which situation do you think is the most emotional?

Dealing with difficult situations

Turn to pictures 1–3 on page 207, which show people dealing with difficult situations.

Candidate B, compare two of the pictures and say why the situations might be difficult to deal with, and how important it might be for the people to deal with them well.

Candidate A, which situation do you think is most difficult for the people to deal with?

PART 3

Turn to the pictures on page 208, which show how technology has changed people's lives.

First, talk to each other about the positive and negative impact of changing technology on people's lives today. Then decide which kind of technology will be less important in the future.

PART 4

Answer these questions:

- What do you think is the most positive change technology has brought in modern life?
- Do you think that life is generally easier now than it was in the past? Why/Why not?
- Some people say that computers are the biggest time-saving device in modern life. What do you think?
- Mobile phones mean that people are always contactable. Is this a good thing?
- What effect do you think social networking sites have had on relationships?

Part 1

You are going to read three extracts which are all concerned in some way with unusual hobbies. For questions **1–6**, choose the answer (**A**, **B**, **C** or **D**) which you think fits best according to the text.

In the exam, mark your answers **on the separate answer sheet**.

The man with a passion for vacuum cleaners

Wherever he goes, James Brown, known to his fellow enthusiasts as Mr Vacuum Cleaner, gets the red carpet treatment. The hum of a Hoover and the drone of a Dyson are music to his ears and recently, frustrated by Britain's failure to recognise the importance of vacuum cleaners, he opened the first museum dedicated to them. Visitors have been turning up to the exhibition on a shopping street in numbers he can't quite explain. Perhaps they come because vacuum cleaner obsession is a more widely-suffered condition than previously suspected, or because Mr Brown's love for the machines is so deep, genuine and, in its way, touching.

'I've been fascinated by vacuum cleaners since I was a small boy,' he says. 'My mum probably thought I'd grow out of it, but once I got my hands on an Electrolux, I knew I never wanted to let go.' By the time he reached his teens, Mr Brown had 30 vacuum cleaners. One by one his other interests – music, sport, books – bit the dust. 'I suppose you could say that vacuum cleaners took over my life,' he says. 'I love the look, the feel, the sound of them. You can't really explain it to people who don't have the same enthusiasm. It's like people love vintage cars or clocks. For me, it was vacuum cleaners.'

1   The writer suggests that James Brown's museum may be popular because

   A   people are attracted by his passion for vacuum cleaners.
   B   he has put so much effort into publicising it.
   C   a lot of people find the whole idea of it amusing.
   D   it enables people who share his interest to meet each other.

2   James Brown says that his fascination for vacuum cleaners

   A   has had one particular disadvantage for him.
   B   does not make sense to some people.
   C   is not as understandable as other people's fascinations.
   D   grew steadily as he got older.

Stair running

Businessman Duncan Bannatyne is facing a challenge that could bring him to his knees. He is joining the growing number of athletes, runners and joggers worldwide who get to the top of skyscrapers the hard way – by running up the stairs. In his case, that means attacking the 920 steps of Tower 42, the tallest building in the City of London, to a daunting height of 183 metres in less than 15 minutes – if he's lucky. Or he may collapse in a heaving mass halfway up.

Tower running is one of the toughest new sports to capture the imagination of fitness addicts all over the world. Now beginning to take off in Britain, it's physically incredibly hard, fiercely competitive and visually amazing, given that it's played out within constructions such as New York's Empire State Building, Taiwan's enormous Taipei 101 Tower and the huge Sydney Tower in Australia.

Last year, Bannatyne joined 600 runners who headed to the top of Tower 42 in a race organised for a charity. Now he is making a second assault, this time with a hugely increased field of 1,200 contestants – a sign of the sport's growing popularity. 'I'd never run up 42 flights before and didn't think I could do it last time,' he says. 'I started off at the run, but after what I thought were three or four floors, I realised I was still only on the first floor. After four floors I couldn't run any more, I had to slow down.' But though it was 'one of the most physical things I've ever done', he eventually reached the top to a burst of elation powerful enough to bring him back for a re-run. 'I'd like to do more tower running,' he says.

3   One of the writer's purposes in the first two paragraphs is to

    A explain the growing popularity of stair running.

    B say what kind of people are attracted to doing stair running.

    C point out how varied the buildings used for stair running are.

    D warn against taking up stair running unless you are very fit.

4   Duncan Bannatyne is going to run up Tower 42 again because he wants to

    A improve on his performance the first time he did it.

    B be part of something that is growing rapidly in popularity.

    C experience again the feeling he had on completing it the first time.

    D use the knowledge he gained when he did it previously.

Caesar, the 'dangerous' pet

Their natural habitat is the marshy wetlands of Central America, where they live on a diet of fish, birds and small mammals. But for one spectacled caiman crocodile, life is a lazy existence in a converted bungalow in southern Britain.

Chris Weller has moved into the loft of his home to allow his pet, Caesar, to roam through the property. It is one of dozens of crocodiles and alligators kept as pets in Britain under the Dangerous Wild Animals Act (DWAA). More than 4,000 animals, from antelope to zebras, are licensed under the Act, which imposes strict security rules on owners to prevent escapes.

Caesar, who is four years old, is already 4.5 feet long. His species can live for 40 years and reach 7 feet. Mr Weller bought him as a one-year-old when he was one foot long. He has spent about £20,000 on his loft and turning the dining room and conservatory of his home into a habitat for his pet, complete with its own pool. Mr Weller says that the downstairs kitchen, bathroom and hallway are 'neutral zones' for them. 'He comes in the kitchen sometimes. When he is hungry, he will come when I call his name. He really likes steaks and salmon, tuna and prawns. I get a lot of it from the supermarket, but it is only the budget ranges.'

Mr Weller has installed a cat-flap device to allow Caesar to move between rooms. Although the crocodile can push open the flap himself, an additional shutter is usually in place to control his movements for safety. 'He grunts at me when he wants me to open the shutter,' Mr Weller says.

5 We learn in the text that Caesar

- **A** has an affectionate relationship with his owner.
- **B** would like to move around the house more than he can.
- **C** does not go into one particular part of the house.
- **D** costs less to feed than he used to.

6 What is the writer doing in the article as a whole?

- **A** criticising some aspects of the situation
- **B** emphasising how strange he thinks the situation is
- **C** expressing approval of what he describes
- **D** presenting the facts without comment

You are going to read an article about a series of books. Six paragraphs have been removed from the article. Choose from the paragraphs **A–G** the one which fits each gap (**7–12**). There is one extra paragraph which you do not need to use.

In the exam, mark your answers **on the separate answer sheet**.

Publishing's natural phenomenon

The 'Collins New Naturalist' series is as famous for its covers as its content.
Peter Marren looks at how the unique jackets have taken on a life of their own.

They fill a large bookcase like a paper rainbow. The *Collins New Naturalist* series (or 'library', as its editors prefer) has been a publishing phenomenon for many decades. It has rolled on, in fits and starts, from the late 1940s and is currently enjoying a sprint, with four new titles in the past 12 months. Numbering 111 books in all, and with plenty more in the pipeline, the *New Naturalist* is probably the longest running specialist series in the world. What is its secret?

| 7 | |

There is nothing quite like them. From the start, they were based not on strictly natural photography but on lithographic prints. The artists preferred bold, simplified forms that were symbolic rather than strictly illustrative.

| 8 | |

These quirky designs were the work of Clifford and Rosemary Ellis, a husband-and-wife artistic partnership who normally signed their work with a cipher: 'C&RE'. They generally used a limited palette of colours broadened by printing one on top of another. Both were well-versed in animal drawing, in Rosemary's case from sketching livestock on the farm where she lived as a girl, in Clifford's from studying animals at the London Zoo.

| 9 | |

But the technology for producing those in colour was in its infancy in the 1940s and the available stock was unimpressive. Instead, with the tacit support of William Collins, the Ellises were commissioned to produce a jacket for the first title, *Butterflies*. Collins liked it. The books' scientific editors, led by James Fisher and Julian Huxley, did not. But, since the jacket was part of the sales process, not the science, Collins had his way. The Ellises then produced a common design for every book in the series.

| 10 | |

They were seen to best advantage when the books were displayed together in the shop, becoming ever more eye-catching as the series took off during the late 1940s and 1950s. The jackets were printed by lithography in three or four colours on expensive art paper. Initially, the artist's life-size sketch was transferred to the printing plate with great skill by artisan printers in London.

| 11 | |

The jackets effectively became an extended work of art, until the Ellises had completed 70 designs (plus 22 more for the series of single-species monographs). Their last one was published the year Clifford Ellis died, in 1985. Fortunately, his shoes were filled by Robert Gillmor, the highly acclaimed bird artist, who since then has produced dazzling jackets to the same overall design. Originally printed by lithography, Gillmor's designs are now based on linocuts, and they evoke the contents of the book as well as ever. To celebrate these unique jackets, Collins commissioned Gillmor and me to write a book discussing each design, one by one.

| 12 | |

Our book, *Art of the New Naturalists*, has now been published. We hope people agree that it commemorates something special: commercial art inspired by natural forms, a riotous dance of biodiversity and imagination.

A Later, an even more demanding production method was devised, which separated out each colour for combining on the press. Great trouble was taken to get each one exactly right, and every design was the product of many weeks of sketching and colour trials.

B For example, the jacket of *The Sea Shore* shows a broken crab's claw resting on the beach; nothing more. The fox on the jacket of *British Mammals* is a green-eyed blur, and the eye of the rabbit it is stalking is repeated three times on the spine.

C In the process, some buried treasures came to light. These included the original artwork, long lost to sight in a warehouse, preparatory sketches and discarded alternate designs. There was even artwork for books that never were; striking jackets for the unpublished *Bogs and Fens, The Fox* and the intriguingly titled *Ponds, Pools and Puddles*.

D This had the title printed on a broad band of colour (at first in handcrafted letters) and the book's number in the series at the top of the spine. A specially designed colophon with two conjoined 'N's smuggled itself inside an oval at the bottom.

E Partly it was, and is, its scientific quality. The series is at the high end of popular natural history, unafraid to tackle difficult cutting-edge science. These books are also collector's items. And the reason they are collected is their jackets.

F The proof of this is that the cover illustrations have become iconic. They have given the books a highly distinctive style that has inspired nature enthusiasts for many decades and they have helped to make the books become highly collectible.

G They came to the series largely by chance. The original plan had been to wrap the books in photographic jackets, in keeping with the publisher's intention to 'foster the natural pride of the British public in their native fauna and flora'.

You are going to read an article about happiness. For questions **13–19**, choose the answer (**A**, **B**, **C** or **D**) which you think fits best according to the text.

In the exam, mark your answers **on the separate answer sheet**.

The impossible moment of delight

A recent survey has examined the well-trodden ground of the relationship between pleasure and money. Many studies have examined this, from any number of starting points, often concluding, in the oldest of old clichés, that money can't buy you happiness or, in more sophisticated terms, that happiness and pleasure often reside, not in riches in absolute terms, but in being richer than the people who happen to live to your left or your right. Other studies have claimed that comparison with the wealth of others leads to a 'set-up for disappointment' and that a good attitude is all that matters.

This most recent study inquired into the wellbeing of 136,000 people worldwide and compared it to levels of income. It found, overall, that feelings of security and general satisfaction did increase with financial status. Money, however, could not lift its possessors to the next level, and was unable to provide enjoyment or pleasure on its own. The survey, published in the *Journal of Personality and Social Psychology*, examined large numbers of people from almost every culture on Earth, and found much the same thing. The stereotype of the rich man who finds life savourless and without pleasure was not invented simply to keep the poor happy with their lot.

Paul Bloom addresses the same issue in his book *How Pleasure Works*. According to Bloom, at the point when people get the thing they really want, they enter a state of perfect pleasure. Both Bloom's book and the enormous survey concentrate on status and on the moment of getting possession of something we want. Are we satisfied and filled with pleasure when we get what we want? Bloom, looking at eager consumers, would say 'yes'; the survey tends to say 'not necessarily'. In my view, it's rare that we can actually pin down the specific moment when the feeling of pleasure is at its clearest.

Take the teenager determined to buy the latest must-have gadget, a woman setting out to get a new handbag, or a prosperous businessman who wants to add to his collection of Japanese *netsuke*. The setting out with the happy intention of spending; the entering of the shop; the examination of the wares; the long decision; the handing over of the money; the moment when the ownership of the goods is transferred; the gloating at home; the moment when the object is displayed to others. All these steps form a process in enjoyment, but almost all of them are redolent with anticipation or with retrospective glee. The moment where bliss is at its peak is over in a flash, and hardly exists at all. Everything else is expectation or memory.

Composers have always known this simple, basic truth: pleasure is half anticipation and half blissful recollection, and hardly at all about the fulfilment of the promise. The great musical statements of ecstasy, such as Wagner's *Tristan and Isolde* or Schubert's first *Suleika* song, are literally all half crescendo and half languid recall. We look forward to pleasure; we look back on it. The moment of pleasure itself is over in a flash, and often rather questionable.

The hairband and geegaw emporium Claire's Accessories has a thoughtful, rather philosophical slogan to tempt its young customers. It sells itself under the strapline 'where getting ready is half the fun'. That is honest and truthful. A group of 14-year-old girls in their party best is nowhere near as successful an enterprise of pleasure as exactly the same girls putting on and trying out and discussing their hopes for the party in advance; not as successful either as talking it over the next day. The party itself, from the beginning of time, has consisted of a lot of standing around and gawping and giggling, and someone crying in the lavatory.

So any notion of fulfilled pleasure which insists on the moment of bliss is doomed to failure. Mr Bloom and the researchers of the *Journal of Personality and Social Psychology* were clearly happiest when undertaking their research, during which time they were looking forward to coming to a conclusion. And now they can sit back and start to say 'Yes, when I concluded my theory of pleasure and satisfaction ...' Even for philosophers of pleasure, another ancient and well-handled cliché about travel and life is true: getting there really is half the pleasure.

13 The writer says that previous studies of happiness have differed on

    A whether having more money than others makes people happy.
    B why people compare their financial situation to that of others.
    C what makes people believe that money brings happiness.
    D how important it is for people to think that they are happy.

14 According to the writer, the most recent survey

    A confirmed a common belief about wealth and happiness.
    B produced results that may surprise some people.
    C provided more accurate information than many other surveys.
    D found that there was no connection between money and happiness.

15 In the third paragraph, the writer says that his own opinion on the subject

    A has been influenced by the results of the survey.
    B is based on his personal feelings rather than on research.
    C differs from what Bloom concludes in his book.
    D might not be widely shared by other people.

16 The phrase 'Everything else' at the end of the fourth paragraph refers to

    A most of the stages of buying something you really want.
    B feelings that are less important than those already mentioned.
    C other situations in which people get what they really want.
    D other feelings at the moment of buying something.

17 The writer says that the musical works he mentions

    A are not intended to produce feelings of intense happiness.
    B sometimes disappoint people who listen to them.
    C perfectly illustrate his point about pleasure.
    D show how hard it is to generalise about pleasure.

18 The writer says that the company Claire's Accessories understands that

    A parties are less enjoyable for girls than getting ready for them.
    B girls enjoy getting ready for parties more than any other aspect of them.
    C looking good at parties makes girls happier than anything else.
    D what girls wear for parties affects their memories of them.

19 The writer concludes that both Bloom and the researchers

    A would agree with his own theory of pleasure.
    B would agree with a certain cliché.
    C have made an important contribution to the study of pleasure.
    D have gone through a process he has previously described.

Part 4

You are going to read a magazine article about interns – young people doing work placements for a limited period, usually without pay. For questions **20–34**, choose from the sections of the article (**A–D**). The jobs may be chosen more than once.

In the exam, mark your answers **on the separate answer sheet**.

Which intern mentions

her feeling when discovering something at work?	**20**
the fact that some of her work can be seen?	**21**
having no idea how to carry out a certain task?	**22**
her feeling about the people she works with?	**23**
having no regrets about a choice she made previously?	**24**
what is considered normal in her area of work?	**25**
the outcome of some of the work she does?	**26**
a desire not to be in the same situation in the future?	**27**
something she regarded as unpredictable?	**28**
a preference concerning the work she does as an intern?	**29**
reasons why it is possible for her to be an intern?	**30**
the attitude of her employer?	**31**
the outcome if she found herself in a difficult situation?	**32**
making useful contacts?	**33**
a change she believes will happen during her work placement?	**34**

The intern's tale

Many workplaces have interns. Is being an intern useful work experience or an unpaid waste of time? Sarah Barnes meets four young women trying to get a foot on the ladder.

A Jessica Turner: intern at the film company Future Films

Working on scripts that you know are going to become films one day is really exciting. We get a broad variety of genres sent to us here. Personally, I love anything that's been adapted from a book, especially if I've read the book. I read scripts, sometimes I attend meetings with writers, and I've also researched potential writers and directors online. Also, I volunteer in my local theatre and help out as an auditorium assistant. It's a great way of seeing different aspects of the industry, meeting people and developing your career. My placement was due to come to an end this month but I've just been offered the paid role of production and development assistant. I'm pleased to be able to stay – I didn't want to leave everyone. It's been tough getting to this point, but you can't expect too much because it's a competitive industry. Because my degree was in film theory, I didn't come away with the practical experience of being able to go on set and know what's what. Maybe I would have progressed more quickly if I had.

B Rasa Abramaviciute: intern at the Vivienne Westwood fashion company

I work in the same department as Vivienne Westwood, so I see her almost every day. She treats everyone equally, whether they are paid staff or interns. My main task is tracing patterns. I was shocked by how big they are; so much fabric goes into making a Westwood dress. When I started, I was working on the archive, so I had the opportunity to see past collections up close. I work five days a week, 10a.m. to 6p.m., but I expect the days to get longer and more stressful as we approach Fashion Week. I will stay for another three months, until we go to Paris for that, and then I will go straight back to university to complete my final year. In fashion, if you want to establish yourself over the competition, you have to work hard and for free, because that's what everyone else is willing to do.

C Hannah Sanderson: intern at the emergency relief charity Merlin

Over the past few years I've been doing volunteer work in Calcutta, Bogotá and Teheran, so it's quite hard to adjust to being back in the UK. Most of my friends are buying houses and have cars and go on holidays. But I never feel I've missed out because I'm doing what I've always wanted to do. I work three days a week, receiving a small sum to cover expenses. Money from my father has gone towards funding my placement and I'm really fortunate that I can live with my mum, although it does mean my commute can take up to two hours. Without my family, I don't think I could be doing this. Next month I am starting a six-month placement in Myanmar, monitoring the health facilities the charity supplies there. After that, I might actually be in a position to earn a salary. If I was 35 and still working unpaid, I would think 'What am I doing?'

D Paula Morison: intern at the Whitechapel Gallery

I came to London six months ago with no plans. I didn't know how long it would take to get a job. I had saved up some money and resigned myself to staying on a friend's sofa for a while, but luck was on my side and I found a job as a seamstress within a couple of weeks. My placement at the gallery came along a week later. I've helped install exhibitions and create gallery publications. One of the most exciting tasks was helping the artist Claire Barclay create the installation that's now on display in the gallery. Because some of the piece is sewn, my seamstress skills came in handy. The hardest thing is at the start, when you don't know anything. Someone asks: 'Can you courier this?' and you have to ask so many questions, like 'Which courier company?' and 'Where are the envelopes?' I'm about to finish my placement and I'm planning my own curatorial project with a friend. It will be a lot of work but I think I have to go for these things now, otherwise I will regret it later. My parents know I'm sensible. If I couldn't afford my rent, I wouldn't just get into a spiral of debt. I would go and get a full-time job and the rest would have to wait.

Part 1

You **must** answer this question. Write your answer in **180–220** words in an appropriate style. In the exam, write your answer **on the separate answer sheet provided**.

___

1   Your school magazine is publishing a series of articles about young people who have chosen to do part-time jobs before going to university. Read the email sent around to all former students and the notes you made on your own experience of doing such part-time work. **Using the information appropriately**, write your article for the school magazine.

Hi all!

We'd like to help our younger students decide whether to do a part-time job before they go to university. Write us an article telling us about your experiences. We'd like our students to be able to judge whether it's worth it or not, what the possible benefits are (apart from the money!) and what kind of things to be wary of.

Thanks for your contribution!

Boring – could have done more.

Time management skills – definite plus.

Adult work experience – can't be bad.

Part-time workers not valued.

Missed out on social time with friends.

Write your **article**. You should use your own words as far as possible.

Part 2

Write an answer to one of the questions **2–5** in this part. Write your answer in **220–260** words. In the exam, write your answer **on the separate answer sheet provided**, and put the question number in the box at the top of the page.

---

2   You see this announcement in an international magazine.

> # The 'Best Friend Ever' award!
>
> We are running a competition to find the best friend ever. Write to us nominating a friend who you feel has done something very special. You should explain what this person has done, what makes him or her so special and why you think they should win the award.

Write your **competition entry**.

3   Your school wants to help its language students improve their communication skills in different languages, and is planning to hold a series of 50:50 conversation evenings for the whole school. Your class has been asked to write an information leaflet publicising the event. In your leaflet you should explain the aim of the evenings, the benefits to the students, describe the activities that will take place and suggest possible future events.

Write your **information leaflet**.

4   Your class has had a discussion on the value of competitive sport to young people. Your teacher has asked you to write an essay on the subject *Doing competitive sport in school creates more problems than benefits*. In your essay you should consider the advantages and disadvantages for students of doing competitive sport in school. Then decide whether there are more problems than benefits.

Write your **essay**.

5   Answer one of the following two questions based on a book you have read. In the exam, you will have to write about one of two specific titles. Write the letter **(a)** or **(b)** as well as the number 5 on your answer sheet.

   (a) You have bought a book after reading some reviews on an internet shopping site. You decide to write your own review of the book to post on the website. In your review you should briefly say what the book was about, explain whether or not you enjoyed it and why, and give your reasons for recommending it or not to other readers.

   Write your **review**.

   (b) A school library wants to buy some new novels that feature strong women characters, and has asked students to write a report recommending suitable novels. Write a report about a novel you have read which features a strong female character, saying what the novel is about, describing the character you think is strong and giving your reasons for recommending the novel for the school library.

   Write your **report**.

Part 1

For questions **1–12**, read the text below and decide which answer (**A**, **B**, **C** or **D**) best fits each gap. There is an example at the beginning (**0**).

In the exam, mark your answers **on the separate answer sheet**.

Example:

0 **A** features **B** aspects **C** factors **D** prospects

0	A	B	C	D

Ceramics Fair

It's a sleepy village, whose main **(0)** .... are a central square with a fountain and an unpretentious restaurant. **(1)** .... the place for an internationally famous exhibition attracting 15,000 visitors, one would think. Yet Bussière-Badil has just that **(2)** .... in the world of ceramics. **(3)** ...., when a pottery fair was first held there over 30 years ago, it was the only one in all of France, and it is still the country's only ceramics fair that **(4)** .... four days.

But why here? There is a seam of clay which runs through the area, but it is red clay of the type used to make tiles and bricks as **(5)** .... pots, so there is no **(6)** .... tradition of art pottery. The idea of the fair started when a Portuguese potter by the name of Miguel Calado **(7)** .... a studio in the village at the **(8)** .... of the mayor, himself a local tile-maker, who was **(9)** .... to put the region on the map.

And he has certainly succeeded. Every year, up to 40 potters from all over France and beyond **(10)** .... on the village to display their wares in a huge purpose-built shed. **(11)** .... on show range from the utilitarian to the decorative, with every nuance in between. And the crowds come to look, to **(12)** .... at the potters' art, and to buy.

1	**A**	Barely	**B**	Seldom	**C**	Hardly	**D**	Unlikely
2	**A**	esteem	**B**	reputation	**C**	respect	**D**	bearing
3	**A**	Nevertheless	**B**	However	**C**	Indeed	**D**	Otherwise
4	**A**	perseveres	**B**	endures	**C**	continues	**D**	lasts
5	**A**	opposed to	**B**	rather than	**C**	instead of	**D**	apart from
6	**A**	certain	**B**	particular	**C**	exact	**D**	individual
7	**A**	turned up	**B**	took up	**C**	made up	**D**	set up
8	**A**	instigation	**B**	advice	**C**	encouragement	**D**	persuasion
9	**A**	convinced	**B**	determined	**C**	dedicated	**D**	committed
10	**A**	gather	**B**	assemble	**C**	converge	**D**	collect
11	**A**	Issues	**B**	Items	**C**	Matters	**D**	Topics
12	**A**	astonish	**B**	fascinate	**C**	amaze	**D**	marvel

Part 2

For questions **13–27**, read the text below and think of the word which best fits each gap. There is an example at the beginning (**0**).

In the exam, write your answers **IN CAPITAL LETTERS on the separate answer sheet**.

Example: | **0** | A | N | Y | | | | | | | | | | | | | | |

Cheating at Computer Games

It's something **(0)** .... gamer will tell you. Computer games shouldn't be so hard that they drive you mad, but **(13)** .... should they be so easy that they **(14)** .... to offer enough of a challenge. Inevitably, however, you get stuck sometimes. What do you do then? Ask the internet, of course. Many other gamers have figured **(15)** .... what to do and posted the solution online. The answer is just a **(16)** .... clicks away.

Purists say this is cheating. They argue that solving a puzzle yourself, **(17)** .... gamers had to do in the old days, might have **(18)** .... longer, but it was more satisfying. **(19)** .... you know that detailed 'walkthroughs' are available online, free **(20)** .... charge, for almost any game, the temptation is to ask for virtual help **(21)** .... the first sign of trouble, **(22)** .... robs players of a true sense of achievement.

I say this is rubbish. **(23)** .... a search and downloading a solution has many merits. It stops me throwing my controller at the screen, and **(24)** .... me more likely to finish games **(25)** .... than giving up when they start to get tricky. So **(26)** .... in all, I get better value for money. The search is also a reminder that I'm a member of a broader community, many of **(27)** .... have been this way before.

Part 3

For questions **28–37**, read the text below. Use the word given in capitals at the end of some of the lines to form a word that fits in the gap **in the same line**. There is an example at the beginning (**0**).

In the exam, write your answers **IN CAPITAL LETTERS on the separate answer sheet**.

Example: | 0 | E | S | S | E | N | T | I | A | L | | | | | | | | | | |

Trolley Bags

Wheeled trolley bags have become an (**0**) .... item of luggage   **ESSENCE**

amongst frequent travellers. The compact version proves particularly

(**28**) .... as a piece of hand luggage. Carried onboard aeroplanes,   **USE**

it allows you to avoid the queues at the baggage check-in counters

on your (**29**) .... journey and waiting at the baggage   **OUT**

(**30**) .... carousel on your way home. These days, there are   **CLAIM**

(**31**) .... guidelines regarding the maximum size for hand luggage   **OFFICE**

on flights, and these stipulated (**32**) .... are continuously subject   **MEASURE**

to change. Policies also vary between airlines and airports

as well as being influenced by your (**33**) .... destination.   **EVENT**

The outcome of all this is that travellers are recommended

to check out the latest luggage (**34**) .... before setting   **RESTRICT**

out for the airport.

What's more, before investing in a trolley bag, it's wise to run

a few checks. You're likely to be negotiating (**35**) ....   **EVEN**

surfaces as well as the smooth flooring of airport lounges,

so bear in mind that larger wheels are better able to absorb

bumps than their smaller (**36**) .... Also check the handle.   **COUNTER**

You're bound to need to lift your bag at some point in

your journey, probably when you are suddenly confronted

with an (**37**) .... flight of steps, and that's not the moment   **CONVENIENT**

to discover that the handle is awkward to hold.

Part 4

For questions **38–42**, think of one word only which can be used appropriately in all three sentences. Here is an example (**0**).

Example:

0 I was on the .... of booking my holiday when my boss said I might have to change the dates.

As the meeting drew to a close, the chairperson moved on to the final .... on the agenda.

Theo couldn't see the .... of getting to the airport too early, as the check-in desk only opened one hour before the flight departed.

Example: | **0** | P | O | I | N | T | | | | | | | | | | | | | |

In the exam, write **only** the missing word **IN CAPITAL LETTERS on the separate answer sheet**.

---

38 The bag that fell overboard on the yacht that day has never been ....

In her first teaching job, Denise .... handling a class of thirty small children quite difficult.

Tim realised that somebody must have .... out what he was planning to do.

39 It's quite .... to see people swimming in the sea in the winter here.

Jane felt that the most .... wildflowers were actually more interesting than the rare ones.

Pete and Luisa share a .... interest in the sport of volleyball.

40 Ingrid decided to wait for a spell of .... weather before attempting to climb the mountain.

Although the two acts both performed well in the talent contest, the judges thought there was a .... winner.

The items you carry on board should be placed in a .... plastic bag, so that everyone can see what's inside.

41 Neil's football kit was wet through, so he asked if he could .... it out to dry somewhere.

The success of the company will eventually .... on its ability to sell is products to all age groups.

The town square used to be the place where teenagers would .... out and meet their friends.

42 The runners set off at a brisk .... at the start of the race.

Steve thought that the film lacked .... and at one point he thought it would never end.

It's difficult to keep .... with the rate of change in computer products.

Part 5

For questions **43–50**, complete the second sentence so that it has a similar meaning to the first sentence, using the word given. **Do not change the word given.** You must use between **three** and **six** words, including the word given. Here is an example (**0**).

Example:

0   Chloe would only eat a pizza if she could have a mushroom topping.

ON

Chloe .... a mushroom topping when she ate a pizza.

The gap can be filled with the words 'insisted on having', so you write:

Example:	**0**	INSISTED ON HAVING

In the exam, write **only** the missing words **IN CAPITAL LETTERS on the separate answer sheet**.

---

43   Even if she runs really fast, Tina won't get to school on time.

HOW

No .... , Tina won't get to school on time.

44   Penny was unwilling to admit that the accident had been her fault.

BLAME

Penny was .... for the accident.

45   Clarice's mother told her not to spend the money under any circumstances.

MUST

'Whatever .... that money, Clarice,' said her mother.

46   Joe was very surprised to see Melanie walk into the room.

TAKEN

Joe .... Melanie walked into the room.

47 In the office, Tom is responsible for all aspects of the updating of the company's website.

OVERALL

In the office, Tom has .... the company's website up to date.

48 It's quite common for students at the school to go on to win Olympic medals.

MEANS

It's .... for students at the school to go on to win Olympic medals.

49 Graham was not the only person who felt disappointed with the food in the restaurant.

ALONE

Graham .... disappointed with the food at the restaurant.

50 'I wouldn't take your car into Central London, if I were you, Simon,' said Rita.

AGAINST

Rita .... taking his car into Central London.

Part 1

You will hear three different extracts. For questions **1–6**, choose the answer
(**A**, **B** or **C**) which fits best according to what you hear. There are two questions for
each extract.

In the exam, write your answers **on the separate answer sheet**.

Extract One

You hear a man talking to a friend who's just arrived at an airport.

1   They disagree about whether the woman's flight

   A   represented good value for money.

   B   managed to keep to the schedule.

   C   offered a good level of comfort.

2   What is the man suggesting for the future?

   A   changing the airline

   B   changing the arrival airport

   C   changing the means of transport

Extract Two

You hear a science teacher telling a friend about her work.

3   What does she say about kids using the internet as a source of information?

   A   It has changed the nature of the teacher's role.

   B   It should only happen with the teacher's guidance.

   C   It can't take the place of the teacher's input on a subject.

4   How does she feel about the type of teaching she does?

   A   keen to keep changing it to meet students' needs

   B   sorry that other teachers don't want to adopt it

   C   convinced that it is proving to be effective

Extract Three

You hear a new album being reviewed on a music radio station.

5   What aspect of the recording made the greatest impression on the woman?

   A   where it was made

   B   the style of the finished product

   C   the range of instruments used on it

6   What does the man feel is different about this band?

   A   the originality of their sound

   B   the consistent quality of the tracks

   C   the way they've blended various musical influences

Part 2

You will hear a student called Jon giving a class presentation about the llama, an animal that comes originally from South America. For questions **7–14**, complete the sentences.

In the exam, write your answers **on the separate answer sheet**.

THE LLAMA

Jon says that llamas and alpacas are generally distinguished by the shape of the

	7

Jon discovered that the wild ancestor of the llama was mostly

| | 8 | in colour.
|---|---|

In ancient times, domesticated llamas most often worked in | | 9 | areas.

Jon says that the word

| | 10 | is most often used by humans when talking about llamas.

Jon found out that well-trained llamas only spit and kick if they feel | | 11 |

Jon describes the noise made by llamas for usual communications as a

	12

Jon says that llama fleece is popular with weavers because it contains no

	13

The commonest products made from llama hair are | | 14 |

Part 3

You will hear an interview with a young film director, Lauren Casio, who is talking about her life and work. For questions **15–20**, choose the answer (**A**, **B**, **C** or **D**) which fits best according to what you hear.

In the exam, write your answers **on the separate answer sheet**.

---

15 Lauren was encouraged to follow a career as a film-maker because her teachers

    A could see that she had potential.

    B found her early attempts highly original.

    C were impressed by her level of motivation.

    D appreciated her ability to work within a budget.

16 How does Lauren respond when asked about critics of film school?

    A She thinks they would benefit from going to one.

    B She defends the record of the one that she attended.

    C She agrees that it's less useful for certain types of work.

    D She regrets that it is the only option for poorer students.

17 Lauren didn't start making full-length feature films sooner because

    A she wanted to be sure of her ability first.

    B she had a bad experience with an early attempt.

    C she wasn't lucky enough to have the opportunity.

    D she didn't manage to find the financial backing she needed.

18 What does Lauren say about the characters in her films?

    A She tries to surprise her audience with them.

    B She likes them to fit into well defined types.

    C She accepts that the men may be more interesting.

    D She sets out to make them as complicated as possible.

19 How does Lauren feel now about the film *Hidden Valley Dreams*?

    A She regrets the setting she chose for it.

    B She regards it as being far from perfect.

    C She's surprised that it's proved so popular.

    D She wishes she'd spent more time on the plot.

20 How does Lauren feel when she goes to give talks in schools?

    A unsure whether to reveal her humble background

    B worried that she might give the kids unrealistic ambitions

    C slightly uncomfortable with the idea of being a role model

    D concerned that she may not command the respect of the students

Part 4

You will hear five short extracts in which people are talking about falling asleep in a public place.

In the exam, write your answers **on the separate answer sheet.**

TASK ONE

For questions **21–25**, choose from the list (**A–H**) the reason each gives for falling asleep in the place they did.

A	to keep someone company	
B	as a result of physical exertion	Speaker 1 [ ] 21
C	to save money	Speaker 2 [ ] 22
D	as preparation for physical activity	Speaker 3 [ ] 23
E	to avoid inconveniencing others	Speaker 4 [ ] 24
F	as a result of some treatment	Speaker 5 [ ] 25
G	to avoid a long walk home	
H	to prove something to themselves	

TASK TWO

For questions **26–30**, choose from the list (**A–H**) how each speaker felt afterwards.

A	embarrassed by the situation	
B	aware of physical discomfort	Speaker 1 [ ] 26
C	offended by the reactions of others	Speaker 2 [ ] 27
D	pleased to have had some rest	Speaker 3 [ ] 28
E	worried about the risk taken	Speaker 4 [ ] 29
F	grateful for a way of passing the time	Speaker 5 [ ] 30
G	happy to have followed local customs	
H	disgusted by the conditions	

PART 1

The interlocutor will ask you a few questions about yourself and on everyday topics such as work and study, travel, entertainment, daily life and routines. For example:

- What jobs are popular with young people in your country nowadays? Why?

- Has the kind of music you enjoy changed since you were younger? Why/Why not?

- When is the best time of day for you to study? Why?

PART 2

Challenging activities

Turn to pictures 1–3 on page 209, which show people doing activities that can be challenging.

Candidate A, compare two of the pictures and say why the people might be finding these activities challenging, and which activity might give people the most satisfaction.

Candidate B, which activity do you think is the most challenging?

Learning about the past

Turn to pictures 1–3 on page 210, which show people learning about the past.

Candidate B, compare two of the pictures and say what are the advantages of learning about the past in these ways, and who might actually learn most about the past.

Candidate A, which do you think is the easiest way to learn about the past?

PART 3

Turn to the pictures on page 211, which show some jobs that require people to have special qualities.

First, talk to each other about why people need special qualities to do these different jobs. Then decide which job would be the most rewarding.

PART 4

Answer these questions:

- Which is more important in any job: qualifications, personality or practical experience?
- What type of jobs should be most highly-valued? Why?
- Should there be a compulsory retirement age or should people be allowed to work as long as they like? Why/Why not?
- Do you think that people can be taught to be good leaders? Why/Why not?
- Some people say that it doesn't matter what job you do – the most important thing is to enjoy doing it. What do you think?

Part 1

You are going to read three extracts which are all concerned in some way with research. For questions **1–6**, choose the answer (**A**, **B**, **C** or **D**) which you think fits best according to the text.

In the exam, mark your answers **on the separate answer sheet**.

English language: lost and found

When does a word become a word? For the staff of the *Oxford English Dictionary*, it is not a philosophical question, but a practical one. Words are space, time and money.

A researcher at Kingston University, London, recently described his fascination at discovering a vault full of millions of 'non words' that had failed to make the grade. They included 'wurfing', the act of surfing the internet at work; 'polkadodge', the awkward dance performed by pedestrians trying to pass each other on the street; and 'nonversation', a pointless chat. 'What you have to remember,' says Fiona McPherson, senior editor of the *OED*'s new words group, 'is that once a word has gone into the dictionary, it never comes out. So words have to pass a few basic tests before they can be deemed to have entered the language. They have to have been around a reasonable amount of time and be in common use.'

First published in 1928, after a gestation period of more than 50 years, the *OED* is authoritative, scholarly, but never complete. As soon as the original dictionary was completed, work began on a second edition, published in 1989. A third edition is now in preparation, though it is anybody's guess when it will see the light of day. 'The internet has made our work both easier and harder,' says McPherson. 'Being able to store words electronically is a godsend. On the other hand, there are so many potential outlets for new words that it is far more difficult to keep track of changes in the language.'

1   The writer uses 'polkadodge' as an example of a word that

   A   may be included in the dictionary at some point in the future.
   B   has not been considered for inclusion in the dictionary.
   C   is used quite commonly but is not included in the dictionary.
   D   has not been regarded as worthy of inclusion in the dictionary.

2   When the writer says 'it is anybody's guess', he is referring to

   A   varying opinions on something.
   B   the difficulty of predicting something.
   C   the number of people involved in something.
   D   how inconsistent something is.

Stone Age discovery

The Stone Age may have started a million years earlier, after archaeologists found evidence that one of our ancestors was using tools much earlier than previously thought.

The find suggested that *Australopithecus afarensis*, the half-ape, half-human nicknamed Lucy when her skeleton was found, was using stone tools 800,000 years before *Homo habilis*, nicknamed The Handy Man and thought to have been the first hominid to have mastered tools. A team led by Zeresenay Alemseged from the California Academy of Sciences discovered two fossil animal bones dating back 3.4 million years in Ethiopia, close to where Lucy was found in 1976. The bones showed evidence of being cut and having the marrow extracted with a stone tool.

'This find will definitely force us to revise our text books on human evolution, since it pushes the evidence for tool use and meat eating in our family back by nearly a million years,' says Mr Alemseged. 'These developments had a huge impact on the story of humanity.' His colleague Shannon McPherron says, 'This is pushing the Stone Age back. It is profound. We can now picture Lucy walking around the East African landscape with a stone tool in her hand, scavenging and butchering meat. We have shown that two key aspects of our evolution, meat eating and stone tool use, took place much further back in our history.'

3   The research described centred on

   A   further analysis of an earlier discovery.
   B   signs of activity previously carried out on a discovery.
   C   comparison between a new discovery and an earlier one.
   D   changes in the condition of a discovery over a period of time.

4   The main point of the text is that

   A   a belief that has long been accepted may in fact be incorrect.
   B   the names given to certain creatures may have to be changed.
   C   little research has previously been done into an aspect of human development.
   D   the order of certain developments in humans has now been established.

EXTRACT FROM A NOVEL

Two miles to the east, Sarah Matson eased herself slowly into a prime vantage point beside a rock. Barely thirty feet away, a noisy colony of Steller's sea lions basked at the water's edge. A dozen or so of the fat, whiskered mammals sat huddled together, while four or five could be seen swimming in the surf. Two young males barked loudly at each other. Several pups slept, blissfully oblivious to the racket.

Pulling a small notepad from her jacket pocket, Sarah began jotting down particulars about each animal, estimating its age and health. After nearly an hour, she replaced the notepad in her pocket, and slowly retraced her steps across the boulder-strewn gulley.

Sarah relished working outdoors. The flaxen-haired thirty-year-old had a slender frame and delicate features, but she had grown up in rural Wyoming and had spent all her summers hiking and horse riding in the Teton mountains. Now, in her role as field epidemiologist for the Center for Disease Control, she was able to combine her passion for the outdoors with her love of wildlife by helping to track the spread of animal diseases that were communicable to humans.

A number of mysterious sea lion deaths had been reported along the western Alaskan Peninsula, and Sarah and two CDC associates had been sent to the Aleutian Islands to determine the extent and range of the die-off. This was her second day on Yunaska, and so far she had failed to find any indications of an ailment in the local sea lion population.

5 The language used in the first paragraph is intended to create an impression of

    A how happy all the sea lions seemed to be.
    B how much sound the sea lions were making.
    C how organised the colony of sea lions was.
    D how appealing Sarah found the sea lions.

6 What do we learn about Sarah and her work in the extract?

    A She was becoming frustrated at the lack of progress in her work.
    B Her assignment was not as interesting as she had expected it to be.
    C She had found a job that suited her perfectly.
    D Her work took up most of her time.

You are going to read a newspaper article about a very young artist. Six paragraphs have been removed from the article. Choose from the paragraphs **A–G** the one which fits each gap (**7–12**). There is one extra paragraph which you do not need to use.

In the exam, mark your answers **on the separate answer sheet**.

Is Kieron Britain's most exciting artist?

Peter Stanford watches an amazing seven-year-old artist at work.

All the time we are talking, Kieron Williamson is busy sketching on the pad in front of him with quick, fluid movements of his pencil. He is copying from a book of pen and ink illustrations by Edward Seago, the twentieth-century British artist, before he adds touches of his own to the sketches.

7

Kieron is clearly caught up in what he is doing, his blonde head a study in concentration as he kneels in the front room of his family home. But he's not so distracted that he doesn't sometimes look me in the eye and put me right. 'You've added a bit more detail here,' I say, as he is reproducing Seago's sketch of an old man in an overcoat. 'Seago's', I explain, 'is lighter.' 'Not lighter,' Kieron corrects me. 'You call it looser. Loose and tight. They're the words.' Seven-year-olds don't often give adults lessons in the terminology of fine art.

8

Kieron actually can and does, and has been hailed as a 'mini-Monet', on account of his neo-Impressionist style, or the next Picasso. Recently, buyers from as far afield as South Africa and America queued up outside his modest local art gallery – some of them camping out all night – to snap up 33 paintings in just 27 minutes, leaving Kieron £150,000 better off. How did it feel? 'Very nice,' he replies politely. 'Did you talk to any of the buyers?' 'Yes, they kept asking me what else I do.' And what did you tell them? 'That I go to school, that I play football for my school and that I am the best defender in the team.'

9

His exhibition – the second to sell out so quickly – has brought him a lot of attention. Several American TV networks have filmed him in the family flat already and today a camera crew is squeezed into the front room with me, Kieron's mum, Michelle, his younger sister, Billie-Jo, and two sleeping cats.

10

'These are ones I did last night when I was watching the television with Billie-Jo,' he says, handing me a sketchbook. It falls open on a vibrant fairground scene. Kieron finds the page in the Seago book that inspired him. There is the same carousel, but he has added figures, buildings and trees in his drawing in the sketchbook.

11

As accomplished as Kieron's paintings are, part of their appeal is undoubtedly the story of precocious talent that goes with them. If he's doing similar work when he's 28, it may prompt a different reaction.

12

But Kieron is having none of it. He looks up sharply from his sketching. 'If I want to paint,' he says, 'I'll paint.'

A An example is his pastel *Figures at Holkham*, an accomplished composition with big blues skies, a line of sand, dunes framing to either side and two figures, one with a splash of red in the centre to draw the eye in. There is such an adult quality to his work that you can't help wondering if someone older has been helping him.

B Standard seven-year-old boy stuff there. Kieron, however, is being hailed as a child prodigy. 'They only come along once in a generation,' artist Carol Pennington tells me later, as she explains how she helped nurture this early-blooming talent, 'and Kieron is that one.'

C Michelle Williamson is aware of this. 'I fully expect Kieron in a few years' time to focus on something else as closely as he is focusing on art right now,' she says. 'Football or motor racing. There may well be a lot more ahead for him than art.'

D Yet, in the centre of the melee, Kieron seems utterly oblivious and just gets on with what he does every day, often rising at 6 a.m. to get on to paper a picture that is bursting to get out of his head. He will be painting every day of the school holidays, relishing the freedom denied him during term time.

E Each one takes him only a few minutes – horses, figures huddling in a tent, men and women in unusual costumes. 'I'm going to do this one, then this one, then this one,' he tells me, 'but not this one – the eyes aren't looking at anyone – or this one – it's too messy.'

F This, it is clear, is no mechanical exercise in reproduction. To underline the point, Kieron takes it back off me and adds a smudge of dark under one of the groups of people.

G But then Kieron Williamson is not your average boy. Aside from his precocious articulacy, he is single-handedly illustrating that familiar remark, made by many a parent when confronted with a prize-winning work of modern art, that 'my seven-year-old could do better than that'.

You are going to read an article about a management theory book. For questions **13–19**, choose the answer (**A**, **B**, **C** or **D**) which you think fits best according to the text.

In the exam, mark your answers **on the separate answer sheet**.

The new management gurus

What can animals tell us about business?

Bees. Ants. Reindeer. Not the usual topic of conversation at an average board meeting. But if Peter Miller's debut book, *Smart Swarm*, is anything to go by, the creatures could revolutionise the way we do business. In the latest in a series of books that challenge leaders to think differently, *Smart Swarm* explores the habits, actions and instincts of animals and how they can be applied to business. The book is set to become the most talked about in management circles after Miller, a senior editor at *National Geographic Magazine*, wrote an article on the subject a few years ago, which was read by 30 million people globally.

It follows a string of 'business thinking' books that have hit the shelves in recent years, all searching for new answers on how to run organisations effectively. *Obliquity*, published in March, told us that the most profitable companies are not the most aggressive in chasing profits, *Wikinomics*, a bestseller, demonstrated new models of production based on community and collaboration. Miller believes his book is the first time anyone has laid out the science behind a management theory. 'The biology of how ant colonies or beehives work are appealing models for organisations and systems that can be applied in a business context,' he says.

So how exactly can bees help run board meetings? 'By the way they work independently before they work together,' Miller says. 'Picture a huge beehive hanging on the branch of a tree, with about 5,000 bees vying for space and protection. They know their colony is getting too big and leaving them vulnerable. They must find a new home – and fast – but in a way that everyone agrees with. In today's business environment, managers need to be able to make the right decisions under huge amounts of pressure. Yet, it is clear that some of the best-paid leaders in some of the biggest organisations can get it dramatically wrong. How is it that they can fail to make efficient business decisions when a swarm of bees can make a critical decision about their hive in just a few seconds?'

According to Miller, 'swarm theory' can help managers in three simple steps: discover, test and evaluate. The bees first realise they have a problem. They then fly into the neighbourhood to find potential new sites. They come back and perform a 'dance' to get other bees to follow them. Eventually, the bees with the best dance attract the most votes – and a decision is made. Back to the board meeting. Managers that encourage debate, and then have a ballot over which idea is best, stand a better chance of getting it right, Miller says. 'The bee example tells you that you need to seek out diversity in your team. You need to have a way of gathering up very different approaches and ideas so you can make sure you pick the right one.'

Ants, in addition, can help businesses organise workflow and people. In an ant colony, there is no leader. Ants are self-organised, and respond to their environment and each other. One ant on its own could not raid a kitchen cupboard, but one ant telling the next one that it's worth following him to find food ends up creating a food chain. 'In an ant colony, you get the right number going in and out searching for food, you get the right number taking care of the babies,' Miller says. 'As a manager, this can tell you your hierarchy, your bureaucracy, is getting in the way of getting the work done.'

The airline industry has already flirted with the idea that ants can help make flying stress-free. Southwest Airlines, an American low-cost airline, was concerned its 30-year-old policy of letting customers choose where they sit once they boarded a plane was slowing down the process. By creating a computer simulation of people loading on to a plane, based on what ants would do, the company was able to show that assigned seating would only be faster by a few minutes. It was not worth scrapping their first-come, first-served policy, which was a key part of the company's brand.

Other animal examples in the book include reindeer, which can act together as a single herd, and schools of fish, which coordinate their movements precisely so they can change direction in an instant. Miller says: 'If you are concerned about surviving the next business cycle, in other words giving your company the resilience and ability to bounce back from challenges that you can't anticipate, then Nature is a great model.'

13 What does the writer say about *Smart Swarm* in the first paragraph?

    A It has already attracted a great deal of attention.

    B It is one of several books on animal behaviour and business.

    C It concerns a topic that a great many people are interested in.

    D It reflects what is already happening in some businesses.

14 Miller believes that his book differs from other 'business thinking' books because of

    A the evidence given in support of the theory.

    B the ease with which the theory can be implemented.

    C its focus on behaviour rather than profit or production.

    D its emphasis on practical action rather than theory.

15 In the third paragraph, the writer says that the behaviour of bees can show managers

    A the consequences of making the wrong decisions.

    B how to pinpoint exactly what a problem is.

    C how to arrive at the correct conclusions very quickly.

    D the need to act decisively when under great pressure.

16 According to the 'swarm theory', managers need to

    A consider the effect of a decision on a variety of other people.

    B be able to persuade others that their proposed decisions are right.

    C regard decision-making as a collaborative process.

    D accept criticism of decisions they have made.

17 The example of ants raiding a food cupboard illustrates

    A the need to create the right kind of hierarchy and bureaucracy.

    B the differences between how managers and employees think.

    C the belief that aims can be achieved in various different ways.

    D the effectiveness of employees making decisions for themselves.

18 Looking at the behaviour of ants caused Southwest Airlines to

    A improve one of its practices.

    B speed up one of its processes.

    C retain one of its policies.

    D increase customer choice.

19 What do we learn about Miller's book in the last paragraph?

    A It focuses both on individual and group behaviour among animals.

    B It is aimed at people who have fear about the future of their companies.

    C It makes connections between business cycles and animal behaviour.

    D It compares animal behaviour with the behaviour of managers.

Part 4

You are going to read an article about the Royal Society, a British scientific institution. For questions **20–34**, choose from the sections of the article (**A–D**). The jobs may be chosen more than once.

In the exam, mark your answers **on the separate answer sheet**.

In which section of the article are the following mentioned?

a belief that a certain development has been of particular use to scientists	**20**
the variety of ways in which the Royal Society encourages people who are not scientists to consider scientific issues	**21**
a rapid reaction to research being made public	**22**
a particular development that requires urgent action to improve it	**23**
the need for non-scientists to discuss certain scientific issues	**24** **25**
a resource for information on past scientific discoveries	**26**
a lack of understanding of scientific matters among people in general	**27**
the need for the Royal Society to maintain its original purpose	**28** **29**
a system that the Royal Society introduced	**30**
the fact that scientists do not always reach firm conclusions	**31**
previous difficulties in finding certain information	**32**
a problem that is not limited to the world of science	**33**
the belief that certain things that are possible are not desirable	**34**

The unstoppable spirit of inquiry

The president of the Royal Society, Martin Rees, celebrates the long history of one of Britain's greatest institutions.

A

The Royal Society began in 1660. From the beginning, the wide dissemination of scientific ideas was deemed important. The Society started to publish *Philosophical Transaction*, the first scientific journal, which continues to this day. The Society's journals pioneered what is still the accepted procedure whereby scientific ideas are subject to peer review – criticised, refined and codified into 'public knowledge'. Over the centuries, they published Isaac Newton's researches on light, Benjamin Franklin's experiments on lightning, Volta's first battery and many of the triumphs of twentieth-century science. Those who want to celebrate this glorious history should visit the Royal Society's archives via our *Trailblazing* website.

B

The founders of the Society enjoyed speculation, but they were also intensely engaged with the problems of their era, such as improvements to timekeeping and navigation. After 350 years, our horizons have expanded, but the same engagement is imperative in the 21st century. Knowledge has advanced hugely, but it must be deployed for the benefit of the ever-growing population of our planet, all empowered by ever more powerful technology. The silicon chip was perhaps the most transformative single invention of the past century; it has allowed miniaturisation and spawned the worldwide reach of mobile phones and the internet. It was physicists who developed the World Wide Web and, though it impacts us all, scientists have benefited especially.

C

Traditional journals survive as guarantors of quality, but they are supplemented by a blogosphere of widely varying quality. The latter cries out for an informal system of quality control. The internet levels the playing fields between researchers in major centres and those in relative isolation. It has transformed the way science is communicated and debated. In 2002, three young Indian mathematicians invented a faster scheme for factoring large numbers – something that would be crucial for code-breaking. They posted their results on the web. Within a day, 20,000 people had downloaded the work, which was the topic of hastily convened discussions in many centres of mathematical research around the world. The internet also allows new styles of research. For example, in the old days, astronomical research was stored on delicate photographic plates; these were not easily accessible and tiresome to analyse. Now such data (and large datasets in genetics and particle physics) can be accessed and downloaded anywhere. Experiments and natural events can be followed in real time.

D

We recently asked our members what they saw as the most important questions facing us in the years ahead and we are holding discussion meetings on the 'Top Ten'. Whatever breakthroughs are in store, we can be sure of one thing: the widening gulf between what science enables us to do and what it's prudent or ethical actually to do. In respect of certain developments, regulation will be called for, on ethical as well as prudential grounds. The way science is applied is a matter not just for scientists. All citizens need to address these questions. Public decisions should be made, after the widest possible discussion, in the light of the best scientific evidence available. That is one of the key roles of the Society. Whether it is the work of our Science Policy Centre, our journals, our discussion meetings, our work in education or our public events, we must be at the heart of helping policy makers and citizens make informed decisions.

E

But science isn't dogma. Its assertions are sometimes tentative, sometimes compelling; noisy controversy doesn't always connote balanced arguments; risks are never absolutely zero, even if they are hugely outweighed by potential benefits. In promoting an informed debate, the media are crucial. When reporting a scientific controversy, the aim should be neither to exaggerate risks and uncertainties, nor to gloss over them. This is indeed a challenge, particularly when institutional, political or commercial pressures distort the debate. Scientists often bemoan the public's weak grasp of science – without some 'feel' for the issues, public debate can't get beyond sloganising. But they protest too much: there are other issues where public debate is, to an equally disquieting degree, inhibited by ignorance.

F

The Royal Society aims to sustain Britain's traditional strength in science, but also to ensure that wherever science impacts on people's lives, it is openly debated. Citizen scientists, with views spanning the entire political and philosophical spectrum, should engage more willingly with the media and political forums. In the words of a recent president of the Society, 'the ivory tower is no longer a sanctuary; scientists have a special responsibility. We should aspire, like our founders, to 'see further' into Nature and Nature's laws, but also to emulate their broad engagement with society and public affairs – no longer just in one city or one nation, but on global scales.'

You **must** answer this question. Write your answer in **180–220** words in an appropriate style. In the exam, write your answer **on the separate answer sheet provided**.

---

1   Your college does not currently have any kind of a cafeteria for the students, and the Principal wants to use a room in the college to set up this facility. The college has done a survey on other colleges and the facilities they provide, and has asked students to provide a proposal for the new cafeteria.

Read the extract from the Principal's email and the results of the survey on which you have made some notes. Then, **using the information appropriately**, write your proposal.

> To all students!
>
> You have asked for a cafeteria in the college, and we have done a survey on the possible facilities we could provide. I'd like the facility to be popular and well-used, so the money it will cost will not be wasted. Tell us what you think is the best way forward!

Self-service

Fast food section.

Hot food to eat in.

Separate coffee bar for snacks. ——— *Coffee not good for everyone!*

Open all day including before school.

Waitress service

Set menu.

Hot and cold food. ——— *Balanced – busy at peak times.*

Fixed opening times.

Health-food delicatessen

Salad options. ——— *Boring!*

Sandwiches.

Vegetarian food.

Open before and after school. ——— *Lunchtime?*

Write your **proposal**. You should use your own words as far as possible.

Part 2

Write an answer to one of the questions **2–5** in this part. Write your answer in **220–260** words. In the exam, write your answer **on the separate answer sheet provided**, and put the question number in the box at the top of the page.

2 A magazine is planning to publish a series of reviews of films that have made a lasting impression on people, and has asked readers to send in reviews of films they want to be included in the series. Write a review of a film you have seen that made a lasting impression on you, saying what it was about and why it made such an impression on you. You should also explain why you think it should be included in the series.

Write your **review**.

3 An international magazine wants to collect information about young people's shopping habits across the world and has asked readers to send in reports on how young people shop in their country. The magazine also wants its readers to find out whether the way young people shop is changing, and what affects the kind of things young people buy.

Write your **report**.

4 You see the following announcement in an international magazine.

> ### What's the best place in the world to live?
>
> Do you live there yourself?
>
> Nominate your favourite place to live, saying what it is like, what you can do there and explaining why it is such a good place to live.
>
> The best entry will win a prize for the town.

Write your **competition entry**.

5 Answer one of the following two questions based on a book you have read. In the exam you will have to write about one of two specific titles. Write the letter **(a)** or **(b)** as well as the number 5 on your answer sheet.

(a) You read the following announcement in an in-flight magazine.

> We're planning a series of reports about books which people might enjoy reading on a long journey. Write a report about a book which you think would be suitable, and we'll publish the best. In your report you should:
>
> • briefly outline the plot
>
> • describe any particularly absorbing scenes or characters
>
> • explain why you recommend it in general, but especially for a long journey

Write your **report**.

(b) As part of your English course you have discussed the question *Are there any colourful and funny characters in modern fiction?* Your teacher has asked you to write an essay on one or two colourful and funny characters in a book you have read. In your essay you should describe one or two characters, outline scenes in which they behave in a funny way and explain why you found them funny or colourful.

Write your **essay**.

Part 1

For questions **1–12**, read the text below and decide which answer (**A**, **B**, **C** or **D**) best fits each gap. There is an example at the beginning (**0**).

In the exam, mark your answers **on the separate answer sheet**.

Example:

0 A fulfil   **B** accomplish   **C** manage   **D** perform

0	A	B	C	D

Book Review
Galapagos: The islands that changed the world

I was lucky enough to **(0)** .... an ambition and visit the Galapagos Islands two years ago. It's only when you experience the place first **(1)** .... that you really appreciate why the early explorers gave this isolated archipelago the **(2)** .... 'The Enchanted Isles'.

(3) .... no substitute for a visit, this superbly attractive book provides a fascinating commentary and scientific background to the Galapagos experience. BBC books have **(4)** .... their usual high-quality job in producing the volume that will accompany their TV series of the same name.

Nothing can compare to exploring the strange landscapes, **(5)** .... up close and personal with the unique wildlife and witnessing the rich biological and environmental history that is so very apparent on the islands. However, this book does **(6)** .... close. The superb descriptive prose of award-winning cameraman Paul Stewart is another plus **(7)** ...., as is the fact that this is punctuated by his iconic photography. This book **(8)** .... in celebrating the weird and wonderful sights and unique life **(9)** .... that are hidden amongst these fascinating islands. It also comes **(10)** .... with a comprehensive gazetteer section. But don't **(11)** .... read this book as an alternative to actually going, use it as the **(12)** .... of inspiration for your own trip, a useful guide once you're there and a stunning reminder on your return.

1	**A** foot	**B** person	**C** flesh	**D** hand
2	**A** label	**B** badge	**C** emblem	**D** token
3	**A** Despite	**B** However	**C** Whilst	**D** Whereas
4	**A** set	**B** done	**C** made	**D** given
5	**A** getting	**B** reaching	**C** arriving	**D** gaining
6	**A** run	**B** come	**C** go	**D** pass
7	**A** spot	**B** point	**C** mark	**D** tip
8	**A** attains	**B** succeeds	**C** achieves	**D** obtains
9	**A** sorts	**B** types	**C** forms	**D** ways
10	**A** complete	**B** entire	**C** intact	**D** joined
11	**A** barely	**B** hardly	**C** merely	**D** scarcely
12	**A** base	**B** cause	**C** origin	**D** source

Part 2

For questions **13–27**, read the text below and think of the word which best fits each gap. There is an example at the beginning (**0**).

In the exam, write your answers **IN CAPITAL LETTERS on the separate answer sheet**.

Example: | **0** | A | S | | | | | | | | | | | | | | | | |

A history of table tennis

Like many other sports, table tennis started out **(0)** .... a mild social diversion. It is actually a descendent, **(13)** .... with lawn tennis and badminton, of the ancient game of tennis. It was popular in England in the second half of the nineteenth century under its present name and various trade names **(14)** .... as Whiff-Whaff and Ping-Pong, **(15)** .... sought to imitate the sound **(16)** .... by the ball striking the table. The game soon **(17)** .... something of a craze and there are many contemporary references to it and illustrations of it **(18)** .... played, usually in domestic surroundings.

(19) .... the early twentieth century, the sport had already acquired some of its present-day complexities, **(20)** .... it was still seen by many as an after-dinner amusement **(21)** .... than a sport. An account published in 1903 found it necessary to warn players **(22)** .... the wearing of evening dress, but went **(23)** .... to give detailed technical advice about the pen-holder grip and tactics.

Over the next 60 years, table tennis developed **(24)** .... a worldwide sport, played by up to 30 million competitive players and by countless millions **(25)** .... played less seriously. **(26)** .... getting faster, more subtle and more demanding all the time, the game has not changed in its essence **(27)** .... the earliest days.

Part 3

For questions **28–37**, read the text below. Use the word given in capitals at the end of some of the lines to form a word that fits in the gap **in the same line**. There is an example at the beginning (**0**).

In the exam, write your answers **IN CAPITAL LETTERS on the separate answer sheet**.

Example: | **0** | I | N | C | R | E | A | S | I | N | G | L | Y | | | | | | |

Dancing is good for you

In recent decades, in both theatre and cinema, dance shows have

become (**0**) .... popular. Meanwhile, the British Amateur Dancesport   **INCREASE**

Association estimates that there are now four million people (**28**) ....   **PART**

in dancing activities in the country every week. But the popularity of

dancing is by no means a recent phenomenon.

Since the dawn of civilisation, dance has been an important part of life,

and dance (**29**) .... struggle to identify the first evidence of dance   **HISTORY**

as it has always been an intrinsic part of human (**30**) ....   **BEHAVE**

The earliest recorded dances, discovered in the 9,000-year-old

Bhimbetka rock paintings in India, were used to tell stories and

celebrate (**31**) .... events, whilst also serving as a way of   **SIGNIFY**

passing on information to future generations.

But why has dance, something which can make someone look utterly

(**32**) .... if done wrong, always seemed to be natural to our DNA?   **RIDICULE**

Experts argue that its psychological and physiological benefits

are the cause. (**33**) .... studies have discovered that dancing is   **NUMBER**

not only an (**34**) .... form of non-verbal communication, but is   **EFFECT**

also a mood-boosting cure that can alleviate (**35**) ...., improve   **DEPRESS**

interpersonal (**36**) .... and cure illnesses. Physically, dancing   **RELATION**

makes us happy because, as with any repetitive exercise, it releases

endorphins. Also it's a socialising event, (**37**) .... us to be physically   **ABLE**

close to people and more emotionally connected to them.

Part 4

For questions **38–42**, think of one word only which can be used appropriately in all three sentences. Here is an example (**0**).

Example:

0 I was on the .... of booking my holiday when my boss said I might have to change the dates.

As the meeting drew to a close, the chairperson moved on to the final .... on the agenda.

Theo couldn't see the .... of getting to the airport too early, as the check-in desk only opened one hour before the flight departed.

Example: | 0 | P | O | I | N | T | | | | | | | | | | | | | | |

In the exam, write **only** the missing word **IN CAPITAL LETTERS on the separate answer sheet**.

---

38 We were asked to choose a .... from a famous novel to read out loud in class.

Keeping the doors open helps the .... of air through the building, and stops it getting too hot.

There's a narrow .... connecting the two parts of the shopping complex, which gets very crowded at weekends.

39 The magazine has decided to .... a series of articles on how to set up your own website.

As he'd missed the airport bus, Jack's neighbour offered to .... him there in his car.

The gadget is useful for travellers because it can .... off either mains electricity or batteries.

40 The village .... at the head of a valley in the National Park.

Thinking about technological change, I often wonder what .... ahead of us in the future.

The responsibility for ensuring the students follow the detailed curriculum .... with the class teacher.

41 Yolanda's a very reliable person, so it's .... to assume that she'll turn up on time.

Diana needed to find a .... place to hide Tom's birthday present, so she could surprise him on the day.

Alma was told that it wasn't .... to leave valuables in her hotel room when she went out.

42 This is .... the best computer game I've ever played.

Flora was a good tennis player and so beat her young opponents ....

David found that he fitted .... into his new circle of friends at college.

Part 5

For questions **43–50**, complete the second sentence so that it has a similar meaning to the first sentence, using the word given. **Do not change the word given.** You must use between **three** and **six** words, including the word given. Here is an example (**0**).

Example:

0 Chloe would only eat a pizza if she could have a mushroom topping.

ON

Chloe .... a mushroom topping when she ate a pizza.

The gap can be filled with the words 'insisted on having', so you write:

Example:	**0**	INSISTED ON HAVING

In the exam, write **only** the missing words **IN CAPITAL LETTERS on the separate answer sheet**.

---

43 The village shop is now being managed by a national supermarket chain.

TAKEN

A national supermarket chain .... of the village shop.

44 This door is an emergency exit and must never be locked for any reason.

ACCOUNT

On .... be locked because it is an emergency exit.

45 Melvin's friend recommended that website where he bought the camping equipment.

ON

Melvin bought equipment from that website .... a friend.

46 We never imagined that Julian might be planning to resign from his job.

OCCURRED

It never .... Julian might be planning to resign from his job.

47 As long as he could see, Kevin really didn't mind where he sat in the stadium.

DIFFERENCE

As long as he could see, ... where he sat in the stadium.

48 Unfortunately, I don't have enough time to visit the gym regularly.

ABLE

If I had more time, ... more regular visits to the gym.

49 Somebody should have told us that the date had been changed.

INFORMED

We .... the change of date.

50 Yolanda's family persuaded her to enter the competition.

TALKED

Yolanda was .... the competition by her family.

Part 1

You will hear three different extracts. For questions **1–6**, choose the answer
(**A**, **B** or **C**) which fits best according to what you hear. There are two questions for
each extract.

In the exam, write your answers **on the separate answer sheet**.

Extract One

You hear two friends discussing a book.

1   What surprised the man about the book initially?

    A   the fact that it was a thriller

    B   the writer's underlying intention

    C   the way the characters interacted

2   The woman feels that the book has made her consider

    A   being more honest with people online.

    B   being more cautious with people online.

    C   choosing online contacts more carefully.

Extract Two

You hear part of a discussion about a jewellery designer.

3   What aspect of the designer's latest collection does the woman admire most?

    A   the flexibility it gives the wearer

    B   the diverse influences in the style

    C   the characteristic use of beadwork

4   She feels that the designer's next collection

    A   represents a brave change of direction.

    B   may turn out to be disappointing.

    C   promises to be very exciting.

Extract Three

You hear part of an interview with the owner of a shopping website.

5 When answering the interviewer's first question, he is

   A justifying a rather hands-on approach.

   B regretting that he lacks certain key skills.

   C admitting that he needs to reconsider his priorities.

6 He feels the hardest part of being an entrepreneur is

   A finding reliable people to work on a project.

   B choosing the best time to launch a project.

   C deciding which project to go with.

Part 2

You will hear a woman called Mara Styles telling a group of people about her holiday at an ecocamp in Patagonia. For questions **7–14**, complete the sentences.

In the exam, write your answers **on the separate answer sheet**.

ECOCAMP HOLIDAY

Mara uses the word [_____ 7] to describe her previous experiences of camping.

Mara says that traditional local buildings in the region were made out of

[_____ 8], skins and fur.

Like traditional buildings, good protection against

[_____ 9] is a feature of the modern ecocamp domes.

Mara particularly appreciated the feeling of [_____ 10] in her dome.

In the communal areas, it was the quality of the

[_____ 11] that impressed Mara most.

Something called a

[_____ 12] helps to protect the ground on which the camp is sited.

Mara chose to go on hikes in the [_____ 13] category.

Mara is particularly proud of her photo of the [_____ 14] which she saw on a hike.

Part 3

You will hear an interview with a sportsman called Greg Marton, talking about his life and the different sports he's taken part in. For questions **15–20**, choose the answer (**A**, **B**, **C** or **D**) which fits best according to what you hear.

In the exam, write your answers **on the separate answer sheet**.

---

15 When talking about teenage ice-hockey, Greg reveals that

    A he now wishes he'd trained harder.
    B he's sorry that he let his father down.
    C he resents the pressure he was put under.
    D he accepts that he lacked the drive to succeed.

16 What led Greg to take up rowing?

    A He followed up a suggestion made by friends.
    B He was frustrated by his performance as a runner.
    C He was told that he had the physical strength for it.
    D He was disappointed not to get on to a degree course.

17 What does Greg say about his initial failure to make the national rowing team?

    A He feels that he wasn't treated fairly.
    B He admits that he was mostly just unfortunate.
    C He disagrees with the way the selection process operated.
    D He recognises that he should have attended training camps.

18 What does Greg suggest about his move to California?

    A He saw it mainly as a way of furthering his career.
    B He was motivated by his desire to try a new activity.
    C He needed convincing that it was the right thing to do.
    D He wanted to concentrate his energies on work rather than sport.

19 Greg says that cycling and rowing both require

    A a commitment to a team effort.
    B a tolerance of intense pain.
    C a willingness to take risks.
    D a good sense of timing.

20 According to Greg, why should cyclists include rowing as part of their training?

    A They might find it as enjoyable as he does.
    B They would develop a similar set of muscles.
    C It might help them to avoid injury in accidents.
    D It provides a break from the monotony of cycling.

Part 4

You will hear five short extracts in which actors are talking about performing in live theatre productions.

In the exam, write your answers **on the separate answer sheet.**

TASK ONE

For questions **21–25**, choose from the list (**A–H**) what each speaker usually does before a performance.

A gets some fresh air	
B puts flowers in the dressing rooms	Speaker 1 21
C focuses on personal souvenirs	Speaker 2 22
D does some exercises	Speaker 3 23
E chats to the audience	Speaker 4 24
F leaves gifts for other cast members	Speaker 5 25
G has a rest	
H checks everything is in place	

TASK TWO

For questions **26–30**, choose from the list (**A–H**) what each speaker says went wrong on a recent production.

A being affected by illness	
B getting a negative audience reaction	Speaker 1 26
C receiving poor reviews	Speaker 2 27
D being disturbed by noise	Speaker 3 28
E having an accident	Speaker 4 29
F finding something unexpected on stage	Speaker 5 30
G attracting a very small audience	
H getting the words wrong	

PART 1

The interlocutor will ask you a few questions about yourself and on everyday topics such as work and study, travel, entertainment, daily life and routines. For example:

* What is your favourite way of travelling short distances? Why?

* Do you ever listen to the radio? Why/Why not?

* What do you do when you go out with your friends?

PART 2

Feeling proud

Turn to pictures 1–3 on page 212, which show people feeling proud in different situations.

Candidate A, compare two of the pictures and say why the people might feel proud in these situations and how important the feeling might be to them.

Candidate B, who do you think will feel proud the longest?

Weather conditions

Turn to pictures 1–3 on page 213, which show people experiencing different weather conditions.

Candidate B, compare two of the pictures and say what effect the weather conditions might be having on the people's mood and how difficult it might be for them to deal with the conditions.

Candidate A, who do you think is most affected by the weather conditions?

PART 3

I'd like you to imagine that a holiday company is constructing a new website. It wants to attract more clients of all ages.

Turn to the pictures on page 214, which show some of the pictures they are considering for the home page.

Talk to each other about what each picture might say about the company. Then decide which picture should be used on the home page of the company's website.

PART 4

Answer these questions:

* Some people say that going away on holiday is a waste of money. What's your opinion?
* What do you think are the advantages and disadvantages of buying a holiday online?
* Do you think that working for a travel company is a good job? Why/Why not?
* Why do you think people enjoy travelling to other countries?
* In future, do you think people will travel more, or less? Why?

Part 1

You are going to read three extracts which are all concerned in some way with flying. For questions **1–6**, choose the answer (**A**, **B**, **C** or **D**) which you think fits best according to the text.

In the exam, mark your answers **on the separate answer sheet**.

Unidentified Flying Objects – The UFO files

UFO – Three letters that produce a feeling of creeping unease in normally rational people – albeit for different reasons. For some of us, nothing is more disturbing than the thought of unexplained objects in the sky. They may be turquoise lights that throb gently among the stars, causing you to stop and squint as you put out the rubbish. Or they may be sinister black projectiles that flash across your windscreen so fast that you nearly crash your car. Either way, there's something out there and the Ministry of Defence needs to know about it (unless it already does but isn't saying). For others, the mere thought of UFOs produces a different kind of fear: that of being cornered at a party by a Ufologist – a UFO enthusiast.

Recently, the British government released previously secret files from the National Archives which prove that, for many years, UFOs were a much bigger deal than we suspected. True believers will go nuts with excitement. The files (Ufologists always talk about 'files', never boring old documents) reveal that for a period of some years, RAF jets were scrambled to investigate UFO reports no fewer than 200 times a year. The files include sketches of extra-terrestrial rockets and spaceships sent in by members of the public. These range from a simple triangle with three lights (one red, which 'pulsed', two white which 'did not pulse') to a small rocketcraft.

---

1   In the extract as a whole, the writer makes a contrast between

   A   his own beliefs about UFOs and the beliefs of other people.
   B   common beliefs about UFOs and the evidence that exists about them.
   C   the kinds of emotion that UFOs arouse in people.
   D   the different ways that a single object can be described.

2   What point does the writer make about the secret files?

   A   They are not as interesting as some people expected them to be.
   B   They contain more detail than some people might expect.
   C   They show that some reports of UFOs were taken more seriously than others.
   D   They indicate that there were a surprisingly high number of reports of UFOs.

The Mail Run

'Welcome to the Mail Run!' says John, sliding into the pilot's seat beside me. With his shock of white hair, crisp suit and aviator shades, he cuts a dashing figure. The plane is the width of a family car and seats just six people. Pre-flight checks are brief: 'There are flotation devices in the seat pockets, but I don't think we're going to need them today!' he says, grinning.

It is mid-morning in downtown Vancouver, and a forest of shiny skyscrapers reflects a sullen sky. On the pontoon, seaplanes bob on the tide. Above the gridlocked traffic, the snow-capped Rockies pierce a dark slab of cloud. John keys the ignition and the de Havilland beaver splutters to life. The propeller blades scythe the air, building momentum until the seaplane jogs on the spot, the engine note a deafening roar. I don my headset. John opens the throttle and we bounce off across the bay, scattering the cormorants.

Our destination is the Southern Gulf Islands, the wooded archipelago that straddles the strait between the mainland and the Pacific breakwater of Vancouver Island. We climb to 500 feet, soaring over the harbour bridge. The city recedes as we head south, skirting virgin beaches backed by pines. Beyond the logging camps of the Fraser River estuary, the snow-melt meets the ocean in murky tidal lines. We follow the sediment, flying out across open water. The route is still called the Mail Run but the planes no longer carry the Islands' post. 'The mail is contracted out now,' explains John, 'so these days we deliver people instead of parcels.'

3   In the second paragraph, the writer describes

    A   the view of the city from the sky.
    B   her feelings before the flight.
    C   the movement of the plane before the flight starts.
    D   a change in the weather on the day of the flight.

4   What do we learn about the Mail Run in the text as a whole?

    A   Its name is no longer appropriate.
    B   Its route has changed.
    C   John has flown it for many years.
    D   People fly on it because of the scenery.

Grandmother's helicopter record attempt

The last time Jennifer Murray attempted a world helicopter record, she crashed on the ice sheets of Antarctica in a tangle of crushed metal. She was seriously injured and lay waiting in piercing cold for a rescue that took hours to arrive. Now she's having another go.

It's precisely the same challenge: circling the globe in a tiny helicopter via both North and South Poles – a feat of skill and endurance never achieved before. Yet here's the truly shocking thing – Murray is a 66-year-old grandmother. So why is she revisiting an attempt that almost killed her last time? 'It's unfinished business,' she explains. 'We've ghosts to lay to rest.'

She holds several flying records of her own. She was the first woman to co-pilot a helicopter around the globe and the first to do it solo. But these were both latitudinal flights. The big one, the truly daunting challenge, is to circle the Earth via the Poles, experiencing the coldest and the hottest landscapes in the process. Attempting the feat with co-pilot Colin Bodill in 2003, Murray crashed in a blizzard on Antarctica in temperatures of -40 degrees. Enough adventure for an entire lifetime perhaps. But the same pair are about to try to finish the job.

It's a trip that underlines the enduring nature of the challenge but also the sheer joy of helicopters. It was certainly the idea of release that drew Murray to them at the age of 54. 'It gave me a whole new perspective on life,' she says. 'Life was two-dimensional before and then became three-dimensional. You are a bird, you can soar, you have the freedom of the sky and it's intoxicating.' But what propelled her to world record attempts? 'I'm someone who loves a challenge, who loves to go off the beaten track. In some ways you could say it's insecurity. I have always wanted to excel at something.'

5   What is emphasised about the world record attempt?

    A   that Jennifer Murray is making it for the second time
    B   that it has not been made by anyone of Jennifer Murray's age before
    C   that the chances of it succeeding are low
    D   that it is attracting a lot of publicity

6   When talking about the trip, Jennifer Murray

    A   plays down the amount of danger involved.
    B   suggests a possible reason why she is doing it.
    C   says that only someone like her would try it.
    D   accepts that others may regard it as foolish.

You are going to read an article about a British TV soap opera called *Coronation Street*. Six paragraphs have been removed from the article. Choose from the paragraphs **A–G** the one which fits each gap (**7–12**). There is one extra paragraph which you do not need to use.

In the exam, mark your answers **on the separate answer sheet**.

The birth of *Coronation Street*

Scriptwriter Daran Little has dramatised the beginnings of the first British soap.
He explains how sneers came before success.

I was 21 and fresh from university when I started work as an archivist on *Coronation Street*. My role was pretty simple: I had to memorise everything that had ever happened in the show and so help the writers with character histories.

7 _____

Now my own dramatised version of how it all began, *The Road to Coronation Street*, is about to go on air. I moved on to become a writer on the show in the early 2000s. But those early black and white episodes will always be close to my heart, and so will the genius who created the show.

8 _____

Last summer, I was sitting and chatting with colleagues about the latest plot twist in *Coronation Street*. While I was doing that, I suddenly realised what a compelling piece of television drama the creation of the programme itself would make.

9 _____

Tony Warren was a one-time child actor with a passion for writing who turned up at the infant Granada Television with a vision for a new form of story-telling – a show about ordinary people and their everyday lives. It had never been done before.

10 _____

It was that Granada had a condition, as part of its franchise, to create locally sourced programmes, an obligation it was not meeting at that time. One of the owners, Sidney Bernstein, was a showman who loved the entertainment business and was keen to develop it. He created Granada television in 1956 and shortly afterwards employed a Canadian producer, Harry Elton, to help nurture talent. It was Elton who employed Tony Warren, and it was these two men who would eventually change the face of British television.

11 _____

It should have ended there. A script written and discarded by a broadcaster, Warren and Elton should have drowned their sorrows and moved on to the next project. But they didn't; they fought to change the bosses' minds. *The Road to Coronation Street* tells the story of how, against all the odds, a television phenomenon was born, and how a group of unknown actors became the first superstars of British television drama. On December 9, 1960, *Coronation Street* was first broadcast. With minutes to go before transmission, Warren was feeling sick, one of the lead actors was missing, and so was the cat for the opening shot.

12 _____

It's a story I'm proud to have brought to the screen.

A Luckily, I wasn't the only one to be persuaded of this, and within a fortnight I had been commissioned to write a script. In a world of prolonged commissioning debates, this was highly unusual – but then the story of *Coronation Street* is also highly unusual.

B At that point, its creator Tony Warren had given it the title *Florizel Street*. The first episode was broadcast live and it was envisaged that there would be just 13 episodes of the show.

C Half a century later, that inauspicious beginning is a far cry from the ongoing success of one of Britain's most-watched soaps. My drama is more than a celebration of that event, it's a story of taking chances, believing in talent and following a dream.

D I first met that person, Tony Warren, as a student, after I wrote asking to interview him. We chatted about the show he had created when he was 23 – a show which broke new ground in television drama and brought soap opera to British television. I was fascinated by his story, and have remained so ever since.

E Tony Warren developed a show set around a Northern back street with a pub on the corner called the Rovers Return. Its characters were drawn from Warren's past. A script was written and sent 'upstairs' to management. He was told, in no uncertain terms, that this wasn't television. It had no drama, the characters were unsympathetic and if it was transmitted, the advertisers would withdraw their custom.

F At that stage, *Coronation Street* had been on air for 28 years and it took me three-and-a-half years to watch every episode that had been made. That's 14 episodes a day, which means that I went a bit stir crazy somewhere between 1969 and 1972 and was a gibbering wreck by the time a lorry crashed in the street in 1979.

G In fact, no original piece of television featuring regional actors had ever been broadcast. Television was ruled by Londoners who spoke with rounded vowels. The only Manchester accents on the screen were employed in a comic context. For broadcasters, the language of the North of England didn't translate to television drama. Besides, even if it did, no one in London would be able to understand it – so what was the point?

You are going to read an article about children learning to cook. For questions **13–19**, choose the answer (**A**, **B**, **C** or **D**) which you think fits best according to the text.

In the exam, mark your answers **on the separate answer sheet**.

Cooking shouldn't be child's play

Take the fun out of cooking with your kids and there's a chance you'll have bred a chef with a great future. Television cook Nigella Lawson has revealed that her own mother put her and her sister 'to work' in the kitchen from the age of five. For the young Nigella, preparing food was certainly not recreational. Sounds intriguing. Will her new series feature her putting young ones through a blisteringly tough regime, sweating as they bone out chickens and being blasted when their souffle collapses? Apparently not, but she makes a good point. 'Parents sometimes feel that they have to get into children's TV presenter mode and make cooking all fun and recreational.' For the young Lawsons it was about getting a meal on the table. She and her sister took it in turns to cook their father's breakfast.

My mother took a similar view. She tutored us in cooking. We never made grey pastry in amusing shapes or had hilarious squirting sessions with icing bags. If we were going to cook, it was for a purpose. At first, the only aim was that it be edible. But my mother noticed the interest my sisters and I had in cooking (in her defence, she never forced us to do it) and set us some challenging tasks. My speciality was sweet pastry. She would look over my shoulder and suggest rolling it thinner 'so the light shines through it'.

Nowadays, this instructive style of upbringing is frowned upon. Learning to make things has to be all about play and each creation is greeted with exaggerated applause. Parents plaster their kitchen walls with their five-year-olds' paintings and poems; they tell their kids how clever and talented they are in the belief that if you do this often enough, clever and talented they will be. But experts say that overpraised children can, in fact, underachieve and that compliments should be limited and sincere. Analysis by researchers at Stanford University in California found that praising too much demotivates children – interestingly, more so with girls than boys.

Playschool cookery exists alongside another culinary crime – making funny faces on the plate. The idea goes that it's nothing but fun, fun and more fun to eat the cherry-tomato eyes, mangetout mouth and broccoli hair. Hmmm, is it? At some point, the cartoon stuff has to go. I have had dinner with grown men who, I suspect, have yet to get over the fact that their fish is not cut out in the shape of a whale. I'd love to meet the comic genius who decided it was somehow good to urge our children to eat food shaped like an endangered species. Nigella Lawson remembers making giraffe-shaped pizzas for her children, only to be asked why they couldn't have ordinary ones like their dad. Smart kids, those.

Sooner or later we have to chuck out all those books that tell you and the little ones what a laugh cooking is and tell the truth. Cooking is a chore – and not an easy one for busy people to keep up. Better to be honest than discover this disagreeable fact later. If my mother had not made cooking something to take seriously, I suspect I would have eaten far more convenience food.

But you can go too far with budding chefs. Nigella might say her early training 'just felt normal', but I am not sure that my childhood culinary regime was an ordinary part of growing up. Perhaps our families were too obsessed with food. We shouldn't be too didactic with our little ones, for children lose out if they never fool around with their parents.

The chef Mary Contini got it right, producing a great children's cookery book, *Easy Peasy*. The recipes were for real meals – Italian-inspired, common-sense food. Dishes have fun names – Knock-out Garlic Bread and Chocolate Mouse, but all the basics are there. The secret of getting children cooking is perhaps a step away from the intense tutorial given to Nigella and myself. My recipe would be two parts seriousness and one part creative fun. The result should be a youngster with a real passion for food.

13 In the first paragraph, the writer suggests that there is a connection between

    A parents' enthusiasm for cooking and children's ability to cook.

    B teaching children to cook and making a popular TV cookery series.

    C childhood experiences of cooking and success as a professional cook.

    D the effort children put into cooking and how much they enjoy doing it.

14 What does the writer say about her mother teaching her how to cook?

    A She sometimes resented her mother's demands on her.

    B Her mother's comments were intended to encourage her.

    C Her mother misunderstood her level of interest in cooking.

    D She wished that her mother would allow her to have more fun doing it.

15 In the third paragraph, the writer points out a contrast between

    A a belief about parental behaviour and the response of children to this behaviour.

    B public praise for children and private opinions of what they do.

    C the kind of praise given to boys and the kind given to girls.

    D what children are good at and what their parents would like them to be good at.

16 The writer mentions certain 'grown men' as an example of people who

    A grew up having a lot of fun while learning to cook.

    B have the wrong idea about how children view food.

    C pass bad ideas about cooking on to their children.

    D think that everything associated with food has to be fun.

17 What does the writer suggest about regarding cooking as 'a chore'?

    A It is something that children are not able to understand.

    B It is not necessary.

    C It can affect the kind of food that people cook and eat.

    D It is a lazy view.

18 The writer says that she differs from Nigella Lawson concerning

    A her aspirations as a cook.

    B her attitude to her family life as a child.

    C the way that children should be taught how to cook.

    D the amount of fun she thinks children should have at home.

19 The writer's main point in the article is that

    A children who are taught that cooking is fun lose interest in it later in life.

    B children should not be given the impression that cooking is an entirely fun activity.

    C for children, cooking needs to be fun first and taken seriously later.

    D it is very hard for children to see cooking from an adult perspective.

Part 4

You are going to read part of a brochure for visitors to Norway suggesting activities they could do during their visit. For questions **20–34**, choose from the sections of the article (**A–D**). The activities may be chosen more than once.

In the exam, mark your answers **on the separate answer sheet**.

In connection with which activity are the following mentioned?

a talk before visitors start doing this activity	**20**
the physical condition required to do this activity	**21**
a belief that this activity is very unpleasant	**22**
the reason why conditions make this activity possible	**23**
people for whom this activity is essential	**24**
something unexpected for many people when they are doing this activity	**25**
a belief that this activity no longer happens	**26**
the moments just before the activity starts	**27**
the length of time most visitors choose for this activity	**28**
a contrast with another activity	**29**
particular skills that are demonstrated to visitors	**30**
two benefits of doing this activity	**31**
something that may cause people a problem when they are learning how to do this	**32**
the enjoyment gained from travelling with others	**33**
what people look like when doing this activity	**34**

Activities for visitors to Norway

Norway offers some truly remarkable ways to explore the great outdoors.

A   Ride a snowmobile

For many who live in Northern Norway, the snowmobile is an everyday means of transport – and nothing less than a lifeline for those in more remote areas. But these vehicles are also great fun to ride and snowmobile excursions are one of the most popular tourist experiences. It's a thrill indeed to roar in convoy through a landscape of wooded trails on the Arctic's answer to a Harley-Davidson motorbike. Anyone with a driving licence for a car may operate one and the basics are easily mastered. The only controls to worry about are a thumb-operated throttle and motorcycle-style brakes. All riders are kitted out with a helmet, warm waterproof overalls, boots and gloves, and given a comprehensive safety briefing. Scores of outfits throughout the region offer snowmobile excursions, from half-day taster sessions to expeditions of up to a week.

B   Go fishing on a frozen surface

Fishing through a hole in the ice may seem like the ultimate Arctic cliché. Many people from Europe's warmer climes may think it is something that exists only in old footage of Eskimo living, but this isn't the case at all. Under the frozen surface, many of Norway's freshwater lakes and fjords are teeming with fish and there are plenty of enthusiasts who devote their days to catching them. Sign up for an excursion and you'll find out how the experts use the auger to drill through the ice, a skimming loop to keep the water from freezing over again and a familiar rod to catch the fish. There's something magical about seeing a tug on the line and a sparkling fish being suddenly whisked out of the icy depths. Some companies offer fishing trips lasting three days or more, involving snowmobile or dog-sled journeys up to remote mountain lakes.

C   Go skiing or snowshoeing

Snowmobiling has high-octane attractions, but to appreciate fully the stillness and peace of the mountains, it's best to use your own feet to get around. There are several ways of doing this. Cross-country skiing is among the most popular Nordic pastimes and there are thousands of miles of trails. A few lessons are essential to pick up the rudiments of the technique. After that, you will discover that gliding around the snowy terrain is not just a great way of getting close to nature, but also fantastic aerobic exercise. Younger explorers will find plenty of opportunities for snowboarding fun. A more sedate manner of exploration (though still invigorating) is on snowshoes. The racquet-like footwear makes it possible to yomp over deep snow. A classic snowshoe safari involves a guided walk to a forest glade, where snacks are served.

D   Try dog sledding

Before the invention of the petrol engine, dog sleds were vital to those who lived inside the Arctic circle, and a trip to a husky farm is something every visitor to northern Norway should experience. Half- or full-day sled safaris are most popular, although overnight and longer tours are also available. Norwegians treat dog sledding as a sport and regularly take part in prestigious races. It's difficult not to feel a frisson of excitement as a team of huskies is harnessed to your sledge. The instinct to run is so strongly bred into the dogs that whenever they realise an outing is imminent, they become as keyed up as domestic pets about to be taken for walkies – howling, leaping in the air and straining at their leashes. When the signal is given to depart, you may well be surprised at the speed that they can reach. Dog sledding is available through various companies at different locations in northern Norway and is suitable for novices, though you should be reasonably fit.

E   Bathe in the Barents Sea

The Barents Sea is the part of the Arctic Ocean that lies north of Norway and Russia, and although the North Atlantic Drift keeps it ice-free through the year, its temperature seldom rises much above freezing point. So it might be imagined that bathing in the frigid waters would be at best masochistic and at worst suicidal, but with the right equipment you can take a dip off the coast of Finnmark. You'll first need to be sealed into a bright orange survival suit, which leaves only the face exposed and lends bathers a rather peculiar appearance. These provide heavy insulation and buoyancy, allowing you to float and paddle around to your heart's content. In Kirkenes, bathing in the Barents Sea is often combined with a king crab safari – the experience bringing new meaning to the phrase 'cold appetiser'.

Part 1

You **must** answer this question. Write your answer in **180–220** words in an appropriate style. In the exam, write your answer **on the separate answer sheet provided**.

1   You have just completed two weeks of work experience at a local company as part of your college course. Your college Principal has asked you to write a report on your experience, saying what was good or bad about it, how valuable it was for making decisions about your future and whether you would recommend it for all the students in the school.

Read the information you received from the company before you did the work, and the notes you have written on it. Then, **using the information appropriately**, write your report for the principal.

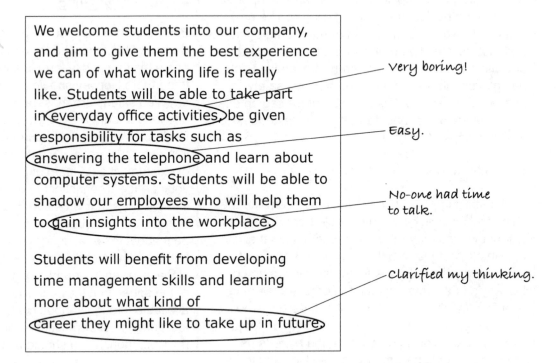

We welcome students into our company, and aim to give them the best experience we can of what working life is really like. Students will be able to take part in *everyday office activities,* be given responsibility for tasks such as *answering the telephone* and learn about computer systems. Students will be able to shadow our employees who will help them to *gain insights into the workplace.*

Students will benefit from developing time management skills and learning more about what kind of *career they might like to take up in future.*

Very boring!

Easy.

No-one had time to talk.

Clarified my thinking.

Write your **report**. You should use your own words as far as possible.

Part 2

Write an answer to one of the questions **2–5** in this part. Write your answer in **220–260** words. In the exam, write your answer **on the separate answer sheet provided**, and put the question number in the box at the top of the page.

2   Your class has been discussing the value of travelling to other countries, and whether watching travel programmes on television is more useful. Your teacher has asked you to write an essay based on your discussion, called *Travel – it's an overrated pastime*. Your essay should consider the benefits and disadvantages of foreign travel.

   Write your **essay**.

3   An international magazine is planning a series of articles on the place of role-models in today's society, and has asked readers to send in articles on the subject. In your article, you should consider the kind of people who make the best role-models, and any responsibilities celebrity role-models have in their lifestyle and behaviour.

   Write your **article**.

4   Your town is planning to hold a music festival next year to attract people of all ages to the town. To make sure that the festival is a success, the organisers have asked people who live in the town for suggestions on how to organise the event and what extra facilities the town might need to provide. Your proposal should also include ideas on transport and accommodation.

   Write your **proposal**.

5   Answer one of the following two questions based on a book you have read. In the exam, you will have to write about one of two specific titles. Write the letter **(a)** or **(b)** as well as the number 5 on your answer sheet.

   (a) A magazine is running a series of articles on books that have been made into films, and has invited readers to send in articles about whether it is better to read the book first, or see the film. You decide to write an article on a book you have read that was also made into a film. In your article, you should explain how the film is different from the book, explain what was good about either the film or the book, and recommend what people should do first: read the book or see the film. You should support your ideas with examples from the book and/or film.

   Write your **article**.

   (b) A new book club wants ideas for books to recommend to readers, and has asked people to send in a review of a book which has a particularly dramatic or surprising ending. You decide to send in a review of a book you have read. In your review, you should briefly outline the plot and the main characters, explain why the ending was so dramatic or surprising and say whether you recommend this book to members of the book club.

   Write your **review**.

TEST 6
USE OF ENGLISH

Part 1

For questions **1–12**, read the text below and decide which answer (**A**, **B**, **C** or **D**) best fits each gap. There is an example at the beginning (**0**).

In the exam, mark your answers **on the separate answer sheet**.

Example:

0 **A** capable   **B** skilled   **C** qualified   **D** competent

0	A	B	C	D
	▬	▭	▭	▭

Mr Espresso

The idea that only an Italian is **(0)** .... of making the world's greatest cup of coffee seems to have been around forever, so universally is it **(1)** .... today. **(2)** .... it is actually a fairly recent phenomenon. Emilio Lavazza, who died in 2010 at the age of 78, can **(3)** .... much of the credit. He taught the world not only how to make coffee, but also how to drink it. That may explain why Italy has still not been invaded by the American coffee-bar chains so ubiquitous **(4)** .... in Europe.

Emilio Lavazza was born in 1932, and was a leading **(5)** .... in the generation of Italian businessmen who **(6)** .... their family firms in the 1950s. These began to expand rapidly, first around the country and then abroad as Italy **(7)** .... its long post-war economic expansion. This was the generation that **(8)** .... the seeds for what has **(9)** .... to be known as 'Made in Italy', the **(10)** .... of companies and brands that make high-quality household and consumer products, from fashion to food to furniture. These products are identified with a **(11)** .... of craftsmanship on the one hand, and the elegant Italian lifestyle on the other. Emilio Lavazza **(12)** .... sure that coffee became an inextricable part of that heritage.

1	**A** consented	**B** agreed	**C** accepted	**D** complied
2	**A** Yet	**B** Though	**C** Whereas	**D** Whilst
3	**A** insist	**B** claim	**C** demand	**D** uphold
4	**A** therefore	**B** wherever	**C** moreover	**D** elsewhere
5	**A** figure	**B** symbol	**C** role	**D** creature
6	**A** enlisted	**B** joined	**C** enrolled	**D** participated
7	**A** entertained	**B** appreciated	**C** benefited	**D** enjoyed
8	**A** set	**B** sowed	**C** laid	**D** buried
9	**A** ended	**B** come	**C** finished	**D** gone
10	**A** cluster	**B** pile	**C** bundle	**D** heap
11	**A** range	**B** connection	**C** variety	**D** combination
12	**A** held	**B** made	**C** took	**D** stood

146   TEST 6, PAPER 3: USE OF ENGLISH

Part 2

For questions **13–27**, read the text below and think of the word which best fits each gap. There is an example at the beginning (**0**).

In the exam, write your answers **IN CAPITAL LETTERS on the separate answer sheet**.

Example: | **0** | W | I | T | H | | | | | | | | | | | | | | |

Drift Diving

Drift diving is diving **(0)** .... a difference. Are you already an experienced diver **(13)** .... fancies a change **(14)** .... splashing around a reef or a wreck? If **(15)** ...., then drift diving may be worth trying. Basically, drift diving **(16)** .... use of the prevailing current in the ocean to propel you along underwater. Depending **(17)** .... the speed of the current, **(18)** .... is measured in knots, drift diving can either be like flying underwater, **(19)** .... simply the lazy person's approach to diving. A slow drift would involve travelling at about one knot, equivalent **(20)** .... just under two kilometres per hour, **(21)** .... it feels much faster when you're down at depth.

With drift diving, of course, there's **(22)** .... need to kick. You're being carried along, and can view all the local sealife as you float by. It feels quite surreal to begin with; you float along **(23)** .... if you were on a conveyor belt. What's **(24)** ...., you often cover **(25)** .... much greater distance than on a conventional dive.

If the current is running fast, say four knots, it can be a very different experience, however, comparable only really to flying. Travelling underwater at speed **(26)** .... your heart pumping as the plants, rocks and sea life suddenly pop **(27)** .... in front of you and whiz past.

Part 3

For questions **28–37**, read the text below. Use the word given in capitals at the end of some of the lines to form a word that fits in the gap **in the same line**. There is an example at the beginning (**0**).

In the exam, write your answers **IN CAPITAL LETTERS on the separate answer sheet**.

Example: | **0** | D | E | V | E | L | O | P | M | E | N | T | S | | | | | | |

The Limits of Technology

Technology changes fast, making it difficult to keep track of

the latest **(0)** .... Yet, there are certain moments when   **DEVELOP**

technology makes a big **(28)** .... on you. Imagine,   **IMPRESS**

for example, seeing television or a helicopter for the first time.

It would be an **(29)** .... experience. One such revelatory   **AWE**

moment occurred while I was on a group camel trek across

the Sahara desert.

We were about fifty miles from the nearest **(30)** ...., feeling   **SETTLE**

that we'd finally managed to get away from it all. Hardly any

technological **(31)** .... had reached this corner of the globe,   **BREAK**

or so it seemed. There were just sand dunes as far as the eye

could see. And yet, despite our **(32)** ...., the silence was   **ISOLATE**

suddenly broken by the somewhat **(33)** .... noise of a frog.   **EXPECT**

Ignoring for the moment the looks of distinct **(34)** .... I got from **APPROVAL**

my fellow travellers, I put my hand in my pocket. The **(35)** .... frog **ANNOY**

was, of course, my ring tone. And when I pressed the button,

there was my boss asking me a simple work question,

(36) .... of the fact that I was thousands of miles away.   **REGARD**

We were beyond the limits of civilisation, yet had not gone

far enough to avoid an **(37)** .... work call from a colleague.   **WELCOME**

Part 4

For questions **38–42**, think of one word only which can be used appropriately in all three sentences. Here is an example (**0**).

Example:

0 I was on the .... of booking my holiday when my boss said I might have to change the dates.

As the meeting drew to a close, the chairperson moved on to the final .... on the agenda.

Theo couldn't see the .... of getting to the airport too early, as the check-in desk only opened one hour before the flight departed.

Example: | 0 | P | O | I | N | T | | | | | | | | | | | | | | | |

In the exam, write **only** the missing word **IN CAPITAL LETTERS on the separate answer sheet**.

---

38 Because he spent so much time practising the piano, Jamie felt he .... out on some other things as a teenager.

From the questions they asked, Deanna could see that the audience had obviously .... the main point of her presentation.

When I went to live abroad, I found I .... some aspects of my own culture more than I expected to.

39 Andy got rather a .... reception when he told his friends that he'd forgotten to book tickets for the concert.

If somebody annoys you, try to keep .... and avoid showing your feelings too much.

Once the hot liquid is .... enough to drink, it can be transferred to individual cups.

40 There's nothing better than an early morning swim to .... your spirits and set you up for the day.

Pressure from local shopkeepers has led the council to .... the ban on parking in the High Street.

Sam was told not to .... the lid of the saucepan while the meat was cooking.

41 There has been a .... rise in crime in the area, which is worrying local residents.

Simon cut his finger on a .... piece of metal that was sticking out of the bed frame.

The house is on quite a .... corner, so traffic has to slow down as it drives past.

42 It was Peter who .... the bad news about the team's defeat to the fans back home.

Sally and Eddie .... off their engagement three times before they eventually got married.

When he was a student, Harry actually .... the college long-jump record on one occasion.

Part 5

For questions **43–50**, complete the second sentence so that it has a similar meaning to the first sentence, using the word given. **Do not change the word given.**
You must use between **three** and **six** words, including the word given. Here is an example (**0**).

Example:

0   Chloe would only eat a pizza if she could have a mushroom topping.

   ON

   Chloe .... a mushroom topping when she ate a pizza.

The gap can be filled with the words 'insisted on having', so you write:

Example: | **0** | INSISTED ON HAVING

In the exam, write **only** the missing words **IN CAPITAL LETTERS on the separate answer sheet**.

---

43   Only time will tell whether Ella was right to change her training programme.

   REMAINS

   It .... whether Ella was right to change her training programme.

44   'Would you lend me your camera, Patrick?' asked John.

   BORROW

   John asked .... camera.

45   Ronan fully intends to write a blog about his round-the-world trip.

   EVERY

   Ronan .... a blog about his round-the-world trip.

46   If nobody objects, today's class will be held on the terrace outside.

   UNLESS

   Today's class will be held outside on the terrace .... objections.

47 Ursula's parents did not approve of her plan to visit a friend in the USA.

MET

Ursula's plan to visit a friend in the USA .... of her parents.

48 The big increase in hits on his website came as a surprise to Philip.

GOT

Much .... a big increase in hits on his website.

49 Barbara likes people to think that she is a good cook.

OF

Barbara likes .... a good cook.

50 We assumed that the agency would email us the theatre tickets.

GRANTED

We .... that the agency would email us the theatre tickets.

Part 1

You will hear three different extracts. For questions **1–6**, choose the answer (**A**, **B** or **C**) which fits best according to what you hear. There are two questions for each extract.

In the exam, write your answers **on the separate answer sheet**.

You hear two friends discussing a rock concert they both went to.

1 How does the boy feel about the main band?

    A disappointed by their performance

    B confused by all the advanced publicity

    C unsure whether he got value for money or not

2 What is the woman doing in her reply?

    A criticising the support band

    B defending the approach of the media

    C agreeing with comments about the main band

You hear part of a sports report about a football club manager.

3 What is the male presenter doing?

    A praising changes that the manager has made

    B suggesting that rumours about the manager are unfounded

    C describing a growing sense of dissatisfaction with the manager's performance

4 In the female presenter's opinion,

    A the manager's strategy is the correct one.

    B the real problem is a lack of talented players.

    C the pressure on the manager is likely to increase.

Extract Three

You hear two friends discussing an exhibition of modern sculpture.

5 What does the woman particularly admire about the artist?

   A the originality of his work

   B the way his art has developed

   C the issues that his sculptures raise

6 What disappointed them both about the exhibition?

   A the pieces of work that had been chosen

   B the information provided for visitors

   C the way it had been laid out

Part 2

You will hear a man called Carl Pitman, giving a group of tourists practical advice about learning the sport of surfing. For questions **7–14**, complete the sentences.

In the exam, write your answers **on the separate answer sheet**.

LEARNING THE SPORT OF SURFING

Carl recommends the [7] as the best place for learning to surf in his area.

Carl uses the term [8] to describe the distance between waves.

Carl advises getting a wetsuit that has a [9] fit.

Carl says it's important to check the quantity of material beneath the

[10] of a new wetsuit.

Carl says that the wetsuit, [11] and footwear all need washing regularly.

According to Carl, a hanger made of [12] is best for storing wetsuits.

Beginners most often damage surfboards through contact with [13]

Carl suggests using a

[14] as the first step in removing wax from a surfboard.

Part 3

You will hear an interview with a writer called Barry Pagham, who writes crime novels. For questions **15–20**, choose the answer (**A**, **B**, **C** or **D**) which fits best according to what you hear.

In the exam, write your answers **on the separate answer sheet**.

---

15 What does Barry say about his first two published novels?

    A They were more successful than he anticipated.
    B They were useful in proving that he could write.
    C It's a shame that they're no longer available to buy.
    D It was a mistake to write an unfashionable type of novel.

16 Barry admits that when he wrote the novel *Transgressions*,

    A he only did it to please his publishers.
    B he didn't expect it to be so well received.
    C he didn't intend to produce any more like it.
    D he never meant it to be sold as a horror story.

17 Looking back, how does Barry view his decision to write his first crime novel?

    A He accepts that he took a big risk.
    B He wishes that he hadn't upset his publishers.
    C He recognises that he behaved unprofessionally.
    D He regrets putting himself under so much stress.

18 Barry tells the story of the arrest of an armed robber to illustrate

    A how true to life his novels are.
    B how dangerous his research can be.
    C how seriously the police take his work.
    D how unpredictably criminals can sometimes behave.

19 What does Barry say about the city where his novels are based?

    A He makes it sound more exciting than it actually is.
    B He regards it as an important element in the stories.
    C He doesn't attempt to create a realistic picture of it.
    D He's surprised that foreign readers want to visit it.

20 How would Barry feel about becoming a policeman?

    A He suspects that he wouldn't be brave enough.
    B He doubts whether he would have the patience.
    C He's sure someone of his age wouldn't be accepted.
    D He suggests that he wouldn't reject the idea completely.

Part 4

You will hear five short extracts in which people are talking about their experiences of travelling.

In the exam, write your answers **on the separate answer sheet**.

TASK ONE

For questions **21–25**, choose from the list (**A–H**) what advice each speaker gives about travelling.

A	plan what you need to take carefully	
B	explore a range of booking methods	Speaker 1 [21]
C	participate in local cultural events	Speaker 2 [22]
D	sample as much local produce as possible	Speaker 3 [23]
E	learn some of the language	Speaker 4 [24]
F	consider how belongings should be packed	Speaker 5 [25]
G	keep a diary of travel experiences	
H	carry sufficient funds with you	

TASK TWO

For questions **26–30**, choose from the list (**A–H**) what mistake each speaker has made about travelling.

A	failing to check documents	
B	booking a hotel in an unattractive area	Speaker 1 [26]
C	failing to research a destination	Speaker 2 [27]
D	forgetting some pieces of luggage	Speaker 3 [28]
E	making a poorly-considered purchase	Speaker 4 [29]
F	not allowing enough preparation time	Speaker 5 [30]
G	turning down a travel opportunity	
H	buying overpriced goods	

PART 1

The interlocutor will ask you a few questions about yourself and on everyday topics such as work and study, travel, entertainment, daily life and routines. For example:

- What do you enjoy most about the work or study you are doing at the moment?
- Is there anything you dislike about travelling? Why?
- What kind of magazines or newspapers do you read regularly? Why/Why not?

PART 2

Working together

Turn to pictures 1–3 on page 215, which show people working together in different situations.

Candidate A, compare two of the pictures and say why it might be important for people to work together in these situations and how difficult it might be for them to do the work alone.

Candidate B, who do you think benefits most from working with other people?

Travelling

Turn to pictures 1–3 on page 216, which show people travelling in different ways.

Candidate B, compare two of the pictures and say why the people might have chosen to travel in these different ways, and how the people might be feeling.

Candidate A, who do you think is having the easiest journey?

PART 3

Turn to the pictures on page 217, which show some things that many people feel should be protected in today's world.

Talk to each other about what should be done to protect these things. Then decide which two things are most important to protect for future generations.

PART 4

Answer these questions:

- Do you think that individuals can do very much to protect things like these? Why/Why not?
- Do you think that children should be taught about conservation at school? Why/Why not?
- Some people say that it's better to spend money on preserving what we've got than on inventing new things. What's your opinion?
- Many young people feel that traditions are old-fashioned and not relevant to them. Do you agree with that view? Why/Why not?
- Do you think governments should work together to protect the environment? Why/Why not?

Part 1

You are going to read three extracts which are all concerned in some way with science. For questions **1–6**, choose the answer (**A**, **B**, **C** or **D**) which you think fits best according to the text.

In the exam, mark your answers **on the separate answer sheet**.

The periodic table

The periodic table – that set of boxes you remember hanging on the wall of your chemistry class – is many things. It's an invaluable tool for organising the building blocks of the universe. Its columns and rows are a microcosm of the history of science. And it's also a storybook, containing all the wonderful and clever, and ugly aspects of being human. From simple hydrogen at the top left to the man-made impossibilities at the bottom that can only be conjured into existence for fractions of a second, the periodic table describes every single known element: the chemical substances that, separately or combined, make up everything we can see or sense around us. We eat and breathe the periodic table: people bet and lose huge sums on it; it poisons people; it spawns wars.

Some elements have been important since the early days of civilisation. However, simply relying on the elements we found around us was never enough. For thousands of years, alchemists attempted to unearth new elements and study their properties. But it was not until the late 1700s that our knowledge of the elements really took off, as chemists developed new ways to purify and isolate elements. Such research was, in terms of the technology of the time, cutting-edge. The discovery of dozens of elements brought new challenges for scientists. Biology had the Tree of Life, which linked the various species and phyla, but did anything similar exist to organise the elements? Or were they inherently chaotic, a jumble of substances that could be arranged equally well by any old trait? The answer, of course, was that there was a pattern, and it's embodied in the periodic table.

1 The writer's aim in the first paragraph is to point out

  A aspects of the periodic table that are seldom noticed.
  B reasons why the periodic table is of great significance.
  C misunderstandings about the periodic table.
  D contrasting opinions of the periodic table.

2 In the second paragraph, the writer refers to a time in the past when people thought that

  A biology was the most important area for scientific research.
  B there was no point in trying to find more new elements.
  C it might not be possible to arrange elements in a systematic way.
  D the Tree of Life would be a good model for organising elements.

Age of discovery in science 'is over'

The age of scientific discovery may be nearing its end as the limits of the human mind make further breakthroughs impossible, according to leading scientists. Experts say the 'low-hanging fruit' of scientific knowledge, such as the laws of motion and gravity, was attained using simple methods in previous centuries, leaving only increasingly impenetrable problems for modern scientists to solve. Uncharted areas of science are now so complex that even the greatest minds will struggle to advance human understanding of the world, they claim. In addition, the problems are becoming so far removed from our natural sensory range that they require increasingly powerful machines to even approach them.

Russell Stannard, the Professor Emeritus of Physics at the Open University, argues that, although existing scientific knowledge will continue to be applied in new ways, 'the gaining of knowledge about fundamental laws of nature and the constituents of the world must come to an end.' He said: 'We live in a scientific age and that's a period that's going to come to an end at some stage. Not when we've discovered everything about the world but when we've discovered everything that's open to understand.' In his new book, *The End of Discovery*, Prof Stannard argues that it is impractical to go on building ever larger machines in the hope of making discoveries. He used the example of 'M-Theory, which could not be tested without a particle accelerator the size of a galaxy'.

3 What does the writer contrast with the 'low-hanging fruit' in the first paragraph?

    A uncharted areas of science
    B our natural sensory range
    C human understanding of the world
    D powerful machines

4 Professor Russell Stannard's view is that soon

    A scientists will turn their attention to issues not previously investigated.
    B methods for discovering the fundamental laws of nature will change.
    C humans will have reached their limit for understanding the world.
    D there will be no new breakthroughs in the world of science.

The Ig Nobel Prizes

Roller-coaster rides relieve asthma. Beards are a health hazard. Promoting workers at random creates more efficient companies. These are all among the 'improbable' scientific discoveries to have won spoof Nobel Prizes this year. The Ig Nobels, designed to honour achievements that first make people laugh and then make them think, are presented in the run-up to the real awards. They are given out at a Harvard University ceremony by the magazine *Annals of Improbable Research*. Marc Abrahams, the magazine's editor, said that scientific research was getting stranger. 'For good and its opposite, humanity is producing more and stronger candidates every year,' he said. 'We like to think that the Ig Nobels make the Nobels shine even more brightly.'

This year the Medicine Prize went to Dutch scientists who discovered that the 'positive emotional stress' associated with riding on a big dipper reduced feelings of shortness of breath among asthma sufferers. Tests on 25 students with asthma found that they suffered fewer breathing problems while on a big dipper. American researchers were awarded the Public Health Prize for finding that bearded scientists posed a risk to their families because bacteria used in the laboratory remained in their facial hair even after washing. Italian physicists won the Management Prize after proving mathematically that randomly promoting employees actually made a company run more efficiently. They found that, contrary to popular opinion, members of 'a hierarchical organisation climb the hierarchy until they reach the level of maximum incompetence'. The best way to avoid this was to promote the best and the worst employees, the model showed.

5 What is said about the Ig Nobel Prizes?

   A They aim to highlight research that gets little or no publicity.
   B They are considered controversial in the world of science.
   C They cast doubt on the winners of the real Nobel Prizes.
   D They are given for research that may have some genuine merit.

6 One of the prizes was awarded for research that suggested

   A a new way of motivating staff.
   B the replacement of a particular system.
   C a possible cause for a medical condition.
   D the reason why a problem is increasing.

You are going to read an article about the hobby of cloudwatching. Six paragraphs have been removed from the article. Choose from the paragraphs **A–G** the one which fits each gap (**7–12**). There is one extra paragraph which you do not need to use.

In the exam, mark your answers **on the separate answer sheet**.

The sky's the limit for cloudwatchers

Christopher Middleton learns to distinguish an altostratus from a cirrus at Britain's first Cloud Bar.

High above the Lincolnshire coastline, a swirl of small white clouds moves slowly across a clear blue sky. In normal circumstances, you'd describe them as wispy and feathery. But because we're standing on the roof of Britain's first Cloud Bar, and it's decked out with wall charts, we assembled skygazers can identify the above-mentioned phenomena as *Cirrus fibratus*. For the moment anyway, since clouds only live for ten minutes (it says on the chart).

7

'It's a fantastic idea, this place,' says off-duty fireman Peter Ward, who's brought his young family here. 'Really inspiring.'

8

At the last count, membership of the Cloud Appreciation Society stood at 23,066, covering 82 nations and all kinds of skywatchers from hillwalkers to airline pilots. 'We think that clouds are nature's poetry,' says the society's founder Gavin Pretor-Pinney, author of *The Cloudspotter's Guide* (sales of 200,000 and still rising). 'Clouds are for dreamers and their contemplation benefits the soul.'

9

'In fact, you don't really need to travel at all to see interesting clouds. You can just lie in your back garden and look upwards,' he says. For many cloudwatchers, the most important factor is not so much geographical location, as your philosophical disposition.

10

'That said, clouds can be tremendously exciting too,' he adds. 'The first cloud I noticed was at the age of four and a half. I saw this magnificent *Cumulonimbus*, with rays of sunshine sprouting out from behind. Even now, I love to see those towering great formations. In my mind, clouds are the last great wilderness available to us.'

11

Cloudpsotters in search of similar experiences flock each autumn to North Queensland in Australia for the tube-shaped phenomenon knows as Morning Glory. 'You go up and surf the wave of air it creates,' says Gavin Pretor-Pinney, whose follow-up book is *The Wavewatcher's Companion*. 'Even more thrilling is to travel through clouds on a hang-glider. The strange thing is, you put your hand inside a cloud, but although it's wet and chilly, there's no actual substance to it.'

12

There's something about clouds which appeals to the soul, Ian Loxley says. 'The line I like best is the one that goes, "Life is not measured by the number of breaths you take, but by the moments that take your breath away."'

A Gavin Pretor-Pinney explains why this is: 'Because of the stately way in which clouds move and the gradual rate at which they develop, contemplating them is akin to meditation,' he says. 'The mere act of sitting, watching and observing slows you down to their pace.'

B Absolutely. And as well as stimulating the imagination, clouds get you out and about. The keeper of the Society's photo gallery, Ian Loxley, has been on cloud-seeking expeditions in places as far afield as Cornwall and Canada, though his favourite location is around his home in the Lincolnshire Wolds.

C The Cloud Appreciation Society website is full of reports of such encounters. Some, like that one, are in mid-air at close quarters, while others are miles below on the ground.

D *Alto* clouds are a good example, They are primarily made up of water droplets, making them appear as grey puffy masses. If you see these on a humid summer morning, watch out for a potential thunderstorm later.

E Yes, spend an hour here and you become an instant expert on telling your *altos* (four to six miles high) from your *cumulos* (anything lower). As for these, they don't start until eight miles up, and they're identifiable because of their long, thin, shape (the name in Latin means a strand of hair).

F And, like all such places, humans want to explore them. Glider pilot Mike Rubin not only flies inside clouds but rides on them. 'You fly underneath, find the thermal lift that is generating this cloud, and climb up by circling inside it,' he says. 'Use the thermals, and on a good day, you can travel hundreds of kilometres.'

G Other beachgoers aren't as convinced that the country has been crying out for a purpose-built pavilion like this, equipped with adjustable mirrors so that you don't even have to look up at the sky. But the world's nephelophile community (that's cloud enthusiasts) would beg to differ, especially now that more changeable autumn weather offers fewer cloudless blue-sky scenarios, and lots more action of the scudding and billowing kind.

You are going to read an extract from a novel. For questions **13–19**, choose the answer (**A**, **B**, **C** or **D**) which you think fits best according to the text.

In the exam, mark your answers **on the separate answer sheet**.

My first day with the family replayed itself in my mind, but in black and white, and the reel grainy and distorted in places. I was seated with the family, nervous, pretending to follow Carl Sagan on TV, covertly assessing their movements and utterances. Peju, seated next to me, suddenly turned and asked casually, 'Lomba, what is the capital of Iceland?'

I discovered later she was going to read journalism at the university and ultimately become a presenter on CNN. She had stacks of cassette recordings of herself reading the news in a cool, assured voice. I looked at her blankly. She was seventeen, and her beauty was just starting to extricate itself from the awkward, pimply encumbrances of adolescence. Her eyes were polite but unrelentingly expectant. Surprised at the question, not knowing the answer, I turned to Bola for help – but he was lost in a loud and argumentative game of Ludo with his mum on the carpet. I shrugged and smiled. 'Why would I know what the capital of Iceland is?'

'Good answer, Lomba,' came the father's voice from behind the *Sunday Guardian*. He was lying on the sofa; he had been listening to us all along.

'Stay out, Daddy,' Peju pleaded, and turning back to me, she proceeded to lecture me on the name and geographical peculiarities of Reykjavik. The next salvo came from Lola, who was going to be a fashion designer. She was twelve and intimidatingly precocious. She had sidled up to me and sat on the arm of my seat, listening innocently to Peju's lecture; but as soon as it was over she took my arm and gave me a cherubic smile. 'Do you know how a bolero jacket looks?'

When I replied, naturally, in the negative, she jumped up gleefully and ran to their room and back with her sketchbook and pencil. She dragged me down to the carpet and quickly sketched a bolero jacket for me. I stared in silence at the tiny hand so sure behind the pencil, and the wispy but exact strokes slowly arranging themselves into a distinct shape.

'The tailor is making one for me. You'll see it when it is ready,' she promised.

'What do you use it for?'

'To dance the bolero – it is a Spanish dance.

'Can you dance it?'

'No, but I'll learn.'

'You'll wear him out with your nonsense, girls,' the father said, standing up and stretching. He yawned. 'Time for my siesta.' He left.

At first, I was discomfited by his taciturnity, which I mistook for moodiness; but in close-up I saw the laughter kinks behind the eyes, the lips twitching, ready to part and reveal the white teeth beneath. I came to discover his playful side, his pranks on the girls, his comradely solidarity with Bola against the others. Apart from his work, his family was his entire life. Now I saw him – in black and white – after work, at home, seated on his favourite sofas, watching CNN or reading the papers, occasionally turning to answer Lola's persistent, needling questions, or to explain patiently to Bola why he couldn't afford to buy him a new pair of sneakers just now. Big, gentle, quiet, speaking only when spoken to. Remember him: conscientious doctor, dutiful father, loving husband and, to me, perfect role model.

But Ma Bola was my favourite, perhaps because she was so different from my mother, who was, coincidentally, the same age as her. Ma Bola was slim, her figure unaltered by years of childbirth.

'Your sister?' people often asked Bola, and he'd look at his mother and they'd laugh before correcting the mistake. Ma Bola was a secretary at the Ministry of Finance – she called her husband 'darling', like white people. Her children were 'dear' and 'honey'. The first time she called me that, I turned round to see if there was someone else behind me. She had laughed and patted me on the cheek. 'Don't worry, you'll get used to our silly ways.' ... Her greatest charm was her ease with people. She laughed so easily; she listened with so much empathy, patting you on the arm to make a point. After a minute with her, you were a captive for life.

'Take care of my husband for me,' she told me often. That was how she sometimes fondly referred to Bola, 'my husband'. 'He can be so impulsive, so exasperatingly headstrong.'

'I will,' I promised.

She went on to tell me how, in traditional society, parents used to select friends for their children. We were alone in the kitchen. She was teaching me how to make pancakes. 'Cousins, usually. They'd select someone of opposite temperament – someone quiet if theirs was garrulous, someone level-headed (like you) if their own was impulsive. They'd make them sworn friends for life, to check each other's excesses. Very wise, don't you think?'

'Very.'

'If I was to select a friend for Bola, it'd be you. But Providence has already done it for me.'

13 Lomba says that he later discovered that Peju

    A was older than he had first thought.
    B frequently asked people surprising questions.
    C was already preparing for her future career.
    D quickly made progress in her career.

14 When Lomba answered Peju's question,

    A she tried to stop her father from giving Lomba the answer.
    B she indicated that she was glad that Lomba did not know the answer.
    C Lomba knew that Bola would not have been able to give him the answer.
    D she supplied him with information he did not know.

15 What does Lomba say about Lola?

    A She was pleased that he didn't know the answer to her question.
    B She seemed younger than she really was.
    C She made him feel much more comfortable than Peju did.
    D He thought at first that she was playing a trick on him.

16 Lomba says that he found out that he was wrong about

    A how the father spent most of his time.
    B what the children thought of their father.
    C the father's priorities in life.
    D the father's sense of humour.

17 When describing Ma Bola, Lomba makes it clear that

    A he got on better with her than with his own mother.
    B he was not familiar with being addressed with the words she used.
    C her physical appearance made him feel comfortable with her.
    D he was envious of her children's relationship with her.

18 When she was talking to Lomba in the kitchen, Ma Bola said that

    A she thought he would be a good influence on Bola.
    B she was becoming increasingly worried about Bola.
    C she wanted him to take on a role he might not want.
    D she realised that a certain tradition was dying out.

19 What is the main topic of the extract as a whole?

    A the speed with which Lomba developed close relationships with the family
    B the contrasts between the personalities of the family members
    C the impression that the family members made on Lomba
    D the difficulties Lomba had in getting used to life with the family

Part 4

You are going to read an article about sea creatures. For questions **20–34**, choose from the sections of the article (**A–D**). The sections may be chosen more than once.

In the exam, mark your answers **on the separate answer sheet**.

In which section of the article are the following mentioned?

the kind of sea creature that people in general find appealing	**20**
how certain creatures reached the sea where they are currently found	**21**
where descriptions of certain sea creatures might be expected to be found	**22**
the replacement of various kinds of sea creature by other kinds	**23**
the likelihood that only a small proportion of all sea creatures is included in the Census	**24**
a situation that is not immediately apparent in the Census	**25**
comparisons between certain sea creatures and certain objects	**26**
the idea that certain sea creatures are consciously attempting to do something	**27**
a doubt about the accuracy of existing information about sea creatures	**28**
the basis on which sea creatures are included in the Census	**29**
an informal term to describe a large proportion of all sea creatures	**30**
a task that would be very difficult to carry out	**31**
the aim of the people carrying out the Census	**32**
a prediction explaining why people's attitude towards certain sea creatures should change	**33**
a physical characteristic of certain creatures that affects their eating habits	**34**

What lies beneath

Marine scientists have discovered strange new species, but their census also reminds us how little we know about sea creatures, says Tim Ecott.

A In the latest Census of Marine Life, the Mediterranean has been identified as one of the world's top five areas for marine biodiversity. The others are the oceans off Australia, Japan, China and the Gulf of Mexico, each containing as many as 33,000 individual forms of life that can be scientifically classified as species. In total, the Census now estimates that there are more than 230,000 known marine species, but that this is probably less than a quarter of what lives in the sea. The Census has involved scientists in more than 80 countries, working over a decade. They hope that by creating the first catalogue of the world's oceans, we can begin to understand the great ecological questions about habitat loss, pollution, over-fishing and all the other man-made plagues that are being visited upon the sea. The truth is that, at present, much of what passes for scientific 'facts' about the sea and what lives in it are still based on guesswork.

B So far, the Census tells us that fish account for about 12 percent of sea life, and that other easily recognisable vertebrates – whales, turtles, seals and so on – are just two percent of what lives beneath the waves. It is the creepy-crawlies that are out there in really big numbers. Almost 40 percent of identified marine species are crustaceans and molluscs – things like crabs, shrimp, squid and sea-snails. The Census continues to add images and data relating to a myriad range of creatures that could have slithered out of the pages of science fiction. None of the writers in that genre could do justice to the shape and form of *Chiasmodon niger* – 'The Great Swallower' – with its cadaverous skull, metallic pink flesh and needlelike teeth, accompanied by an enormous ballooning stomach that allows it to swallow animals bigger than itself. And surely there is something enchanting about the 'Yeti crab' (*Kiwa hirsuta*), another new discovery from the Pacific, with a delicate, porcelain-smooth carapace and arms longer than its body, encased in 'sleeves' of what look like ginger fur.

C In shallower waters, the iridescent pink fronds of *Platoma algae* from Australia resemble the sheen of a pair of pink stockings. Juvenile Antarctic octopuses, speckled brown, mauve and orange, look like exquisitely carved netsuke ornaments, perfectly proportioned and endearing for their donnish domed heads. For its bizarre variety and for its enduring mystery, we must learn to treasure the sea. It is easy to be captivated by intelligent, seemingly friendly sea creatures such as dolphins, or even by the hunting prowess of the more sinister sharks. The Marine Census helps us understand that it is the less glamorous, less appealing and less dramatic creatures that are the great bedrock of life on which the oceans depend. As Nancy Knowlton, one of the Census scientists, observes, 'Most ocean organisms still remain nameless and unknown' – and how would we begin to start naming the 20,000 types of bacteria found in just one litre of seawater trawled from around a Pacific seamount?

D Hidden within the Marine Census results is a dark message. Maps showing the density of large fish populations in tropical waters reveal that numbers of many of the biggest open ocean species have declined by more than 50 percent since the 1960s and specific species, including many of the sharks, by as much as 90 percent. The Census also points to the effect of the so-called 'alien species' being found in many of the world's marine ecosystems. The Mediterranean has the largest number of invasive species – most of them having migrated through the Suez Canal from the Red Sea. So far, more than 600 invasive species have been counted, almost 5 percent of the total marine creatures in the Mediterranean. The annoying jellyfish on Spanish beaches may be sending us a message, or at least a warning. There is evidence that a global jellyfish invasion is gathering pace. As Mediterranean turtles lose their nesting sites to beach developments, or die in fishing nets, and the vanishing population of other large predators such as bluefish tuna are fished out, their prey is doing what nature does best; filling a void. Smaller, more numerous species like jellyfish are flourishing and plugging the gap left by animals higher up the food chain. Clearly it is unwise to talk as if the jellyfish have some kind of plan. But many marine experts have been saying for several years that we need to start loving jellyfish, because in the not too distant future, they may be the most plentiful marine species around.

Part 1

You **must** answer this question. Write your answer in **180–220** words in an appropriate style. In the exam, write your answer **on the separate answer sheet provided**.

---

1   As part of your language course, your school organises regular exchange visits for students to stay with families in other countries. Your school magazine is planning to publish articles from students who have been on these visits.

Read the programme for your visit and the notes you made on it. Then, **using the information appropriately**, write your article for the school magazine. You should also explain what was good or bad about the trip as a whole.

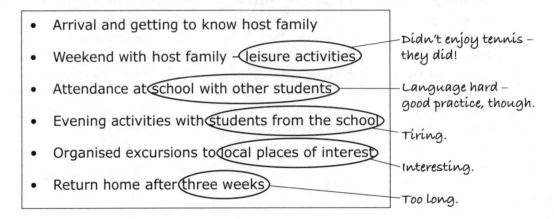

Write your **article**. You should use your own words as far as possible.

Part 2

Write an answer to one of the questions **2–5** in this part. Write your answer in **220–260** words. In the exam, write your answer **on the separate answer sheet provided**, and put the question number in the box at the top of the page.

2   You have received a letter from a younger friend asking for your advice.

> I'm really worried – I've got to decide whether to go to university miles away from all my mates and family, or not bother and take a job locally working for a computer company (you know I love anything technical!) It might possibly lead to promotion in the long-term but I know that university has loads of benefits. Have you ever regretted going to university? What did you gain or lose from it? What should I do?

Write a **letter** to your friend.

3   An English-speaking friend is writing a book about how different places are encouraging people to ease the problems associated with pollution, and has asked you for a contribution. Write a contribution, explaining

- what problems your town has with pollution
- what initiatives your town has taken
- how successful these initiatives have been
- what you think people can do as individuals to help with the problem

Write your **contribution** to the book.

4   You see the following announcement in an international travel magazine.

Do you use buses or trains?

We are running a survey on facilities and services provided at bus and train stations around the world, and would like to find the best and the worst. Send us a report on a bus or train station you have used,

- describing what was good or bad about the bus or train station
- outlining any problems you have experienced
- suggesting any ways in which the bus or train station could be improved

Write your **report**.

5   Answer one of the following two questions based on a book you have read. In the exam, you will have to write about one of two specific titles. Write the letter **(a)** or **(b)** as well as the number 5 on your answer sheet.

(a) Your college magazine wants students to share books they enjoy reading again and again, and has asked students to submit reviews of their favourite book. In your review you should briefly outline the plot and the main characters, and explain what it is about the book that makes you want to read it many times.

Write your **review**.

(b) In your class you have discussed books that have themes that are particularly important or relevant in society today. Your teacher has asked you to write an essay about a book you have read. In your essay you should explain why you chose this book, how its theme is important and relevant to society today, and what we can learn from the book.

Write your **essay**.

Part 1

For questions **1–12**, read the text below and decide which answer (**A**, **B**, **C** or **D**) best fits each gap. There is an example at the beginning (**0**).

In the exam, mark your answers **on the separate answer sheet**.

Example:

0 A founded   **B** originated   **C** embarked   **D** entered

0	A	B	C	D
	▬	▭	▭	▭

Renewable Energy Comes of Age

The British Wind Energy Association was **(0)** .... 30 years ago by a group of scientists. At that time, the **(1)** .... 'alternative energy' was used to describe the generation of wind, water and solar power. These days, we tend to **(2)** .... to them as 'renewable energy' and the use of this name **(3)** .... a real change in their status. These sources of energy, **(4)** .... from being alternative, have now become mainstream and are **(5)** .... to make a significant contribution to the country's energy needs in the future.

Two closely linked developments **(6)** .... behind this **(7)** .... in status. Firstly, over the past decade or so, the price of oil and gas has been rising **(8)** ...., reflecting the extent to which reserves of these fossil fuels are becoming **(9)** .... However, price is only part of the explanation. **(10)** .... as important is the growing consensus that carbon emissions must be curbed. The scientific evidence for climate change is now irrefutable, and both policy makers and the **(11)** .... public are finally in agreement that doing nothing about the prospect of global warming is no longer a viable option. Renewable energy represents one real way of **(12)** .... both issues.

1	**A** caption	**B** title	**C** term	**D** label
2	**A** consider	**B** refer	**C** mention	**D** regard
3	**A** regards	**B** reproduces	**C** reminds	**D** reflects
4	**A** far	**B** away	**C** apart	**D** long
5	**A** set	**B** held	**C** put	**D** stood
6	**A** sit	**B** reside	**C** lie	**D** recline
7	**A** move	**B** shift	**C** switch	**D** jump
8	**A** equably	**B** serenely	**C** habitually	**D** steadily
9	**A** depleted	**B** decreased	**C** depressed	**D** debased
10	**A** Just	**B** Still	**C** Much	**D** Yet
11	**A** deeper	**B** greater	**C** larger	**D** wider
12	**A** coping	**B** engaging	**C** addressing	**D** dealing

Part 2

For questions **13–27**, read the text below and think of the word which best fits each gap. There is an example at the beginning (**0**).

In the exam, write your answers **IN CAPITAL LETTERS on the separate answer sheet**.

Example: | **0** | W | E | R | E | | | | | | | | | | | | | | | | |

The Demise of the Motor Car

In the earliest days of motoring, cars **(0)** .... hand-built by craftsmen. They cost **(13)** .... much that they were never expected to be anything **(14)** .... than playthings for the rich. Then, along **(15)** .... Henry Ford with his dream of making a car for the great multitude, so low **(16)** .... price that almost everyone would be able to own **(17)** .... Ford's invention of the mass-produced car transformed Western civilisation. It changed the shape of our cities **(18)** .... accelerating migration to the suburbs. It **(19)** .... rise to vast new factory-based industries making vehicles and their components. It opened **(20)** .... unprecedented leisure and holiday opportunities by letting people travel wherever they wanted. What's **(21)** ...., it gave us shopping malls, theme parks, motels and fast-food outlets.

(22) .... a long time, people loved their cars. Many still **(23)** .... For some, they are a status symbol – a very visible, and mobile, demonstration of their wealth. For **(24)** ...., they are an extension of their personality, or of the one they **(25)** .... most like to project. Many more derive **(26)** .... a powerful feeling of independence from having a car parked outside the door that, paradoxically, they become dependent on it.

But car ownership is not **(27)** .... it was. Ever worsening traffic congestion means that mobility is correspondingly reduced, and the advantages of owning a car diminish.

For questions **28–37**, read the text below. Use the word given in capitals at the end of some of the lines to form a word that fits in the gap **in the same line**. There is an example at the beginning (**0**).

In the exam, write your answers **IN CAPITAL LETTERS on the separate answer sheet**.

Example: | **0** | E | N | T | I | T | L | E | D | | | | | | | | | |

Do Green Products make us better People?

A recent report in the journal *Psychological Science* was **(0)** ....   **TITLE**

Do Green Products Make us Better People? The answer, **(28)** ....   **ACCORD**

to two Canadian psychologists, was most **(29)** .... not.   **DEFINITE**

After conducting a series of experiments, they reached the

conclusion that those who buy **(30)** .... ethical products   **SUPPOSE**

were just as likely to be cheats and **(31)** .... as those who did not.   **CRIME**

They described this paradox as 'moral balancing' or 'compensatory

ethics'. In other words, there was no direct correlation between

a social or ethical conscience about one aspect of life, and

(32) .... in another.   **BEHAVE**

Despite being an occasional buyer of organic vegetables, I myself

take great **(33)** .... from the study because it fits in with a   **SATISFY**

long-held hypothesis of my own. It is what I call the theory of

finite niceness. We use the word 'nice' to describe those people

we encounter who seem **(34)** .... and kind. Yet, it is not a word   **CHARM**

we use often to describe those to whom we are closest, because

we know that there is a **(35)** .... in their characters. We   **COMPLEX**

understand them and realise that they are people who **(36)** ....   **DOUBT**

have both faults and virtues, and that these do **(37)** .... come   **VARIABLE**

out in different ways.

Part 4

For questions **38–42**, think of one word only which can be used appropriately in all three sentences. Here is an example (**0**).

Example:

0   I was on the .... of booking my holiday when my boss said I might have to change the dates.

As the meeting drew to a close, the chairperson moved on to the final .... on the agenda.

Theo couldn't see the .... of getting to the airport too early, as the check-in desk only opened one hour before the flight departed.

Example: | 0 | P | O | I | N | T | | | | | | | | | | | | | |

In the exam, write **only** the missing word **IN CAPITAL LETTERS on the separate answer sheet**.

---

38   Over the years, interest in the singer's private life has .... off, but he still produces great music.

Since becoming such a keen cyclist, Gerry's .... behind slightly with his college work.

Dan was annoyed when he realised that he had .... into a trap, and had been talked into spending his money unwisely.

39   The theatre has been open for 50 years and is .... for complete refurbishment.

Liam thought the team's poor performance was .... to a lack of support from the crowd.

The coach to Melbourne was .... to arrive in about five minutes.

40   Kim had a .... suspicion that people had been talking about her as she entered the room.

Scientists are suggesting a .... link between the two experiments, which is very exciting news.

Simona was not sure whether she'd be .... enough to lift the heavy box on her own.

41 Help with his Maths homework was the latest .... that Chris was doing for his brother.

When she applied for promotion, Cathy's experience of sales worked in her ....

Would you be in .... of a change to the club's membership rules?

42 Damian didn't much .... whether he went to the beach or not that day.

The students were told to .... out when they were crossing the busy road outside the college.

Della was asked if she'd .... looking after her younger sister when they went to London.

Part 5

For questions **43–50**, complete the second sentence so that it has a similar meaning to the first sentence, using the word given. **Do not change the word given.** You must use between **three** and **six** words, including the word given. Here is an example (**0**).

Example:

0   Chloe would only eat a pizza if she could have a mushroom topping.

ON

Chloe .... a mushroom topping when she ate a pizza.

The gap can be filled with the words 'insisted on having', so you write:

Example:	0	INSISTED ON HAVING

In the exam, write **only** the missing words **IN CAPITAL LETTERS on the separate answer sheet**.

---

43   The new computer game was every bit as good as Caroline had expected.

UP

The new computer game .... expectations.

44   Because he thought it might break down, Dan always kept a mobile phone in his car.

CASE

Dan kept a mobile phone in his car .... down.

45   Should you see Jack this evening, give him my regards.

HAPPEN

If you .... into Jack this evening, give him my regards.

46   Although the manager refused to buy us a new photocopier, she was still popular.

HER

The manager was still popular .... to buy us a new photocopier.

47 Paul wishes that he hadn't started arguing with his best friend.

HAD

Paul regrets .... with his best friend.

48 Lots more people have been shopping online this year.

SHARP

There .... the number of people shopping online this year.

49 The launch of the new product is scheduled for the end of August.

DUE

The new product .... at the end of August.

50 Nobody knows how soon there will be another volcanic eruption.

SAYING

There .... another volcanic eruption is likely soon.

Part 1

You will hear three different extracts. For questions **1–6**, choose the answer (**A**, **B** or **C**) which fits best according to what you hear. There are two questions for each extract.

In the exam, write your answers **on the separate answer sheet**.

Extract One

You hear two students discussing a part-time design course they are doing.

1   What aspect of the course do they appreciate most?

    A   the way it is delivered

    B   the attitude of the staff

    C   the content of the sessions

2   Which aspect does the woman feel could be improved?

    A   feedback on assignments

    B   access to certain resources

    C   pre-course information for students

Extract Two

You hear part of an interview with a young man who has been travelling in many remote parts of the world.

3   What does he say about his luggage?

    A   He's yet to find the best way of carrying things.

    B   He's learnt to leave out unnecessary pieces of equipment.

    C   He's become very good at packing the absolute minimum.

4   When asked what he's learnt from travelling, he says that

    A   he now longs for his comfortable lifestyle at home more.

    B   he appreciates why others don't feel able to do what he's done.

    C   he regrets visiting places where people are less fortunate than him.

Extract Three

You hear part of an interview with the lead singer in a rock band.

5   How does he feel about the criticism of his band's latest album cover?

    A   He thinks it's been exaggerated.

    B   He admits it's the reaction he wanted.

    C   He resents the suggestion that the cover was unoriginal.

6   He thinks much of the criticism was due to

    A   a lack of respect for his band in the music business.

    B   a foolish comment he made to a journalist.

    C   a misunderstanding of his real intentions.

Part 2

You will hear a student called Kerry giving a class presentation about a type of bird called the swift. For questions **7–14**, complete the sentences.

In the exam, write your answers **on the separate answer sheet**.

THE SWIFT

Kerry says that the Latin name for the swift translates to the words

| **7** | in English.

Kerry describes the noise made by swifts as a | **8**

Kerry says many people think that the bird's shape most resembles a | **9**

Kerry thinks that the swifts' natural nesting site is on | **10**

Kerry was surprised to learn that

| **11** | is a common material found in swifts' nests.

Kerry has observed swifts flying fast to avoid | **12**

Kerry says that swifts tend to be strangely | **13** | when they are in Africa.

In the past, a rich family's | **14** | often used the swift as a symbol.

Part 3

You will hear an interview with a professional kayaker called Glenda Beachley, who is talking about her sport. For questions **15–20**, choose the answer (**A**, **B**, **C** or **D**) which fits best according to what you hear.

In the exam, write your answers **on the separate answer sheet**.

15 What does Glenda find most enjoyable about kayaking?

    A It requires a range of skills.
    B It is a test of physical strength.
    C It requires her to work out problems.
    D It gives her a feeling of independence.

16 Glenda advises young novice kayakers to

    A vary their training routine.
    B choose a club very carefully.
    C concentrate on enjoying the sport.
    D keep trying to beat their friends in races.

17 When Glenda talks about what's called 'wild-water' racing, she suggests that

    A she sees it as more a test of stamina than speed.
    B the hardest part is keeping to the prescribed route.
    C her chances of success in races depends on the weather.
    D her main motivation comes from entering competitions.

18 When asked about the dangers of kayaking, Glenda says that

    A a certain level of fear is desirable.
    B you have to learn from your mistakes.
    C a calm assessment of the risks is essential.
    D over-confidence can get you into difficulties.

19 What advice does Glenda have about equipment?

    A Only the most expensive equipment is likely to be durable.
    B Expert help is needed to make the right decisions.
    C People should get whatever looks most comfortable.
    D Doing research is important to get the best value for money.

20 Glenda says that her best kayaking memories involve

    A exploring new places with her friends.
    B performing well in international events.
    C meeting people from a variety of backgrounds.
    D finding unexpectedly good stretches of river to run.

Part 4

You will hear five short extracts in which people are talking about leaving their own country to study abroad.

In the exam, write your answers **on the separate answer sheet.**

TASK ONE

For questions **21–25**, choose from the list (**A–H**) why each speaker decided to study in another country.

A	to explore an alternative career	
B	to extend skills already acquired	Speaker 1 [ ][21]
C	to satisfy family expectations	Speaker 2 [ ][22]
D	to turn a dream into reality	Speaker 3 [ ][23]
E	to learn another language	Speaker 4 [ ][24]
F	to be nearer to places of historical interest	Speaker 5 [ ][25]
G	to escape from a dead-end job	
H	to pursue a simpler lifestyle	

TASK TWO

For questions **26–30**, choose from the list (**A–H**) what each speaker says they gained from the experience.

A	a feeling of being at home	
B	a new attitude towards money	Speaker 1 [ ][26]
C	a completely new interest	Speaker 2 [ ][27]
D	the opportunity to make useful contacts	Speaker 3 [ ][28]
E	a more relaxed attitude towards other people	Speaker 4 [ ][29]
F	a greater sense of motivation	Speaker 5 [ ][30]
G	friends with the same interests	
H	a new sense of independence	

PART 1

The interlocutor will ask you a few questions about yourself and on everyday topics such as work and study, travel, entertainment, daily life and routines. For example:

- If you could do any job, what would it be? Why?
- What types of holiday do you most enjoy? Why?
- Do you watch different kinds of television programmes now to those you watched in the past? Why/Why not?

PART 2

Learning

Turn to pictures 1–3 on page 218, which show people learning in different situations.

Candidate A, compare the pictures and say what the benefits are of learning in these different situations and how enjoyable the learning process might be.

Candidate B, which situation do you think is best for learning something quickly?

Making choices

Turn to pictures 1–3 on page 219, which show people making choices in different situations.

Candidate B, compare the pictures and say how easy it might be for the people to make a choice in these situations and how important it is for them to make the right choice.

Candidate A, which choice do you think is most difficult for the people to make?

PART 3

I'd like you to imagine that a magazine is publishing a series of articles on jobs many people think are glamorous.

Turn to the pictures on page 220, which show some of the jobs they are planning to include.

Talk to each other about the advantages and disadvantages of doing these different glamorous jobs. Then decide which job should be the focus of the first article in the series.

PART 4

Answer these questions:

- Do you think the media gives a false impression of how enjoyable some jobs are? Why/Why not?
- What's the best way to find out what a job is really like?
- What do you think should be the most important consideration when choosing a career?
- Do you think that some jobs are over-paid? Why/Why not?
- Is it a good thing to be ambitious? Why/Why not?

Assessment

Throughout the test, candidates are assessed on their own individual performance and not in relation to each other. There are two examiners.

The assessor awards marks according to five analytical criteria:

- Grammatical resource
- Vocabulary resource
- Discourse management
- Pronunciation
- Interactive communication.

The interlocutor awards a mark for Global Achievement.

Grammatical Resource

This refers to the accurate and appropriate use of a range of both simple and complex forms. Performance is viewed in terms of the overall effectiveness of the language used in spoken interaction.

Vocabulary Resource

This refers to the candidate's ability to use a range of vocabulary to meet task requirements. At the CAE level, the tasks require candidates to speculate and exchange views on unfamiliar topics. Performance is viewed in terms of the overall effectiveness of the language used in spoken interaction.

Discourse Resource

This refers to the candidate's ability to link utterances together to form coherent speech, without undue hesitation. The utterances should be relevant to the tasks and should be arranged logically to develop the themes or arguments required by the tasks.

Pronunciation

This refers to the candidate's ability to produce intelligible utterances to fulfil the task requirements. This includes stress and intonation, as well as individual sounds. Examiners put themselves in the position of a non-ESOL specialist and assess the overall impact of the pronunciation and the degree of effort required to understand the candidate.

Interactive Communication

This refers to the candidate's ability to take an active part in the development of the discourse. This requires an ability to participate in the range of interactive situations in the test, and to develop discussions on a range of topics by initiating and responding appropriately. This also refers to the deployment of strategies to maintain interaction at an appropriate level throughout the test so that the tasks can be fulfilled.

Global Achievement

This refers to the candidate's overall effectiveness in dealing with the tasks in the four separate parts of the CAE Speaking test. The global mark is an independent impression mark which reflects the assessment of the candidate's performance from the interlocutor's perspective.

Reproduced with the kind permission of Cambridge ESOL

Part 1

In Part 1, you answer questions on personal topics such as likes, dislikes, routines, work, holidays, and so on.

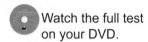 Watch the full test on your DVD.

- Answer your own questions. Don't contribute to your partner's answers.

- Give answers that are interesting, but not too long.

- Don't answer just *yes* or *no* – always give a reason for your answer.

- Imagine that you are in a social situation and meeting someone for the first time. Think about how you might answer general social questions such as:

- What kind of magazines or newspapers do you read regularly? Why?
- Do you ever listen to the radio? Why/Why not?
- What's the best time of day for studying? Why?
- What do you like to do when you go out with your friends?
- Are you an organised kind of person? Why/Why not?
- Do you think that it's good to have a daily routine? Why/Why not?

Responding to questions

I really enjoy … because …

I'm afraid I don't really like … because …

My favourite … is … because …

In future, I'd really like to …

In my family there are …

I think my friends might say … but in my opinion …

I don't know what to say – it's a difficult question, but probably I'd say that …

I don't think I really have a preference, although if I had to choose …

Part 2

In Part 2, you compare two pictures and say something else about them. You have to speak for about a minute.

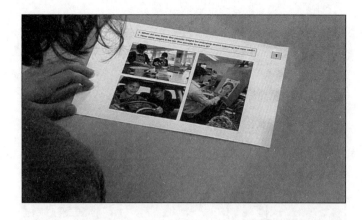

- Listen to the interlocutor's instructions, and only ask for them to be repeated if you really didn't understand. Remember that the questions are written on the paper to help you.

- Look at the questions written at the top of the page so that you don't forget the last two parts of the task. These give you the chance to speculate and show a range of language.

- Spend about 20 seconds comparing the pictures and the remaining time dealing with the rest of the task. This will help you to organise your talk.

- Only compare two of the pictures, otherwise you will run out of time and not complete the task.

- Don't describe what you can see. Don't repeat the question in your answer as you will lose time.

Comparing the pictures

Whereas the people in the first picture are very busy, those in the second picture are …

The first picture shows a workplace. **Conversely**, the second …

The people in the second picture are enjoying themselves more than …

Expressing opinions

I think that …

It seems to me that …

What I think is …

I think it's quite clear that …

I feel quite strongly that …

Speculating

What I would probably say about the people is that …

The people seem to me to be …

Perhaps they are feeling … because …

It's possible that they are … since …

I'm really not sure, but I think that …

Organising your talk

Both pictures show people who are …

To find similarities and differences, I'd say that …

To add to what I said about …

On top of that, I'd say …

Against that is the fact that …

Part 3

In Part 3, you discuss a task with your partner. You have to respond appropriately to what your partner says, and discuss the visuals in turn.

Exam help

- Concentrate on saying as much as you can about the issue each visual represents before moving on to the next. Don't waste time describing the visuals.

- Make sure that you and your partner take it in turns to initiate discussion.

- Respond to what your partner says before moving the discussion on to the next idea.

- Don't worry if you can't talk about all the pictures and don't reach a decision.

Useful language

Agreeing/disagreeing

You made a good point when you said …

That's an interesting point.

I take your point.

You said … but I'm afraid I can't agree.

I can't see how that's relevant to the question.

I can't see what you're getting at really.

Suggesting

Why don't we think about …?

This seems to me to be a good idea.

We could link this to …

Justifying and clarifying

I'm sure that's right, because …

What I meant by that is …

What I said was …

So what you really mean is …

Initiating and moving on to another picture

I'm not sure what this actually is. What do you think?

What do you think about …?

What does this add?

How about considering this one?

Shall we go on to the next picture?

Asking for opinions

What do you think?

Are you with me on that one?

Anything to add?

Do you feel the same?

Part 4

In Part 4, you discuss abstract questions related to Part 3. You should give fuller answers than in Part 1, and you can discuss ideas with your partner if you want.

- The interlocutor may ask you a direct question or may ask a question to you both. Even if the interlocutor asks your partner a question, you can still add your own ideas once your partner has answered. You don't have to agree with your partner.

- If you're not sure of the answer to your own question or have no ideas, use fillers to gain time to think, or ask your partner what they think.

- There are no 'right' answers to these questions – you are simply being asked to express your opinions.

Useful language

Using 'fillers' to have time to think

Let me think about that …

That's a good question! Just a minute. … What I think is …

I've never really thought about it before, but what I would say is …

That's an interesting question!

Responding to a question

What I think about that is …

It seems to me that …

This question is really interesting because …

I've actually thought about this before, and I feel that …

Developing an answer

So if I really think about it, I could also say that …

It also occurs to me that …

What I said doesn't mean that …

To add to what I've already said …

It's true that …, but I think that …

To go into it a bit further, I'd say that …

GENERAL IMPRESSION MARK SCHEME

BAND 5

For a Band 5 to be awarded, the candidate's writing has a very positive effect on the target reader. The content is relevant* and the topic is fully developed. Information and ideas are skilfully organised through a range of cohesive devices, which are used to good effect. A wide range of complex structures and vocabulary is used effectively. Errors are minimal, and inaccuracies which do occur have no impact on communication. Register and format are consistently appropriate to the purpose of the task and the audience.

BAND 4

For a Band 4 to be awarded, the candidate's writing has a positive effect on the target reader. The content is relevant* and the topic is developed. Information and ideas are clearly organised through the use of a variety of cohesive devices. A good range of complex structures and vocabulary is used. Some errors may occur with vocabulary and when complex language is attempted, but these do not cause difficulty for the reader. Register and format are usually appropriate to the purpose of the task and the audience.

BAND 3

For a Band 3 to be awarded, the candidate's writing has a satisfactory effect on the target reader. The content is relevant* with some development of the topic. Information and ideas are generally organised logically, though cohesive devices may not always be used appropriately. A satisfactory range of structures and vocabulary is used, though word choice may lack precision. Errors which do occur do not cause difficulty for the reader. Register and format are reasonably appropriate to the purpose of the task and the audience.

BAND 2

For a Band 2 to be awarded, the candidate's writing has a negative effect on the target reader. The content is not always relevant. Information and ideas are inadequately organised and sometimes incoherent, with inaccurate use of cohesive devices. The range of structures and vocabulary is limited and/or repetitive, and errors may be basic or cause difficulty for the reader. Register and format are sometimes inappropriate to the purpose of the task and the audience.

BAND 1

For a Band 1 to be awarded, the candidate's writing has a very negative effect on the target reader. The content is often irrelevant. Information and ideas are poorly organised, often incoherent, and there is minimal use of cohesive devices. The range of structures and vocabulary is severely limited, and errors frequently cause considerable difficulty for the reader. Register and format are inappropriate to the purpose of the task and the audience.

BAND 0

For a Band 0 to be awarded, there is either too little language for assessment or the candidate's writing is totally irrelevant or illegible.

*Candidates who do not address all the content points will be penalised for dealing inadequately with the requirements of the task.

Candidates who fully satisfy the Band 3 descriptor will demonstrate an adequate performance in writing at CAE level.

Reproduced with the kind permission of Cambridge ESOL

Proposal (Part 1)

You **must** answer this question. Write your answer in **180–220** words in an appropriate style. In the exam, write your answer **on the separate answer sheet provided**.

Your college is planning to hold a careers day for students who are about to complete their courses, giving them information about jobs and advice on possible training courses. The Principal has asked you to write a proposal setting out what should happen on the day and how it should be organised, with reasons to support your ideas.

Read the information from the website forum which students wrote after a previous event, and the email from the Principal, on which you have noted some ideas. Then, **using the information appropriately**, write your proposal for the Principal.

> Need practical stuff – 'question and answer' panels with business people?
>
> More info on vocational courses – especially unusual jobs. Nothing to inspire us!
>
> Same old ideas from college advisors. Didn't stay long!
>
> Started too early – had lectures so could only go to the afternoon session.
>
> No networking opportunities – need contacts, not just information

In your proposal, please take into account the points raised in (last year's forum) – I'm particularly concerned that students don't feel we're giving them what they need – we must make the day interesting, (relevant) and (practical). Could you consider (ways) of doing this?

external speakers

hands-on workshops?

practice interviews?

timing? 2 days?

Write your **proposal**. You should use your own words, as far as possible.

Part 1

- Read all the input information carefully so that you include all the necessary points in your answer.
- Plan your answer before you start to write.
- Don't lift words from input texts as they may be in the wrong register.
- Think about the type of text you are writing, and make sure that you use the correct layout and register for the target reader.
- Remember that Part 1 is transactional, and the reader will usually need to do something after they have read your answer. This message must be conveyed clearly.

Proposal

- The purpose of a proposal is to give information and not engage the reader so techniques like rhetorical questions are not appropriate.
- A proposal is usually for the future, and recommendations may be expressed using modal verbs.
- The style is usually semi-formal or formal.
- It's a good idea to use headings so that you present information clearly.
- Don't use too many bullet-points as you need to show a range of language. Bullet points are useful for recommendations because they are clear and easy to find in the proposal.
- Support your recommendations with reasons.

Headings make it easy for the target reader to read the proposal quickly and get the important information.

Background information

This proposal is for a careers day to be held for students about to leave the college. Previous events have not been successful, and the recommendations are based on student comments.

Student feedback

Students felt that previous events had not addressed their practical needs, and that they were not given any new information. Events were held at the wrong time as many students were unable to attend because they had lectures. Students also wanted more opportunities for practical experience and the chance to make contacts in the business world. Most importantly, students were bored and wanted something more inspiring.

This section gives information from the website and prepares for the recommendations.

Recommendations

- Invite external speakers rather than relying on college lecturers to provide information. This would not only be more interesting for students but would also enable them to meet people who could be useful future contacts.
- Provide practical workshops during the event, in which students could be given advice on presenting themselves in CVs and in interviews. It would be useful to role-play interviews with external speakers.
- Run the event over two days rather than one, perhaps on a weekend. All students would then be free to attend.
- Investigate some unusual jobs and invite people to talk about them, to motivate students.

When bulleted, recommendations can start with an imperative, but it is important to provide back-up reasons or examples.

Conclusion

If these recommendations are implemented, the careers day should be interesting, relevant and practical.

Making formal recommendations

It would be a good idea to …

One suggestion would be to …

It would be useful to …

I would recommend that …

It might be possible to …

Giving supporting information

This would mean that …

This would not only … but also …

In this way …

This addresses the issue of …

This would enable … to …

Conclusion

In the light of …

If these recommendations were to be implemented …

While there may be issues still to resolve, following these suggestions would mean …

Contribution to a longer piece (part 2)

You have been asked to write a contribution to a college prospectus giving advice for new students about the kind of social and sporting activities that are on offer in the college. Your contribution should include advice on the best ways of making new friends, and recommendations for useful and interesting activities to take up.

Write your **contribution to the college prospectus**. Write your answer in **220–260** words in an appropriate style.

Sample answer

The style is formal because it is for a prospectus. An introduction is important to introduce the section in the prospectus.

West College provides numerous opportunities for students to make the most of their time outside study hours. The following information will be useful for students starting out in college life.

Making new friends

Making social contacts can be a problem for new students, who sometimes find it a lonely and daunting experience. There are many social clubs that new students can join, including a debating club and a dance club. Joining a club is the best way to meet people and make friends, and the debating club in particular is a good way of developing new skills that will be useful in later life.

Students can find out about clubs like these in the Student Union building, where there are information sheets available on when and where club meetings take place and who to contact.

Interesting and useful activities

This sentence introduces the sports clubs and makes it easy for students to see what type of information is in this section.

There are a range of sports activities on offer to suit all abilities and interests.

The college runs teams in football, tennis and hockey, and there are regular matches against other colleges. Any student can join the training sessions and try out for the teams, and although not all students can be selected, they will meet like-minded people with shared interests.

There are less intense, more social sporting activities such as table tennis and bowling, and opportunities to go outside the college to do extreme sports such as wall climbing. Information about these can also be found in the Student Union building, along with relevant costs.

While not all students may be interested in sport, it is important for students to stay fit and healthy during their time here, so clubs like these provide many benefits apart from meeting people.

Headings make it easy for students to find the information.

Include an appropriate conclusion.

Exam help

Part 2
- Read through all the questions before choosing which one to answer. You should think about what type of writing you are best at, and then any ideas you have for each topic.

Contribution to a longer piece
- Read the context carefully. Once you have identified the reason you are writing, and the type of publication you are contributing to, you will be able to choose an appropriate layout and style for your answer. Use headings if appropriate.
- Plan your ideas carefully before you start to write and make sure that you have an appropriate beginning and ending.
- Make sure you include all the required information and/or discuss all the required points.
- Don't include irrelevant information or use inappropriate techniques for the type of publication.

Useful language

Introducing new sections

The following will be useful for …

Information about this can be found …

There are numerous opportunities to …

Many people find the following information useful …

Explaining factual situations

Once you have … you will be able to …

There are numerous opportunities to … such as …

In my experience, …

What happens in this area is …

To clarify what the situation is …

Competition entry (Part 2)

Best Film Ever Competition

We are planning to produce a limited edition set of DVDs of the ten best films of all time, and would like your suggestions for films to include in the set. Write to us describing your chosen film, outlining the plot and explaining why the film should be included in the set of DVDs. The best entries will win a DVD player.

Write your **competition entry**. Write your answer in **220–260** words in an appropriate style.

Sample answer

> *This introduction gets the reader interested before revealing what the film is.*

I am a great fan of science fiction films, and although I know these particular films are now old, the original trilogy is so iconic that I don't see how any set of the best DVDs ever could fail to include them. Of course, I'm talking about *Star Wars*.

> *Don't give too much detail about the plot – just enough to give the idea of what happens.*

Who doesn't know the plot? Evil Darth Vader is building the massive Death Star space station to help the Empire overcome the Rebel Alliance, which has been formed to fight back against tyranny. Vader captures Princess Leia, who has stolen the plans to the Death Star and hidden them in the robot R2-D2, who is later bought by Luke Skywalker. Luke accidentally triggers a message put into the droid by Leia, asking for assistance. Luke later trains to be a Jedi and with his friends sets out to crush the Empire. What follows is an action-packed roller coaster, crammed with special effects and enthralling plot twists.

> *Use interesting and dramatic language to support your points.*

The film has to be included in the set of DVDs because everything about it was fresh and new at the time, the special effects were totally spectacular and, amazingly, it still has the power to thrill the audience today. The music is instantly recognisable, and still sends a shiver down my spine. The characters are powerful and interesting and have made stars of some of the actors. The technical effects were well ahead of their time and have influenced many films since they were first seen on screens all over the world.

> *This conclusion challenges the judges not to choose this entry, and is a useful technique.*

Do you really think any set of 'The best films ever' would be complete without this trilogy?

Exam help

Competition entry

- Read the context carefully in order to decide what style to use, but it will probably be semi-formal. You need to organise your ideas clearly as you are presenting your nomination to the judges.
- Use a range of interesting vocabulary and think of interesting details that support your ideas to persuade the judges to choose your entry.
- You can use techniques like rhetorical questions and exclamation marks to emphasise your points.
- Remember that the point of the answer is to win the competition. This means that you have to write in such a way as to persuade the reader that your answer is the best. You could include a conclusion giving the final reason why your entry should win the competition.

Useful language

Making nominations

I would recommend …
The … has to be included …
I can't see how … can be ignored
This is an iconic film/book …
It's well ahead of its time …
It's been very influential …

Using interesting and dramatic language

It's totally spectacular and amazing …
It still has the power to thrill …
It sends a shiver down my spine …
The music is instantly recognisable …

Concluding a competition entry

For all the reasons given, I recommend …
It must be clear that this is the … to win the competition.
How could the … be considered complete without this …?

Reference (Part 2)

A friend has applied for a job in the office of an English Language College that teaches students from all over the world, and you have been asked to provide a reference. The advertisement has asked for applicants who are good with people and have good communication skills. Applicants should also be well organised and be team players.

In your reference, you should include information about your friend's relevant work experience and personal qualities, and your reasons for recommending them for the job.

Write your **reference**. Write your answer in **220–260** words in an appropriate style.

Sample answer

Reference for Sarah Holmes

State your relationship with the person clearly at the start.

▶ I have known Sarah personally as a friend for seven years, and have worked with her for five. During that time she has proved herself to be a trustworthy and supportive friend, and a reliable colleague.

Sarah is a competent administrator, and understands systems. She has worked in the HR department for several years, and knows the importance of efficient organisation. This would be an asset in a school environment. She is known as a hard-worker, and never objects to working overtime when necessary.

Her overall skills set is impressive, and very appropriate for working in a school office. Even more importantly, she gets on well with everyone, and is an excellent team player.

List her professional qualities.

▶ I feel that Sarah would be an ideal person for the job. Firstly, she has excellent communication skills, and is patient and supportive at all times. In my own experience, she deals well with clients from all over the world, and understands the importance of customer relations. She would be an excellent person to deal with young people studying at an International School, and would be equally at home dealing with the teachers. Secondly, she works well under pressure, and thrives in a busy working environment. Thirdly, as already stated, she has good administrative skills and her work in the HR department makes her eminently suitable for a job in an International College.

For all these reasons, I have no hesitation in supporting Sarah's application for the job. ◀

Conclude with a summary of your recommendation.

Exam help

Reference

- Read the context carefully in order to identify what the job is and what the potential employer is looking for in an employee. Make sure that you cover all the relevant points and don't give too much personal information about the person.
- Include a clear conclusion stating whether you recommend the person for the job, and why.
- Use a clear formal style, but try to make the person sound interesting to the potential employer. A reference should be an objective assessment of a person's suitability for a job.

Useful language

Introducing the person

… and I have worked together for …

I have known … since …

I have worked with … for … and have always found her to be …

I am happy to write a reference for …

Describing personal qualities

As a colleague, … is supportive and friendly

It is clear that … has a talent for …

… has proved herself to be a trustworthy and reliable person

… takes a level-headed and sensible approach to her work

Concluding a reference

I have no hesitation in recommending …

I am sure that you would not regret employing …

I support …'s application without reservation.

Review (Part 2)

Your local book club has asked its members to recommend novels for club members to read and discuss. Write a report about a novel which you would like to recommend, briefly outlining the plot, describing any particularly good features of the novel and explaining why you recommend it for the book club.

Write your **review**. Write your answer in **220–260** words in an appropriate style.

Sample answer

State the purpose of your report clearly.

▶In this report I will assess the value of *Through a glass, darkly* by Donna Leon as a potential book for our club members to read and discuss.

First, the plot. Donna Leon writes crime novels that take place in Venice and she is very good at evoking a sense of place. The action takes place on Murano, the famous Venetian island where people make glass. A friend of the local policeman (who is the main character) has been arrested while protesting against the chemical pollution of the Venetian lagoon by factories. The investigation reveals threats by a glass factory owner against his own son-in-law, and what follows involves a mystery, a murder; and raises serious questions about the future of Venice.

If you choose not to use headings, make sure your sections are clearly linked.

▶So why do I recommend it? Firstly, the book is one of a series, which is an advantage as members of the club may like to try some of the others. Secondly, the story is not only believable, but engaging and gripping, and is an enjoyable read. Most importantly for the club, however, is the fact that it focuses on important current issues. It challenges readers to think about the pollution of the Venetian lagoon, and what the future of Venice's glass industries might be as they are undercut by cheaper imitations. The issues raised would be very productive and challenging for club members to debate.

Within sections, if you choose not to use bullet points, use clear connectors to link your ideas.

To conclude, I feel that members of the club would enjoy the book as a crime novel, and find the issues it raises worth discussing.

Include a final section summarising your conclusions.

Exam help

Set text questions

If you choose to answer the question on the set text, make sure that you know it well enough to be able to support your answer with examples from the book.
You don't have to write literary criticism!

- You will be able to prepare vocabulary and ideas for the set text.
- The set text questions will be in the same genre as the other questions in Part 2. Make sure that you follow the guidelines for those task types. The only difference is that you support your ideas from the set text and not from your own imagination.

Report

- Read the context carefully to decide what style to use. It will probably be semi-formal.
- Try to think of interesting and appropriate details to support your ideas.
- Remember that the purpose of a report is to inform the reader in order for the reader to make some kind of decision. You should make recommendations, and give your own personal opinion in order to help the reader to their decision.
- You can use bullet points and headings, but remember that you need to show a range of language. You should decide what format and layout is most appropriate for the context and who you are writing the report for.
- Include a conclusion, possibly with a final evaluation.
- If the report is about a film or a book, don't give away the ending as this will spoil it for your reader!

Useful language

Introducing the report

The aim of this report is to …

In this report, I will …

This report presents …

Making recommendations

In the light of … it seems to me that the best approach to take is

I would recommend … as …

I would suggest …

I definitely recommend this book/film because …

Finishing the report

For the reasons stated, I feel that …

In conclusion, I feel that …

In short, I feel confident in recommending …

Letter (Part 1)

You **must** answer this question. Write your answer in **180–220** words in an appropriate style. In the exam, you write your answer **on the separate answer sheet provided**.

Last year, you spent four months working for an international company that organises winter holidays. Your friend Juan has contacted you to ask whether he should apply for the same job this year.

Read the extract from Juan's letter and the notes from your diary. Then, **using the information appropriately**, write a letter to Juan saying whether you think he should apply for the job, giving reasons for your opinion.

> I love skiing and I'd like to try snowboarding too – without paying for it! I could earn money before going to university and I'd get to learn another language. It sounds pretty easy really.
>
> Should I go for it?
>
> Juan

December 15th: Busy day – clients needed to get equipment. Paid for my own ski pass!

December 20th: Snow conditions poor – lots of complaints. Organised other activities. Pretty stressed.

January 10th: Good snow but had to do paperwork. Clients of mixed nationalities so using English.

March 29th: Skied all day – fantastic! Leaving tomorrow ...

Write your **letter** to your friend. You do not need to include postal addresses. You should use your own words as far as possible.

Sample answer

Hi Juan,

Great to hear from you. So you're thinking of applying for my old job – there are positive things I can tell you about it, but there are loads of down sides as well.

I know how much you love skiing, like me – but in this job you don't get much time to do it. You said you want to snowboard – well, to be honest, you'll be lucky to get more than a couple of days on the slopes. And you have to buy your own ski pass, which is pricey – no freebies there! ◄ - - - - - [*Try to use interesting language.*]

It's pretty stressful because you have to deal with clients the whole time, getting equipment sorted, things like that. When snow conditions are poor, you have to entertain them! They may not be very pleased about that! When I was there they complained a lot. It's true I did get the chance to practise English as the clients were from different countries, but on the whole that was the only plus. I hated the paperwork, ◄ - - - [*Add your own ideas to the input information and extra details to create interest.*] which was really time-consuming, and pretty frustrating when conditions were good and I could've been on the slopes! Filing is not my thing, and there was a lot of it.

I don't really know what to advise. You won't get much skiing, it's stressful, but it's paid employment and the language is a bonus.

It's your call! Let me know if I can do anything. ◄ - - - [*Finish with an appropriate phrase – in this case, it is an informal letter. If you were writing a formal letter, you would finish with 'Yours sincerely' or 'Yours faithfully'.*]

All the best

Carlo

Exam help

Letter

- The style of a letter could be semi-formal, formal or informal depending on the purpose of the letter and the context. Make sure you read the instructions carefully, and identify the target reader and reason for writing. Keep the style consistent throughout.

- Use clear paragraphs and appropriate opening and closing phrases.

Useful language

Beginning an informal letter

Thanks so much for your email …

Sorry not to have contacted you earlier …

Thought it was time I dropped you a line …

Referring to a previous letter

You said in your letter that you want to …

Last time you wrote, you mentioned …

I remember that you spoke about …

Ending an informal letter

I think that's all for now. Do write soon!

Once again, thanks for contacting me.

Give my love to …

Speak to you soon.

Ending a formal letter

Yours sincerely (if beginning with 'Dear Sir/Madam')

Yours faithfully (if beginning with the person's name)

Article (Part 2)

You see the following announcement in an international magazine.

> Have you been to an interesting and unusual celebration recently? For example, an eighteenth birthday, or a wedding that was a bit different? Write an article and tell us about it, explaining why it was interesting and unusual, and whether you enjoyed it. We will publish the most interesting articles in the next edition!

Write your **article**. Write your answer in **220–260** words in an appropriate style.

Sample answer

Try to have an interesting introduction to engage the reader immediately.

Not what I expected!

Have you ever been to a celebration that turned out to be totally different from what you'd expected? How did you feel? My own experience may strike a chord with you all!

It was a celebration concert that my friend took me to as a birthday present. I hadn't particularly wanted to go, as the band's music wasn't really my thing but I knew it would be a special occasion as it was their final performance before they went their separate ways. Tickets were hard to get, but my friend had been lucky and got two on the internet. Although I knew that she had paid a lot for them, I had no idea what was in store for me.

I'm sure you've all been to a big, live concert and so you can imagine the atmosphere – it was electric! When we arrived, I had expected to be shown to a cheap seat far away from the stage – that's my usual position at such events. And I'd even brought my binoculars! But the usher took us to our seats right on the side of the stage and once the music started it was amazing! I felt as though I was right there with the band. And to cap it all, once it was over we were taken backstage and I got to meet them all. It was unlike anything I've experienced before, and I thoroughly enjoyed it.

I still don't feel that their music is for me, but the experience was something special and unforgettable. Now I have to think of something equally good for my friend's birthday!

Think of an interesting title.

Use humour and techniques like exclamation marks to make it exciting for the reader.

Don't give away what is to come – keep the reader in suspense!

Finish with a humorous comment or punchline.

Exam help

Article

- Plan your ideas carefully before you start to write and remember that the focus of an article is usually to interest or inform the reader, and to entertain.

- Think of an interesting title.

- Try to involve the reader by using techniques like rhetorical questions at the beginning, though don't use too many in the article as they can become boring. You can talk to the reader directly.

- The style of an article depends on the context, type of publication and who the reader is. It may be semi-formal or informal.

- Use interesting examples or anecdotes to support your ideas.

- Try to finish in an interesting way, possibly using some kind of joke or punchline.

Useful language

Rhetorical questions

Have you ever done anything like this?

So is this really true?

So what do I really think about the whole thing?

Talking directly to the reader

We're all supposed to hate reality shows, but do we really?

I'm fairly sure that you will all agree with me when I say …

Why not think about it? You'll find that …

Finishing in an interesting way

How fantastic would that be!

After all, we're all in this together!

Speaking for myself …

It goes without saying that …

It just couldn't have been better!

Essay (Part 2)

Following a class discussion on how technology has affected the way we live today, your teacher has asked you to write an essay discussing the statement 'We would all be better off without technology!'. You should consider how technology has affected communication, relationships and working life.

Write your **essay**. Write your answer in **220–260** words in an appropriate style.

Sample answer

Introduce the topic in general terms, using rhetorical questions to lead in to the discussion.

Use clear connectors, and one topic for each paragraph.

Indicate that you are aware of the opposite point of view.

Technology is such a feature of everyday life that it is difficult to remember what we did without it. But is this a change for the better? Would we actually be better off without it?

Firstly, communication has been totally transformed by technology. We can communicate with anyone anywhere in the world at any time of day or night, and it is rare to meet a person who doesn't own a mobile phone. Of course it is useful to be able to contact someone when we need to, but is this always a good thing? We have lost the ability to be content with our own company, and life is more stressful because of it.

Secondly, technology has affected the way we make relationships and our expectations of them. It is common to find people who have more friends on the internet than they do in real life, and spend more time chatting to cyber friends than to real-world friends. Although it is good to feel part of a wider community, this must have a negative effect on people's ability to relate to others on a personal level.

Finally, working life has changed out of all recognition. People sit in open-plan offices but work at computer screens, not with each other – not a satisfying working environment. On the other hand, computers enable people to work from home, which creates a healthy work/life balance.

To sum up, I feel that although technology has negative effects, it is impossible to go back. So we must make the best of it and, on balance, we would not be better off without it.

Don't give your own opinion until the final paragraph. Make sure that your argument has made this a logical conclusion.

Exam help

Essay

- Make sure that you have enough ideas about the topic to write 220-260 words. The point of an essay is to present an argument clearly and provide evidence for your point of view. You might be asked to agree or disagree with a statement, or write about a given topic.

- Read the question carefully and plan your answer in clear paragraphs. You need to organise your ideas clearly as you are presenting an argument, so use suitable connectors.

- An essay is usually written for your teacher, so use a formal or semi-formal style. However, it is appropriate to use rhetorical questions to lead into your argument or ideas.

- Use a range of vocabulary and try to think of interesting details to support your ideas.

- Try to present a balanced argument, showing that you are aware of all the possible issues.

- Don't begin your essay giving your opinion, but finish with a conclusion summarising your own point of view.

Useful language

Introduction

It is often said that …

This is a hotly-debated topic.

This is a topic that is often discussed but rarely solved.

Many people feel that …

Linking ideas

While many may agree with this, it may still be a mistake.

Conversely, it may be inappropriate for this situation.

On the contrary, it is seen by many as a brilliant solution to the problem.

While I can see some benefits, these may be outweighed by the disadvantages.

Giving opinions

It seems to me that …

In my opinion, this is …

From my perspective, this seems to be …

To be honest, I feel that …

Conclusion

To sum up, it seems to me that …

On balance, I feel that …

Taking all the arguments into account, I would say that …

Information sheet (Part 2)

You are organising a new sports club at your college, and want to produce an information sheet about the club in order to get people interested and attract members. In your information sheet, you need to tell people about the sporting activities they can do, the costs involved, the advantages of joining and any future plans the club may have.

Write your **information sheet**. Write your answer in **220–260** words in an appropriate style.

Sample answer

Use headings to make the information sheet clear and easy to read.

Your new sporting life starts here!

Ever felt something was missing from life? Well, it's here! The new Sports Club opens on Saturday.

What you can do

We're planning loads of sporting activities to suit all shapes and sizes. Do you like team games? We're setting up hockey and football teams. Come along to the Sports Hall on Saturday to put your name down for trials. Don't worry if you think you're no good – let us decide that for you!

Perhaps individual games are more your scene? Tennis and badminton may be the answer. No need to plan ahead or commit for a long time – just turn up when you want to play or book a court a few days ahead. You can hire equipment at a reasonable cost, or buy your own from the College Shop.

Looking for a thrill? Skateboarding provides that, along with roller-blading. Register your interest in these on Saturday morning.

Make sure you provide practical information so readers know what they have to do to take part.

Why join?

Use bullet points for clarity, but make sure you use a range of language.

- Get fit – always a good thing!
- Meet people – a great way to make contact with people outside your study group
- Fresh air – don't spend all your time inside on the computer!
- Cheap fees – just a small enrolment fee of £50 that you can pay on Saturday. After that, you can decide if you want to stay with us and pay the £25 each semester – it's pretty cheap for what you get!

Plans for the future

We will become the best college sports club in the area! We're already planning new sports including:

- boxercise – guess what that is!
- jazz dance – lots of fun!
- kitesurfing – a thrill a minute!

Any more suggestions?

Come and check us out!

Try to be original and eye-catching in your approach.

Report (Part 2)

A college magazine is running a series of book reviews featuring books which have particularly good titles. Write a review for the magazine about a book you have read which you think had a good title. You should briefly say what your book is about, explain why you think its title is particularly good and whether you would recommend it to other students at the college.

Write your **report**. Write your answer in **220–260** words in an appropriate style.

Sample answer

> Don't spend too much time telling the story – it is important to answer the rest of the question. Don't give away the end as this is a review and you want other people to read the book!

Set in California during the Great Depression, John Steinbeck's novel *Of Mice and Men* tells the story of two friends, George and Lennie. Lennie is a large, strong man with the intellectual capabilities of a child, and George looks after him. Like many poor men at this time, George and Lennie travel from farm to farm looking for work, although they dream of owning their own land.

We learn that on their last farm, Lennie, who likes touching soft things, saw a girl wearing a red dress and tried to touch it, but the girl was scared and accused him of attacking her. The two men moved on to another farm where, again, circumstances combine against them.

> Give your own opinion clearly.

The title is interesting – it probably comes from a poem which says that the best plans can go wrong however important or unimportant you are. In my opinion, it could also mean that Lennie can't cope in a man's world, or that the two men have aspirational dreams and these are what lift them above the other working men. The novel deals with themes of loneliness, friendship, alienation, kindness, compassion and the importance of having dreams and ambitions. To me, these are themes that are the same for unimportant people (mice) or important people (men).

I really recommend this book because it makes you think about what is important in life. It is fascinating to read, and you get totally involved with the lives of the two men. Although it is sad, you still feel that there are worthwhile things in life.

Exam help

Set text questions
- If you choose to answer the question on the set text, make sure that you know it well enough to be able to support your answer with examples from the book. You don't have to write literary criticism!
- You will be able to prepare vocabulary and ideas for the set text.
- The set text questions will be in the same genre as the other questions in Part 2. Make sure that you follow the guidelines for those task types. The only difference is that you support your ideas from the set text and not from your own imagination.

Review
- Read the context carefully in order to decide what style to use, but it will probably be semi-formal.
- Use a range of interesting vocabulary and try to think of interesting and appropriate details to support your ideas. Remember that the purpose of a review is to inform the reader about the content of the book or film you are reviewing, and give your own personal opinion so that the reader can choose whether to read or see the book or film.
- You can use techniques such as rhetorical questions and exclamation marks to emphasise your points.
- Include a conclusion explaining whether you do or don't recommend the book or film, possibly with a final evaluation. Don't tell them the ending as this will spoil the film or book!

Useful language

Introducing the plot
The story concerns …
Set in Italy in the eighteenth century, the book/film tells the story of …
The main plot is about …
In brief, the story goes through a day in the life of the main character, …

Commenting critically
I found the plot rather …
The characters are completely believable/unbelievable because …
One strength/weakness of the book/film is …
The novelist/director has succeeded in … but the … is less successful.

Recommending
I would definitely recommend this book/film because …
For those who enjoy this type of book/film, this will be a hit.
Go and see this film – you won't be disappointed!

- What do you think the people might be enjoying about learning the new skill?
- How easy might it be for the people to master it?

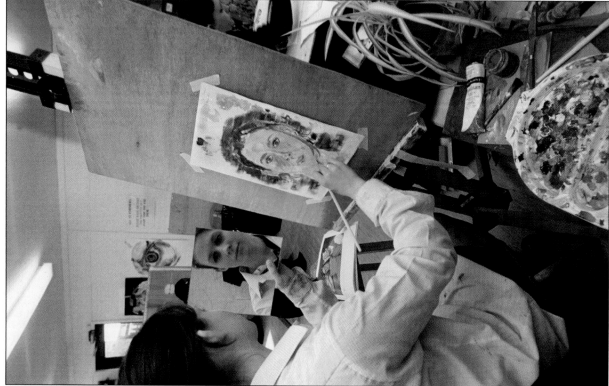

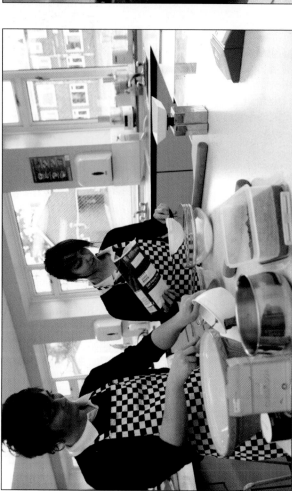

Candidate B

- Why are the people entertaining others in these different places?
- How important might it be for the people to provide good entertainment?

- Why are these things important to some people in today's world?
- Which two things will continue to be important to people in the future?

Candidate A

- How might people benefit from playing games like these?
- How might the players be feeling?

- How important might it be for the people to relax?
- How relaxing might the situations actually be?

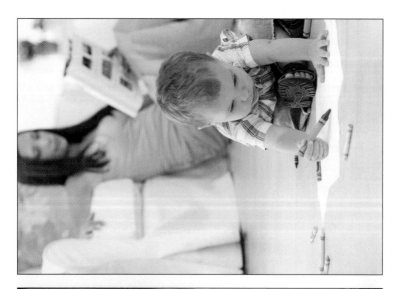

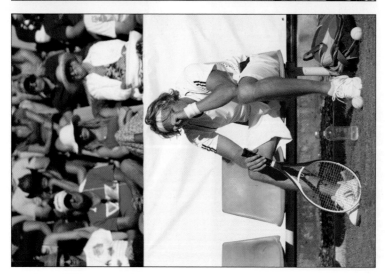

- What satisfaction do people get from having things like these?
- Which two things would provide the most long-lasting satisfaction?

- Why might the people be feeling like this in these situations?
- How long might the feeling last?

Candidate B

- What might be difficult for the people to deal with in these situations?
- How important might it be for them to deal with the situations well?

- What is the positive and negative impact of different aspects of technology on people's lives today?
- Which kind of technology will be less important in the future?

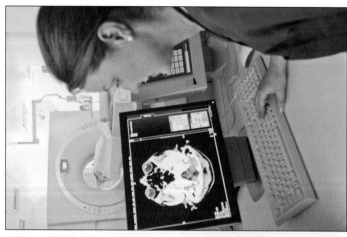

Candidate A

- What might the people find challenging about doing these activities?
- Which activity might give people the most satisfaction?

- What are the advantages of learning about the past in these ways?
- Who might actually learn most about the past?

- Why do people need special qualities to do these different jobs?
- Which job would be the most rewarding?

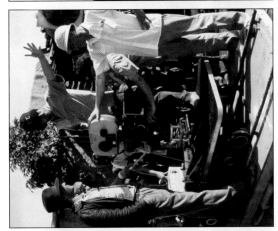
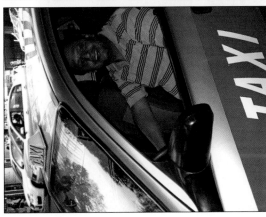

- What might make the people feel proud in these situations?
- How important might the feeling be to them?

Candidate B

- What effect might the weather conditions have on the people's mood?
- How difficult might it be for them to deal with the conditions?

- What might each picture say about the company?
- Which picture should be used on the home page of the company's website?

Candidate A

- How important might it be for the people to work together in these situations?
- How difficult might it be for them to do the work alone?

- Why might the people have chosen to travel in these different ways?
- How might the people be feeling?

- What should be done to protect these things?
- Which two things are most important to protect for future generations?

Candidate A

- What are the benefits of learning in these different situations?
- How enjoyable might the learning process be?

Candidate B

- How easy might it be for the people to make a choice in these situations?
- How important might it be for them to make the right choice?

- What are the advantages and disadvantages of doing these different glamorous jobs?
- Which job should be the focus of the first article in the series?

TEST 7, PAPER 5: SPEAKING

UNIVERSITY of CAMBRIDGE
ESOL Examinations

Do not write in this box

Candidate Name
If not already printed, write name in CAPITALS and complete the Candidate No. grid (in pencil).

Candidate Signature

Examination Title

Centre

Supervisor:
If the candidate is ABSENT or has WITHDRAWN shade here ⊏⊐

SAMPLE

Centre No.

Candidate No.

Examination Details

0	0	0	0
1	1	1	1
2	2	2	2
3	3	3	3
4	4	4	4
5	5	5	5
6	6	6	6
7	7	7	7
8	8	8	8
9	9	9	9

Candidate Answer Sheet

Instructions

Use a PENCIL (B or HB).

Mark ONE letter for each question.

For example, if you think B is the right answer to the question, mark your answer sheet like this:

0 A B C D E F G H

Rub out any answer you wish to change using an eraser.

1	A B C D E F G H	21	A B C D E F G H
2	A B C D E F G H	22	A B C D E F G H
3	A B C D E F G H	23	A B C D E F G H
4	A B C D E F G H	24	A B C D E F G H
5	A B C D E F G H	25	A B C D E F G H
6	A B C D E F G H	26	A B C D E F G H
7	A B C D E F G H	27	A B C D E F G H
8	A B C D E F G H	28	A B C D E F G H
9	A B C D E F G H	29	A B C D E F G H
10	A B C D E F G H	30	A B C D E F G H
11	A B C D E F G H	31	A B C D E F G H
12	A B C D E F G H	32	A B C D E F G H
13	A B C D E F G H	33	A B C D E F G H
14	A B C D E F G H	34	A B C D E F G H
15	A B C D E F G H	35	A B C D E F G H
16	A B C D E F G H	36	A B C D E F G H
17	A B C D E F G H	37	A B C D E F G H
18	A B C D E F G H	38	A B C D E F G H
19	A B C D E F G H	39	A B C D E F G H
20	A B C D E F G H	40	A B C D E F G H

A-H 40 CAS

denote Print Limited 0121 520 5100

DP594/300

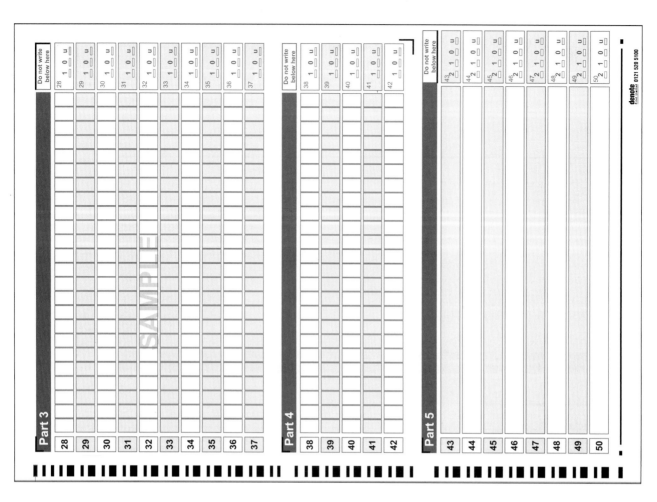

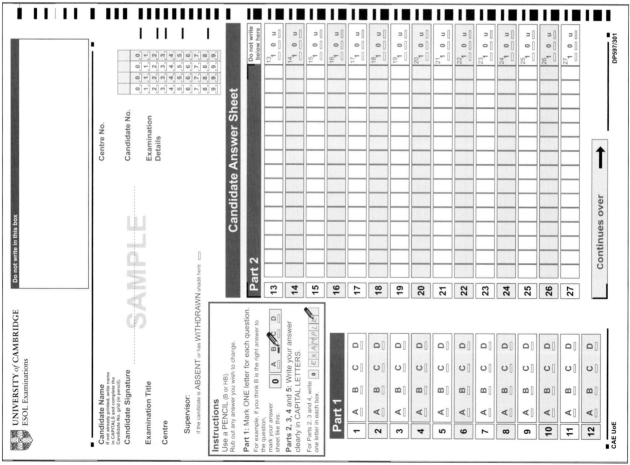

© Cambridge ESOL Photocopiable

USE OF ENGLISH

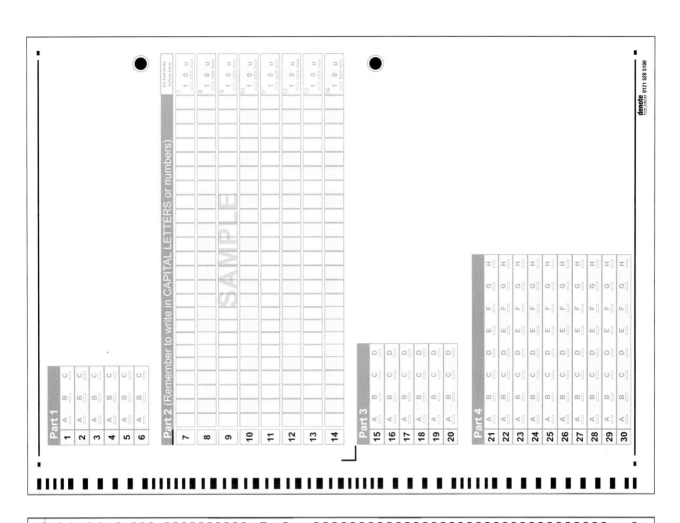

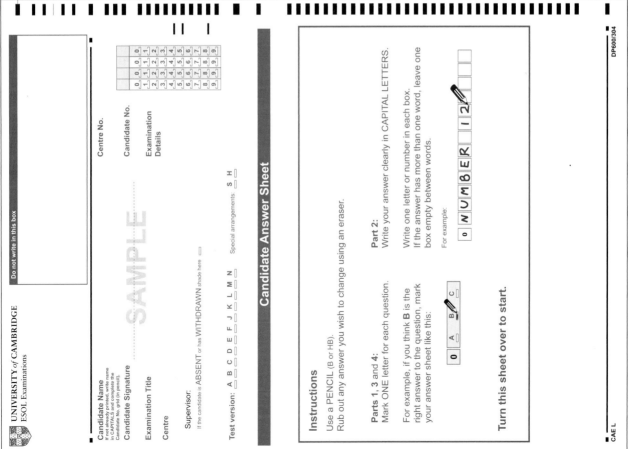

CAE: Top 20 Questions

1 How many marks are needed to pass the exam?

▶ To pass the exam with a grade C, you need around 60% of the total marks.

2 Do I have to pass each paper in order to pass the exam?

▶ No. Each paper doesn't have a pass or fail mark. The final grade, A, B, C, D or E, is arrived at by adding the weighted marks from all the papers together.

3 Are marks deducted for wrong answers?

▶ No. If you're not sure, make a guess, you may be right.

4 Am I allowed to use a dictionary?

▶ No.

5 In Paper 1 (Reading), Part 4 has more questions, so is it more important?

▶ No. The four parts are equally weighted. In Parts 1, 2 and 3, each question = 2 marks, whereas in Part 4, each question = 1 mark.

6 In Paper 1 (Reading), how long should I take on each question?

▶ This is up to you. You can do the tasks in any order and knowing how to use your time well is part of the test.

7 In Paper 2 (Writing), what happens if I don't use all the information given in Part 1?

▶ You will lose marks. The examiners are looking for both correct information and good language. So read the question, the input text and the handwritten notes very carefully.

8 In Paper 2 (Writing), how should I lay out the addresses?

▶ Don't include the addresses. If you do include them, the examiners will ignore them, as this is not part of the task.

9 In Paper 2 (Writing), what happens if I write too many or too few words?

▶ The word count is given as a guide only. Don't waste time counting; the examiners don't, they are more interested in your English! It is unlikely that answers under the lower limits will contain enough information/ ideas to fulfil the task. Overlong answers are more likely to contain mistakes. Plan your time so that you write about the right amount and have time to check what you have written.

10 In Paper 3 (Use of English), what happens if I get the right answer, but make a small mistake in a key word transformation?

▶ There are 2 marks for each answer, so you could still get 1 mark even if there was a small error.

11 In Paper 3 (Use of English), Parts 2, 3 and 4, if I am not sure, can I give two alternative answers?

▶ If there are two answers, and one of them is wrong, no marks are given. So, it's better to decide which of your answers is best!

12 In Paper 3 (Use of English), Parts 2 and 3, do contractions count as one word or two?

▶ Two, e.g. *don't* = two words, *do + not*.

13 What happens if I misspell a word in Paper 3 (Use of English), Parts 2 and 5?

▶ All spelling must be correct in Paper 3.

14 What happens if I misspell a word in Paper 4 (Listening)?

▶ All answers need to be correctly spelt at this level, although both US and British variants are accepted.

15 How many times will I hear each recording in Paper 4 (Listening)?

▶ Each recording is played twice.

16 In Paper 4 (Listening), Part 2, do I have to use the words in the recording or other words?

▶ The word(s) you need to write are heard in the recording, but you won't hear them in the exact sentences you see on the page.

17 In Paper 4 (Listening), Part 2, what happens if my answer is too long to fit on the answer sheet?

▶ Most answers are single words, numbers or groups of 2–3 words. If you think the answer is longer, then it is probably the wrong answer. If you write information which is not the answer in addition to the answer, you will not get the mark, as you have not shown that you know exactly what the answer is.

18 In Paper 5 (Speaking), do I have to go with another student? Can I choose my partner?

▶ You cannot be examined alone as the ability to discuss with another student is being tested in Part 3. In some centres you can choose your partner, in others not. You should ask the local organiser. Don't forget that in Parts 1, 2 and 4 of the test, you talk to the examiner, not to your partner.

19 Is it a good idea to prepare what you are going to say in Part 1?

▶ It's a good idea to practise, but don't forget that the examiners give marks for natural communication in English. If you give a prepared speech which doesn't answer the examiner's question, you will lose marks.

20 What if my partner makes lots of mistakes, or doesn't talk in Part 3?

▶ Don't worry. The examiners will help if necessary. Don't forget, you are not in competition with your partner. If you can help them, this will impress the examiners. Remember that Part 3 is about interaction, so you have to ask and answer questions as well as say what you think.

Answer Key

Part 1:

1 B: 'Their dream of family life had turned into a nightmare' and 'they knew something had to change'.

2 C: The only reference to other people's opinions is in the first sentence, where the writer says that 'those of us' (people like the writer) who like home comforts would regard the family's lifestyle as 'unimaginable'. The writer is suggesting that the reader might feel like this too.

3 C: At this point she realised that what they had in common was mothers not speaking English and spending time in homes like Mina's mother's.

4 B: Even though she couldn't speak English and needed her daughter to translate, she 'insisted on offering me hospitality and her manners sure beat those in Oak Brook' (she was much more polite than people in Oak Brook).

5 A: The researchers said that 'an absence of affection seems to be a bigger problem than high levels of conflict', meaning that siblings having arguments is less important than having affection for each other. Affection between siblings has many positive effects on them, even if they also argue a lot.

6 D: Siblings help each other to be 'kind' and 'generous'; arguments between them teach them 'skills that come in handy as they grow up'; affection between them makes life easier for them and provides 'a big protective factor'; sisters make their siblings less likely to suffer from a range of bad feelings; siblings have 'positive effects' on each other and sisters have 'the most positive influence'.

Part 2: Learning to be an action hero

7 F: link between the fact that the writer 'can't reach much past my knees' and how difficult he is finding this and that belief that the reader will think 'this sounds a bit feeble' – that the writer is weak and incapable of doing the exercise well.

8 D: link between 'get there' in D and 'a very particular, very extreme kind of fitness' before the gap; 'get there' = achieve that kind of fitness.

9 A: link between 'it had all started so well' before the gap and the first thing they did in the session, which was 'a piece of cake' (very easy) for the writer.

10 E: link between 'a few' in E and the 'movements for building strength in your back and arms' on the chinning bar mentioned before the gap.

11 G: link between the bar mentioned before the gap and Steve jumping on to that bar at the beginning of G; link between 'from one to another' and the various bars mentioned in the paragraph before the gap.

12 B: link between the 'one comforting piece of knowledge' mentioned in B and what that piece of knowledge was – that the writer will 'never suffer from an anatomical anomaly'.

Part 3: Is the internet making us stupid?

13 C: Patricia Greenfield 'reviewed dozens of studies on how different media technologies influence our cognitive abilities' and looked at the results of these studies as a whole.

14 B: The University experiment tested how well the students 'retained the lecture's content'; an earlier experiment showed that the more types of information are placed on a screen, the less people can remember.

15 B: Greenfield concluded that 'growing use of screen-based media' had resulted in 'new weaknesses in higher-order cognitive processes' and listed several mental processes that have been affected (abstract vocabulary, etc.).

16 C: It was expected that the people who did a lot of multitasking would 'have gained some mental advantages' from their experience of multitasking but this was not true. In fact, they 'weren't even good at multitasking' – contrary to the belief that people who do a lot of multitasking get good at it.

17 C: The writer says that the 'ill effects' are permanent and the structure of the brain is changed. He quotes someone who is very worried about this and regards the long-term effect as 'deadly'.

18 D: The writer uses Ap Dijksterhuis's research to support his point that 'not all distractions are bad' – if you are trying to solve a problem, it can be better to stop thinking about it for a while than to keep thinking about it all the time.

19 A: 'The cacophony of stimuli short-circuits both conscious and unconscious thought, preventing our minds from thinking either deeply or creatively' and we stop being capable of 'contemplation, reflection and introspection'; 'unconscious thought does not occur' and our brains become 'simple signal-processing units'.

Part 4: The way we worked

20 B: 'Search your high street for a typewriter repairman and your chances of a result at all are ribbon-thin.'

21 D: 'The craze for buying newly available arts and crafts from Japan was at its height in the second half of the nineteenth century.'

22 A: 'Mention them to people and they'll look quizzical,' Roberts says, 'but next time they see you, they'll have started to spot them.' ('them' = the work done by sign-painters).

23 C: 'In 1888, thousands of matchgirls at the Bryant and May factory in London famously went on strike to protest over conditions.'

24 B: They serve 'septuagenarian retirees', 'technophobes', 'novelists' and 'people weaned on digital keyboards who see typewriters as relics of a distant past'.

25 D: When warned that someone might steal his techniques, he says that 'no one wants to' copy him or learn to do what he does.

26 C: 'Over subsequent decades, the long hours, tiny pay packets and exposure to toxic chemicals were addressed'.

27 A: His father told him 'these things will come back' and 'the more technology comes into it, the more you'll be seen as a specialist' and his words showed 'a lot of foresight'.

28 B: They repair typewriters by using 'the vast collection of spare parts they've accumulated over the years'.

29 C: 'The majority of staff are still female'; 'it's still mainly female'.

30 D: 'Shiny, affordable substitutes, like shellac, began to eat away its aura' – cheaper alternative materials contributed to making lacquerwork less appealing and popular.

31 A: As his trade is a 'rare one', people employ him in all sorts of places.

32 B: 'It amazes us the price the old manual machines sell for on the internet'.

33 D: 'One magazine reprinted several slabs of an eighteenth century manual on the subject as a how-to guide.'

34 C: 'The industry largely relocated its production to other countries where labour was cheaper.'

Part 1

Question 1 (proposal)

Style: Proposal format, and formal language. Your paragraphs must be clearly divided, and should include recommendations for a possible outline for the day and how it should be organised. You can use headings, numbering or bullet points, but remember to use a range of structures and formal language.

Content: Include the following points from the notes, but don't repeat the actual words from the blog as they are too informal for a proposal. You should:
- provide a little background information about the previous event.
- recommend what should happen on the day, with reasons based on the notes and blog.
- suggest how the day should be organised.

Part 2

Question 2 (contribution to a longer piece)
Style: Semi-formal, as this is a contribution to a prospectus. Use clear paragraphs, and present your points clearly.
Content: You must include:
- information about social and sporting activities available.
- advice about the best ways of making new friends.
- recommendations for useful and interesting activities to take up.

You should include a conclusion rounding off your contribution.

Question 3 (competition entry)
Style: Semi-formal, but with colourful language that will interest readers and persuade them that you should win the competition. Use clear paragraphs, and finish with a conclusion giving reasons why your entry should win.
Content: You must include:
- your choice of DVD.
- an outline of the story.
- reasons why that DVD should be included in the set of the best films of all time.

Question 4 (reference)
Style: Formal, avoiding colloquial expressions. You may use a letter format, but remember to use a formal style. You must use clear paragraphs, which could be one paragraph for each of the content points below. You should have an introduction saying how long you have known your friend, and a conclusion stating whether you recommend your friend for the job, and why.
Content: Consider the skills identified for the job, especially dealing with people and using communication skills. You must include the following information about your friend:
- personal qualities.
- relevant work experience.
- any other relevant skills or experience they may have.

Question 5a) (report)
Style: Semi-formal language. Your paragraphs must be clearly divided. You can use headings, numbering or bullet points, but remember to use a range of structures and formal language. As this is a report on a book for a club, it might be better to write the report as block text though headings would still be appropriate.
Content: You should:
- outline the plot briefly.
- describe any good features of the novel.
- recommend it with reasons.

Question 5b) (essay)
Style: Formal or semi-formal. You should try to be objective because you are presenting a point of view, giving your reasons and/or providing evidence for your teacher. Use clear paragraphs, one for each scene from the novel. Include an introduction that introduces the novel, and a conclusion that summarises your personal point of view.
Content: You should:
- introduce the novel.
- describe two dramatic scenes from the novel.
- explain what you think makes them dramatic.

Conclude with your overall opinion of the novel.

Test 1, Paper 3, Use of English (Page 18)

Part 1: The Mysterious Isle

1   C: The other words do not complete the fixed phrase.
2   B: Only this answer creates the correct phrasal verb.
3   D: Only this word can be used in the context to mean 'the exact place'.
4   A: The other words cannot be followed with 'out of'.
5   C: Only this phrase indicates what's already been mentioned.
6   B: Although the meaning of the other words is similar, they do not collocate with 'intact'.
7   D: Only this word collocates with 'permanent' to describe an island.
8   A: Although the meaning of the other words is similar, they do not collocate with 'realised' in this context.
9   D: Only this answer collocates with 'opportunity'.
10 B: Only this word can be followed by the object and an adjective.

11 C: The other words are not followed by the preposition 'from' plus noun phrase.
12 A: The other words are not used to describe a party.

Part 2: Choosing Binoculars

13 great/good (quantifier) collocates with 'deal'
14 however/though (linker) indicates a contrast
15 in (preposition) follows the verb 'invest'
16 it (pronoun) part of fixed expression
17 more (comparative) part of linking expression
18 their/his/her (possessive pronoun) refers to everyone
19 which (determiner) to indicate one of many possible
20 on (preposition)
21 is (verb) part of a cleft sentence
22 give (verb) collocates with 'test run'
23 (Al)though/While(st) (linker) introduces a contrast
24 able (adjective) part of fixed grammatical expression
25 for (preposition) part of the phrasal verb
26 make (verb) part of the fixed expression
27 all (quantifier) part of the fixed expression

Part 3: The Inventor of the Bar Code

28 irregular (adjective to negative adjective)
29 length (adjective to noun)
30 outlets (verb to plural compound noun) part of common collocation
31 checkout (verb to compound noun)
32 encoded (verb to adjective) part of noun group
33 potentially (noun to adverb)
34 inspiration (verb to noun)
35 application(s) (verb to noun)
36 workable (verb to adjective)
37 arrival (verb to noun)

Part 4

38 took: collocation, collocation, phrasal verb
39 quickly: pre-modifying adverb, modified adverb, modified adverb
40 link: dependent preposition, collocation, specific word
41 charging: specific word, specific word, specific word
42 high: collocation, fixed expression, collocation

Part 5

43 (already) started by the time: past perfect
44 had great/a good deal of/a great deal of/a lot of difficulty: adjective to noun phrase
45 gave a faultless performance: verb to noun
46 was on the point of calling: fixed expression
47 came as a disappointment: adjective to noun
48 feels the effects of: dependent preposition
49 was weeks before: cleft sentence
50 almost/(very) nearly/all but run out of paper: phrasal verb

Test 1, Paper 4, Listening (Page 26)

Part 1

1   A: 'What companies want is people who can come up with ideas. I get a buzz from that side of it.'
2   C: M: 'Hours aren't fixed and can be long in relation to the salary.'; F: 'The job's not the big earner that people assume it is.'
3   A: 'I've always been competitive, and I work harder than anyone else … I copy the person who beat me. I won't stop till I better them.'
4   C: 'Although I'm not such an experienced cyclist … I jumped at the chance to try it'.
5   C: 'My own experience is much like that of other callers.'
6   B: 'Choose what you plant carefully.'

Part 2: The albatross

7   Arabic
8   21/twenty-one
9   (the) wind
10 shoulder(s)
11 smell

12 (little) mice
13 feathers
14 bottle caps/tops

Part 3

15 B: 'And the production company's put together an impressive team … that's what really pushed me to do it actually.'
16 D: 'I have no choice but to trust these guys, and I've no complaints so far.'
17 C: 'me doing … something interesting and active. Without that we don't have a programme.'
18 A: 'I think they're missing the point.'
19 D: 'As to whether there's a lost city down there, that's a bigger question that'll take years to answer. But we may have moved a step nearer answering that.'
20 D: 'Now that scene could've been cut but we thought it'd be a useful reminder of how archaeology usually works.'

Part 4

21 B: 'sitting about in front of a screen…. (I) never really felt fit.'
22 F: 'it was the sort of people you had to work with. You needed a bit of light relief, but nobody there could see the funny side of my anecdotes.'
23 H: 'it was having to do everything by yesterday that got me down.'
24 E: 'We were all packed into this really small area.'
25 A: 'I'd no commitment to it anymore.'
26 B: 'I really feel that the people who employ me are grateful – that's worth a lot to me.'
27 C: 'when I suggest a new style to a client.'
28 G: 'I'm actually a bit better off as a nurse …. because I had been expecting a cut in my standard of living'.
29 F: 'that makes me determined to do it as well as I can.'
30 D: 'People look up to you when you say you're a plumber' … It means you can do things they can't.'

Test 2, Paper 1, Reading (Page 34)

Part 1

1 D: It is commonly thought that people 'wilfully' (consciously, intentionally) 'put on' (pretend to have something they don't really have) an American accent when they sing pop music.
2 A: People 'lapse naturally' into an American accent; it 'feels more natural'; they do it 'automatically'; it would 'sound peculiar' to sing with their own accent; an American accent is 'the default' and it 'actually requires effort' not to sing with that accent.
3 C: If something 'brings shivers to the spine', it causes a powerful feeling for a short time, it has a strong emotional effect.
4 D: In 'just two years' (only two years, emphasising that this is a short time), he has progressed from having 'almost zero knowledge of music' to being an exceptional singer, reaching a very high level on the piano and becoming a very good player of a range of other instruments, 'none of which he had touched' before.
5 C: The researchers tested what people who had done 'serial recall' tasks could remember to see how background music affected their performance.
6 D: In the tests, people who heard background music did less well than people who didn't. This suggests music 'adversely affects' (has a bad effect on) performance at work because it is 'a distraction' (it stops people from concentrating properly).

Part 2: Fluttering down to Mexico

7 D: link between 'these creatures' and 'this mass of insects' in D, 'butterflies' and 'millions of them' before the gap and 'They' after the gap.
8 G: link between 'Their journey here' before the gap and the description of that journey in G.
9 C: link between the butterflies being 'in search of nectar' (for food) and drinking from pools of water before the gap and what they do after they have therefore 'Fed and watered' at the beginning of C.
10 F: link between beliefs for 'centuries' about the arrival of the butterflies and what was discovered about this more recently, in the 1970s.

11 A: link between 'this' at the beginning of A and the fact that the migration route is 'endangered'. The first sentence of A explains why the migration route is endangered and A gives the results of this. In 'This is why' after the gap, 'This' refers to the problems caused for the butterflies.
12 E: link between 'these' at the beginning of E and the four areas of the reserve that are open to the public mentioned before the gap.

Part 3: Take as much holiday time as you want

13 B: The main topic of the paragraph is how greatly the holiday policy at Netflix differs from what normally happens with regard to holidays in organisations and companies.
14 C: They said that the standard holiday policy was 'at odds with' (did not fit logically with, did not make sense with) 'how they really did their jobs' because sometimes they worked at home after work and sometimes they took time off during the working day.
15 D: The company decided: 'We should focus on what people get done, not how many hours or days are worked.'
16 A: Rules, policies, regulations and stipulations are 'innovation killers' and people do their best work when they are 'unencumbered' by such things – the rules, etc. stop them from doing their best work.
17 B: One 'regard' in which the situation is 'adult' according to the writer is that people who aren't excellent or whose performance is only 'adequate' lose their jobs at the company – they are 'shown the door' and given a 'generous severance package' (sacked but given money when they leave).
18 D: Nowadays, 'Results are what matter'. How long it takes to achieve the desired results and how these results are achieved are 'less relevant'.
19 A: If companies have lots of rules for the workforce because they don't trust them (they 'assume bad faith' – they believe that their employees are dishonest and not willing to do what is required), the employees will try to break those rules or avoid obeying them. If companies 'assume good faith', this encourages employees to have the right attitude.

Part 4: Seeing through the fakes

20 E: 'Anyone can label a picture a fake or a copy.'
21 F: 'museums and galleries constantly question, revise, reattribute and re-date the works in their care.'
22 C: 'All became clear when art historians did further research'. The research explained why the painting used a pigment that was not available to artists until later.
23 F: 'the mistaken belief that museums have anything to gain by hiding the true status of the art they own.'
24 A: 'the study of any work of art begins with a question: is the work by the artist to whom it is attributed?'
25 E: The painting had 'under drawing in a hand comparable to Raphael's when he sketched on paper' and the 'pigments and painting technique exactly match those the artist used in other works'.
26 B: 'how little was known about Melozzo 90 years ago, and how little could be done in the conservation lab to determine the date of pigments or wood panel'.
27 D: 'X-rayed the picture and tested paint samples, before concluding that it was a rare survival of a work by Uccello dating from the early 1470s.'
28 F: 'If they make a mistake, they acknowledge it'
29 A: 'museum professionals' and 'conservation scientists'
30 E: 'infrared photographs that reveal the presence both of major corrections'
31 B: 'a costume historian pointed out the many anachronisms in the clothing.'
32 D: 'I well remember how distressing it was to read an article in which the former director of the Metropolitan Museum of Art, Thomas Hoving, declared that Uccello's lovely little canvas of *St George and the Dragon* was forged.'
33 B: 'Today, we find it incredible that anyone was ever fooled'
34 C: The pigment viridian was 'newly developed' in the 1820s and made available only 'to selected customers' at that time in Paris.

Test 2, Paper 2, Writing (Page 43)

Part 1

Question 1 (letter to a friend)
Style: Letter, informal language as Juan is a friend. You should use clear paragraphs, and include an appropriate greeting, opening and ending.
Content: Include the following points raised in Juan's email, referring to the notes in the diary:
What Juan wants to get from the job, including information about:
- whether he will be able to do winter sports free.
- whether he will be able to make money.
- whether it is a good opportunity to learn the language.

Remember to give final advice on whether the job would be good for him and whether he should apply. You can include ideas of your own, but don't write too many words, or include irrelevant details.

Part 2

Question 2 (article)
Style: Either semi-formal or informal, but as you are trying to interest and entertain the magazine readers you should use colourful language and features like rhetorical questions to capture the reader's interest. Use clear paragraphs, and give your article a title.
Content: You should:
- describe what the event was and give some details about it.
- explain why it was interesting and unusual, including some anecdotes or details.
- explain whether you enjoyed it, with reasons.
- provide an interesting/amusing conclusion.

Question 3 (essay)
Style: Formal or semi-formal. You should try to be objective because you are presenting a point of view, giving your reasons and/or providing evidence for your teacher. Use clear paragraphs, one for each issue. Include an introduction that leads in to the topic of technology, and an conclusion that rounds off your argument and states your personal point of view.
Content: You should include your ideas on the effects of technology on:
- communication.
- relationships.
- working life.

Conclude with your opinion on whether we would be better off without it.

Question 4 (information sheet)
Style: Semi-formal as this is an information sheet for students. You should present facts as clearly as possible. You can either use paragraphs (one for each point) with or without headings, or bullet points. If you use bullet points, remember that you still have to show a range of language, so don't make them too simple and don't use them in every paragraph.
Content: Include information about:
- sporting activities people can do.
- costs involved.
- advantages and benefits of joining the club.
- the club's future plans.

Remember to include details to support your ideas.

Question 5a) (review)
Style: Semi-formal moving towards informal as this is a review in a college magazine. The purpose of the review is to tell people about the book, explain why you think the title is a good one and give your opinion of it, with reasons. You will need to use the language of description or narration, and evaluation. Use clear paragraphs – introduction, description, evaluation and conclusion with recommendations.
Content: Remember to:
- describe the book or briefly narrate the story, giving its title.
- explain why you think it is such a good title.
- explain why you would or would not recommend it to other students in the college.

Question 5b) (article)
Style: Either semi-formal or informal, but as you are trying to interest and entertain the magazine readers, you should use colourful language and features, like rhetorical questions to capture the reader's interest. Use clear paragraphs, and give your article a title.
Content: You should:
- give a brief explanation about the book itself.
- identify and describe the character you have chosen, with reasons and details.
- explain why the character changed your way of thinking.
- provide an interesting/amusing conclusion.

Test 2, Paper 3, Use of English (Page 47)

Part 1: Seaside Artist

1 D: Although the other words have a similar meaning, only the right answer can be used in this context.
2 B: Only the right answer creates the correct phrasal verb.
3 D: The right answer is a strong collocation that is a commonly used term.
4 A: Only the right answer creates a parallel meaning to 'like' earlier in the sentence.
5 C: Only the right answer can be followed by 'afield' to create the fixed expression.
6 D: Only the right answer can introduce this type of clause.
7 C: The other words cannot be preceded by the verb 'to be' and followed by the infinitive.
8 B: The other words do not follow the preposition 'by'.
9 A: The other words are not followed by the preposition 'with'.
10 B: The other words cannot be used after 'to get' without an article.
11 B: Only the right answer creates the correct phrasal verb.
12 C: The other words do not collocate with 'advice'.

Part 2: Early Stone Tools

13 make (verb) collocates with the noun 'use'
14 than (preposition) links two parts of the comparison
15 after (adverb) time marker
16 back (preposition) phrasal verb
17 to (preposition) follows 'similar'
18 which/that (relative pronoun) introduces a defining relative clause
19 As (adverb) part of fixed phrase
20 In (preposition) part of fixed phrase
21 may/might/could (modal verb) expresses a strong possibility with 'well'
22 What (determiner) part of cleft sentence
23 or (conjunction) sets up an alternative explanation with 'whether'
24 by (preposition) comes before 'chance'
25 way (noun) fixed linking expression
26 rather (adverb) part of fixed phrase used to introduce a contrast
27 when/whenever/once (adverb) time marker

Part 3: Marathon Dreams

28 coverage (verb to noun)
29 endurance (verb to noun)
30 admiration (verb to noun)
31 exhaustion (verb to noun)
32 regain (verb to iterative verb)
33 possibly (adjective to adverb)
34 discouraging (noun to negative adjective)
35 overnight (noun to compound noun)
36 commitment (verb to noun)
37 advisable (verb to adjective)

Part 4

38 picked: phrasal verbs
39 fresh: collocations
40 head: collocations
41 use: collocation, collocation, fixed expression
42 issue: collocations

Part 5

43 what makes some cars (determiner + verb)
44 has been widely blamed (passive + adverbial collocation)
45 strength of the wind (noun + verb)
46 wishes (that) she could/was able to/were able to (wish for regrets)
47 expected to turn out for /up for/ up to /up at (passive + phrasal verb)
48 my complete/total dissatisfaction (adjective + noun)
49 chances of tomorrow's match being/chances that tomorrow's match will be (plural noun + preposition)
50 is ages since I have had (direct speech + syntax)

Test 2, Paper 4, Listening (Page 55)

Part 1

1 B: M: 'It was the prospect of shopping for new stuff I couldn't face! F: 'Tell me about it!'
2 A: 'It's heavily linked to wanting to be the centre of attention, to clothes giving them a strong personal identity or whatever. It's basically a way of showing off'.
3 B: 'I had a cockiness, ... I'd hear a hit record and think: "I could do that."'
4 A: 'If after my first hit I thought I'd made it, I was soon disabused of that notion'.
5 A: 'One time I danced in a culture show, and the dance director at my school, she asked: 'Are you interested in really training? Like, you seem to have talent.'
6 C: 'So much so, that I was on the point of rebellion on more than one occasion – though I'm happy to say that particular storm never actually broke.'

Part 2: Radio reporter

7 Communication Studies
8 marketing assistant
9 intimidated
10 Trainee Scheme
11 (live) interviews
12 journalism
13 news
14 flexibility

Part 3

15 C: 'It was pure chance that a friend asked me to design a set for a student musical he was directing'.
16 D: 'What you need to do is to put all the training in the background and get some hands-on experience – an apprenticeship's great for doing that, and I spent three years doing one.'
17 C: 'Having an affinity with a play is pretty vital. If you don't care about it, there's no point in doing it because you'll never come up with good ideas.'
18 A: 'Actually, it helps me to keep coming up with new ideas if I'm constantly changing my focus from one show to another.'
19 D: 'That's a bigger question that'll take years to answer. But we may have moved a step nearer answering that.'
20 A: 'On stage, ... requires the type of thinking I love best ... I don't get that buzz working on a movie, I'm afraid.'

Part 4

21 E: 'My wife said I'd never make it, which only made me more determined actually.'
22 D: 'As a graduation gift, it was a lovely way of marking the achievement.'
23 B: 'My girlfriend wanted to go ... I went along with the idea for her sake.'
24 G: 'Like me, they'd mostly seen that chap on TV at the site and decided to go too.'
25 C: 'I was looking to do a bit of serious walking to see what I was capable of.'
26 C: 'For me the highpoint was how friendly the others were.'
27 A: 'What made it for me ... was the actual design of the place.'
28 B: 'What blew me away ... was looking out from the low walls of the site over the mountains.'
29 E: 'I hadn't expected the actual walk up to the site to be so impressive.'

30 G: 'I'll never forget the meal the night before the final ascent.'

Test 3, Paper 1, Reading (Page 63)

Part 1

1 C: He says that 'as soon as I get home', he's going to go into the woods and start tracking animals on his own because the course was 'inspirational'.
2 B: A rabbit 'pops up' and 'scampers off' and then they look at the 'fresh print' it has left.
3 D: Malcolm tells the writer that students 'can get despondent if they think they're falling behind' – feel very unhappy if they believe they are making slower progress than the others.
4 A: Malcolm says the students are 'surprised at how well they do and how quickly'; Darren Moody builds his wall quickly and very well but 'everyone else is close behind' – all the others do the work almost as quickly as him.
5 A: He describes a 'tiny maze of corridors' that are very crowded, says it's very hot and humid and describes the smell as 'otherworldly' (in this context, this means 'very bad' because it comes from a lot of people's perspiration).
6 B: He has seen the way other people dance and is not impressed (they are 'rather average'); he is 'not too worried' therefore because he doesn't think it will be difficult for him ('how hard could it be?' = it won't be very hard), and he thinks it won't be as challenging as kickboxing or a triathlon.

Part 2: The 'Britain in Bloom' competition

7 D: link between 'do a lot' and 'too much'. D contains an example of a place that did something to please him that in fact didn't please him.
8 G: link between what the competition was like 'In the early days' and what it is like now (it's now 'much more sophisticated' and 'much more competitive' than it was when it started).
9 E: link between the criticisms of the competition in E and 'such criticisms' after the gap.
10 A: link between the statement that the 'old tricks' no longer work and 'This' at the beginning of A; what people used to do in order to win doesn't enable them to win any more and A explains that this is because of changes to the judging criteria; link between 'these developments' after the gap and the changes described in A.
11 F: link between one place that regards the competition as important (Stockton-on-Tees) and a place that has won the competition (Aberdeen); link between 'With so much at stake' after the gap and the description of what is 'at stake' (the fact that winning gives a place a very good image) in F.
12 C: link between 'Some of this' at the beginning of C and the stories of 'dirty tricks' before the gap; Jim is saying in C that some of the stories about rivals doing damage to the flowers of other competitors are 'exaggerated' and not completely true.

Part 3

13 B: The last sentence of the paragraph means: There was nobody better than an American to 'document' (record, in this case with photographs) the way society in Ireland was changing and becoming more like American society. People in Ireland were happy to employ an American to take pictures that looked like the images in 'an expensive American advertising campaign'.
14 D: She had previously 'harboured higher aspirations' (aimed to do work that was more artistic and creative) but she 'didn't mind' doing wedding and portrait photography and compared her situation with that of Dutch painters who did similar kinds of work to make money in the past.
15 D: She preferred analogue cameras, which were 'the old-fashioned method'. It is implied that she spent a lot of time in the darkroom following this 'old-fashioned' method to produce the wedding photographs.
16 C: He asked her 'What's up?' (What's the problem?) and she decided that 'she would tell him' (= tell him what the problem was) 'eventually, but not yet'.
17 A: She describes feeling a connection with the past when she visited the cairns and he says 'You Americans and your history', meaning that she was talking in a way typical of Americans and their attitude to the history of places like that.

18 D: When she said 'I know it' she was agreeing with him that, because they were both photographers, they were only interested in things they could see, their area of interest was limited to 'surface' (only what is visible).

19 B: She didn't want people in Ireland to think she was 'just another daft' (foolish, silly) 'American looking for her roots' (she didn't want people to think she was the same as so many other Americans, who wanted to learn about their ancestors and feel a connection with Ireland in the past).

Part 4: On the trail of Kit Man

20 B: 'discomfort, bad food and danger were seen as part of the authentic outdoor experience'.

21 D: 'this involves not only acquiring new clobber, but new jargon'.

22 C: 'The whole idea of going into the wild is to get away from the things that tie you in knots at home.'

23 A: 'Worried about getting lost? Relax with a handheld GPS unit, featuring 3D and aerial display, plus built-in compass and barometric altimeter.'

24 E: 'Many in the adventure business say gadgets have encouraged thousands who would otherwise not have ventured into the great outdoors.'

25 B: 'Kit Man and his kind stand accused by the old-schoolers of being interested only in reaching the summits of gadgetry.'

26/27 A: 'bleeping'.
D: 'ringing', 'beeping', 'clicking', 'whirring'.

28 C: 'All this technology, I mean, it might look fantastic on paper, but when there's a real problem, it's almost certainly going to let you down.'

29 E: 'there's research from Germany's Institute for Biological Cybernetics, which suggests that, left to their own devices, humans are doomed to wander round in circles.' People 'cannot trust our own senses' to find their way and avoid getting lost.

30 C: 'Who'd want to be stranded out in the wild with a gadget freak?'

31/32 B: 'basic pioneering disciplines – map-reading, camp-laying, First Aid – have declined, to be shakily replaced by the virtual skills offered by technology'.
C: 'people who depend on technology are woefully ill-prepared in other ways. You still need to be able to read a map and do the basic stuff.'

33 A: 'At next month's Outdoors Show in Birmingham, all this kit and more will be on display for an audience which seemingly can't get enough of it.'

34 E: 'Evidence from the American market also suggests that technology has had a positive environmental impact'.

Test 3, Paper 2, Writing (Page 72)

Part 1

Question 1 (report)
Style: Report format, and formal language as the report is for your manager. You can use headings, numbering or bullet points, but remember to use a range of structures and formal language in the report. Your paragraphs must be very clearly divided.
Content: You should describe the session briefly, and make recommendations for improving it.
Include the following points from the notes, but add ideas and suggestions of your own for improvements:
- too much information.
- presentation on company structure good.
- flexible hours system unclear.
- not enough benefits.
- working day too long.

Remember to make recommendations for your manager in the final paragraph.

Part 2

Question 2 (letter)
Style: Informal, but not too colloquial. Use letter layout with clear paragraphs.
Content: You should include information about:
- accommodation available.
- possibilities for sport.

- the possibility of finding part-time work to help him learn the language.

This information should be the main part of the letter but don't forget to include a friendly beginning and ending following the usual conventions of informal letters. 'Dear … All the best/Best wishes …'

Question 3 (review)
Style: Semi-formal moving towards informal. The purpose of the review is to contribute to a list of the best TV series of all time. You need the language of description or narration, and evaluation. Use clear paragraphs – introduction, description/narrative, evaluation and conclusion with reasons for your nomination.
Content: You need to include:
- a description of the TV series, maybe with some examples of good episodes.
- evaluation/reasons why you like it.
- reasons why it should be included in the list.

Question 4 (proposal)
Style: Proposal format, and formal language. Your paragraphs must be very clearly divided. You can use headings, numbering or bullet points, but remember to show a range of language.
Content: You should explain what the current facilities for language students are, and make recommendations for improvements with reasons. Remember that the college doesn't want to spend too much money.

Question 5a) (article)
Style: Either semi-formal or informal, but as you are trying to interest and entertain the magazine readers, you should use colourful language and features such as rhetorical questions to capture the readers' interest. Use paragraphs, and give your article a title.
Content: You should:
- give brief details about your favourite novel.
- outline the plot briefly.
- explain whether the novel would make a good film or not.
- provide an interesting/amusing conclusion.

Question 5b) (essay)
Style: Formal or semi-formal, and objective as you are presenting a point of view to your teacher, with reasons and/or evidence for your ideas. Use clear paragraphs, include an introduction that leads in to the topic and a conclusion that states your point of view.
Content: You should include:
- a brief description of the book.
- a description of the memorable character you have chosen.
- an explanation of why the character is memorable.
- an interesting conclusion.

Remember to support your ideas with examples of incidents, scenes or events from the book.

Test 3, Paper 3, Use of English (Page 74)

Part 1: Caving

1 C: Only the right answer creates the collocation.
2 B: The other words do not create the phrasal verb.
3 D: Only the right answer creates the collocation.
4 A: The other linkers aren't used in this type of sentence.
5 B: Only the correct answer creates the meaning in context.
6 D: Only the right answer creates the collocation.
7 B: Only the right answer is a verb used for water.
8 D: The other words don't create meaning in context.
9 A: Only the right answer creates the collocation.
10 B: Only the right answer completes the fixed expression.
11 B: Only the right answer creates the collocation.
12 C: Only the right answer creates the collocation.

Part 2: Why are sunglasses cool?

13 with (preposition) follows 'associated'
14 that/which (relative pronoun) introduces defining relative clause
15 why (determiner) fixed phrase with 'should'
16 but (conjunction) fixed expression with 'anything'
17 whose (possessive pronoun) refers to 'eyes'
18 of (preposition) part of fixed expression with 'fame'
19 At (preposition) part of expression

20 yet/still (adverb of time) precedes verb in infinitive
21 came (phrasal verb)
22 called (fixed phrase)
23 as (adverb)
24 in (preposition) part of multi-word verb
25 If (linker) introduces the clause in the conditional sentence
26 being (verb) present participle
27 was (verb) fixed phrase

Part 3: Customer reviews

28 accompanied (noun to verb)
29 arguably (verb to adjective)
30 professional (noun to adjective)
31 financial (noun to adjective)
32 unedited (verb to negative adjective)
33 analysis (verb to noun)
34 reliable (verb to adjective)
35 feedback (verb to compound noun)
36 (re)adjustments (verb to noun)
37 recommendation (verb to noun)

Part 4

38 hard: adverb collocations
39 gathered: specific meanings
40 heart: fixed expressions
41 natural: fixed expression, collocation, collocation
42 deal: fixed expressions

Part 5

43 had no choice but to (fixed expression)
44 the race was about to (direct to indirect speech with 'about to')
45 led to the singer being ('led' + passive form)
46 sooner had Alex finished his homework (negative head inversion)
47 bored if I spend ('boring' to 'bored' + condition phrase)
48 doesn't approve of her (reporting verb)
49 provided him with (new subject + verb + dependent preposition)
50 a few people managed to predict ('few' / 'many')

Test 3, Paper 4, Listening (Page 81)

Part 1

1 C: F: 'I find that a tough one to answer, don't you?' M: 'It's hardly an easy thing to articulate.'
2 C: 'There's a difference between the actual experience and the sanitised reality printed on the page. And that's what I want to look into.'
3 B: 'It wasn't easy at first and I soon discovered that I wasn't really cut out to be an interviewer – so I wasn't comfortable in the role.'
4 C: M: 'But it really depends on the party and the crowd – you've got to give them what they want.' F: 'No two sets are ever the same in that respect and that's the beauty of it. I'm all for being flexible.'
5 B: 'I focused on cake-making there because it's quite artistic, but also scientific. I like that idea.'
6 A: 'So I've learnt to follow my instincts, and fortunately we're beginning to see a firm customer base emerging as a result.'

Part 2: Computer game designer

7 developer
8 animation
9 book covers
10 user interfaces
11 Star City
12 narrative
13 difficulty level
14 dedication

Part 3

15 D: 'I knew it wouldn't be a long-term thing for me.'
16 B: '… went knocking on doors to try to sell our socks to retailers. We had a lot slammed in our faces.'
17 D: 'We really made a point of scrutinising our potential retail partners.'
18 A: 'I've talked most team members into using their homes as testing labs, some more enthusiastically than others.'
19 A: 'We don't sell anything through it.'
20 C: 'Focus on your strengths.'

Part 4

21 G: 'I only really went along to the salsa group to keep my boyfriend company.'
22 E: 'acting skills … I thought if I joined, it'd be a chance to pick some up.'
23 H: 'We're doing golf this term; are you up for it or not?'
24 C: 'I thought a club would be a way of getting in touch with like-minded students on other courses.'
25 A: 'So when a doctor I met at the hospital said they did Tai Chi at lunchtimes there, why didn't I give it a try?'
26 H: 'I could've done with someone telling me how I was doing actually.'
27 F: 'I think everyone needs to be given something to get their teeth into.'
28 C: 'but I do find some of the people you meet there a bit superior.'
29 B: 'I feel kind of duty bound to be there to make sure there's always a match.'
30 D: 'I just wish they'd run a session at the university.'

Test 4, Paper 1, Reading (Page 87)

Part 1

1 A: 'Perhaps they come … because Mr Brown's love for the machines is so deep, genuine, and, in its way, touching' – his passion affects and attracts them.
2 B: 'You can't really explain it to people who don't have the same enthusiasm.'
3 B: We are told that 'athletes, runners and joggers' do it and that 'fitness addicts' find it appealing.
4 C: When he got to the top the first time, he experienced 'a burst of elation' (intense happiness) 'powerful enough to bring him back for a re-run.'
5 C: Various parts of the house are 'neutral zones' for them. Both Caesar and his owner go into them and use them. Some parts are for Caesar (the dining room and conservatory) but Caesar cannot go into the loft, which is for his owner only.
6 D: He simply gives the facts of the situation and does not express a personal opinion about any of what he describes.

Part 2: Publishing's natural phenomenon

7 E: link between 'it' in 'Partly it was, and is' in E and 'its secret' before the gap ('it' = 'its secret').
8 B: B gives examples of covers that had the 'simplified forms that were symbolic' mentioned before the gap.
9 G: link between 'They' at the beginning of G and the two people who are the subject of the paragraph before the gap (Clifford and Rosemary Ellis); link between the 'original plan' described in G and what actually happened, described after the gap ('those' after the gap = 'photographic jackets' in G).
10 D: link between 'This' at the beginning of D and 'the common design' mentioned before the gap; link between 'They' after the gap and the covers described in D.
11 A: link between 'an even more demanding production method' and the production method described before the gap; link between 'Initially' and 'Later'.
12 C: link between 'In the process' and the writing of the book mentioned before the gap; Gillmor and the writer found the interesting things described in C while they were writing the book about the covers.

Part 3: The impossible moment of delight

13 A: Some studies conclude that happiness comes from being wealthier than the people near you, but others say that happiness comes from having a 'good attitude' and not from 'comparison with the wealth of others'.

14 B: The survey found that the common idea of rich people not being happy is true and that it was not invented simply so that poor people would be 'happy with their lot' (to persuade the poor that their position is OK and that they shouldn't envy the rich).

15 C: Bloom thinks people are in 'a state of perfect pleasure' at the moment when they get something they want, but the writer believes that it's hard to 'pin down' (define, be certain about) the moment when people feel happiness most clearly. So he does not agree with Bloom that it's possible to say exactly when people are at their happiest.

16 A: 'Everything else' means the times when happiness is not 'at its peak'. Happiness is only at its highest for a very brief time; the rest of the time is spent with feelings of 'expectation' or 'anticipation' before getting something and 'memory' or 'retrospective glee' after getting it.

17 C: These musical works fully illustrate his point that happiness is half expectation and half memory because half of them involves the music building up to a high point and half of them involves peaceful 'recall' after that high point.

18 A: The company's slogan stating that 'getting ready is half the fun' is 'honest and truthful'. Girls are happier getting ready for a party than when they are at the party, where they often do not have a good time (they may be 'standing around' or 'crying' at the party).

19 D: He believes they were at their happiest when they thought about completing their research and after completing it. This means that his main point about people being happiest before and after getting or doing something they want applies to the researchers and Bloom too.

Part 4: The intern's tale

20 B: She was 'shocked' when she discovered how big the 'tracing patterns' were and how much fabric was used to make each dress.

21 D: Her 'seamstress skills came in handy' when working on the 'installation that's now on display in the gallery' – she contributed to the work of art by doing some sewing that appears in it.

22 D: She didn't know how to send something by courier and had to ask lots of questions in order to do this.

23 A: She 'didn't want to leave everyone', meaning that she liked all the people she worked with.

24 C: Her friends have money for houses, cars and holidays and she doesn't, but 'I never feel I've missed out because I'm doing what I've always wanted to do' – she is glad she chose this kind of work.

25 B: She says that if you are an intern, 'you have to work hard and for free, because that's what everyone else is willing to do'.

26 A: She knows that some of the scripts she works on 'are going to become films one day'.

27 C: 'If I was 35 and still working unpaid, I would think 'What am I doing?''

28 D: She says that when she arrived in London, she 'didn't know how long it would take to get a job'.

29 A: 'Personally, I love anything that's been adapted from a book, especially if I've read the book' – she prefers working on film scripts based on books.

30 C: She has money from her father that 'has gone towards funding my placement' and she can live with her mother; 'Without my family, I don't think I could be doing this.'

31 B: She works at Vivienne Westwood's company and Vivienne Westwood 'treats everyone equally, whether they are paid staff or interns'.

32 D: 'If I couldn't afford my rent, I wouldn't just get into a spiral of debt. I would go and get a full-time job and the rest would have to wait' (she would wait before trying to achieve her career aims).

33 A: Working as a volunteer at her local theatre is 'a great way of seeing different aspects of the industry, meeting people and developing your career' – she can meet people who may be useful to her in her career.

34 B: 'I expect the days to get longer and more stressful as we approach Fashion Week.'

Test 4, Paper 2, Writing (Page 96)

Part 1

Question 1 (article)
Style: Semi-formal; remember that you are writing for your school magazine.
Content: Use information from your notes and the email. You should include information about:
- your experiences of doing part-time work.
- benefits and drawbacks of doing such work.
- what to be wary of.
- whether you think it's a good thing for the other students to do.

This question is compulsory, so even if you have not done much part-time work yourself, you can still answer the question by using the given information.

Part 2

Question 2 (competition entry)
Style: Semi-formal, but with colourful language to interest the reader and persuade the magazine editor that you should win the competition. Use clear paragraphs, and include a conclusion giving reasons why your entry should win.
Content: You should:
- identify and describe your friend.
- explain what your friend has done.
- explain what you think makes your friend so special.
- give reasons why your friend (and your entry!) should win the award.

Question 3 (information leaflet)
Style: Semi-formal as this is an information sheet for students. You should present facts as clearly as possible. You can either use paragraphs (one for each point) with or without headings, or bullet points. If you use bullet points, remember that you still have to show a range of language, so don't make them too simple and don't use them in every paragraph.
Content: Include information about:
- what 50:50 conversation evenings are.
- the aim of the evenings.
- advantages and benefits to the students.
- the activities planned for the evenings.
- possible future events.

Remember to include details to support your ideas.

Question 4 (essay)
Style: Formal or semi-formal, and objective as you are presenting a point of view, with reasons and/or evidence. Use clear paragraphs, one for each issue, and include an introduction that leads in to the topic and a conclusion that rounds off the argument and states your point of view.
Content: You should consider both the advantages and disadvantages of doing competitive sport in school, and discuss which one outweighs the other. Remember to state your opinion in the conclusion. You can agree or disagree with the statement.

Question 5a) (review)
Style: Semi-formal moving towards informal as this is a review on a website. The purpose of the review is to tell people about the book, and give your opinion of it. You will need the language of description or narration, and evaluation. Use clear paragraphs – introduction, description, evaluation and conclusion with recommendations.
Content: Remember to:
- describe the book or narrate the story.
- give reasons why you did or did not enjoy it.
- explain why you would or would not recommend it to others.

Question 5b) (report)
Style: Formal language as the report is for the school library. Your paragraphs must be very clearly divided. You can use headings, numbering or bullet points, or block text, but remember to use a range of structures.

Content: Include:
- a brief description of the plot.
- a description of a strong female character.
- a recommendation for including the book in the school library with reasons.

Test 4, Paper 3, Use of English (Page 98)

Part 1: Ceramics fair

1 C: The other words do not express the idea.
2 B: Only the right answer successfully refers back to 'famous' in the previous sentence.
3 C: The other linkers do not create meaning in this sentence.
4 D: The other words need a preposition in this context.
5 A: Only the right answer can follow 'as'.
6 B: The other words do not collocate with 'tradition'.
7 D: The other phrasal verbs do not mean 'established'.
8 A: Only the right answer can follow 'at'.
9 B: The other words cannot be followed by the infinitive.
10 C: Only the right answer can be followed by 'on'.
11 B: The other words are not things which could be 'on show'.
12 D: Only the right answer can be followed by 'at'.

Part 2: Cheating at computer games

13 nor (conjunction) complements 'neither' earlier in the sentence
14 fail/cease (verb)
15 out (phrasal verb)
16 few (quantifier)
17 as (adverb)
18 taken (verb indicating a period of time)
19 When(ever)/Once (linker)
20 of (preposition) part of fixed phrase
21 at (preposition) part of fixed phrase
22 which (relative pronoun) introduces a clause
23 Doing (verb) collocation
24 makes (verb)
25 rather (part of linking expression)
26 all (determiner) part of fixed phrase
27 whom (relative pronoun) follows 'of' and refers to people

Part 3: Trolley bags

28 useful (verb to adjective)
29 outward (preposition to adjective)
30 reclaim (verb to part of compound noun)
31 official (noun to adjective)
32 measurements (verb to plural noun)
33 eventual (noun to adjective)
34 restrictions (verb to plural noun)
35 uneven (adjective to negative adjective)
36 counterparts (noun to plural compound noun)
37 inconvenient (adjective to negative adjective)

Part 4

38 found: specific meaning, specific meaning, phrasal verb
39 common: specific meaning, collocation, collocation
40 clear: collocation, collocation, specific meaning
41 hang: phrasal verbs
42 pace: collocations

Part 5

43 matter how fast she runs: fixed phrase + inversion
44 not willing/unwilling to take the blame: lexical change + collocation
45 you do, you must not spend: fixed phrase + modal verb
46 was taken completely by surprise when: modified adjective to modified verb collocation
47 overall responsibility for keeping: adjective to noun phrase
48 by no means uncommon: fixed phrase negative adjective
49 was not alone in feeling: fixed phrase + complement
50 advised Simon against: reported verb + preposition

Test 4, Paper 4, Listening (Page 105)

Part 1

1 B: F: 'It left half-an-hour late.' M: 'Anyway, the pilot obviously made up time. I'd only just turned up and there you were.'
2 B: 'You could have flown into the little airport down the coast even with this airline.'
3 A: 'What they can't manage to do on their own is question it – have a critical view of its accuracy and usefulness. That's where the teacher comes in.'
4 C: 'We had a meeting last week to see how it was going and nobody wanted to change anything!'
5 B: 'What really blew me away was the fact that it's unaffected in a way you'd scarcely think possible.'
6 A: 'What makes them kind of unique is that they don't seem to be trying to sound like anyone but themselves.'

Part 2: The llama

7 face
8 light brown
9 mining
10 curious
11 threatened
12 (gentle) hum
13 grease
14 rugs

Part 3

15 A: 'I made some short films, and on the strength of that, some of the staff suggested I went in that direction.'
16 B: 'The fact that people I was at that school with are now making their way in the film world is also testimony to its value.'
17 A: 'I knew I wasn't. I wasn't prepared to squander time and money doing something I hadn't yet got the experience and expertise to carry off.'
18 D: 'I've always wanted to create characters with a bit more to them than that: people with a depth that might allow an audience to see a different side to their characters.'
19 B: 'There's a lot of things I'd change if I were to make that film again.'
20 C: 'I have mixed feelings about the whole notion of being someone to look up to, of being a role model.'

Part 4

21 C: 'To keep within our tight budget.'
22 F: 'a foot massage. … then dozed off in the chair halfway through'.
23 B: 'We were so desperately tired that we got our heads down right there on deck for some sleep.'
24 D: 'I knew it'd be a long night of dancing … so I thought I'd better take a rest.'
25 G: 'The last bus had already left and we were some distance from the nearest town … we just all fell asleep right there.'
26 F: 'At least it made the night go quickly.'
27 B: 'I woke up with a stiff neck, and the pain lasted several days.'
28 H: 'A huge, smelly vessel moored up beside us.'
29 C: 'They were quite sniffy and a bit embarrassed.'
30 G: 'They told me people living there often did that at weekends, so I felt good.'

Test 5, Paper 1, Reading (Page 111)

Part 1

1 D: It is a word that has 'failed to make the grade' – it has been considered but it does not pass the 'basic tests' for inclusion and is not 'deemed to have entered the language'.
2 B: The writer means that it is impossible to be certain about when the third edition will be published, and one reason for that is that the internet has made it 'far more difficult to keep track of changes in the language'.

3 B: The archaeologists looked at some bones found near where Lucy was found and discovered that the bones had been cut and that marrow had been removed from them.

4 A: The main point is that 'one of our ancestors was using tools much earlier than previously thought'; the evidence in the second paragraph supports this and the archaeologists say that their discovery means that text books will have to be changed because meat eating and tool use 'took place much further back in our history' than was previously commonly believed.

5 B: They were 'noisy', two of them 'barked loudly' and in general there was a 'racket' from them.

6 C: 'in her role as field epidemiologist for the Center for Disease Control, she was able to combine her passion for the outdoors with her love of wildlife.'

Part 2: Is Kieron Britain's most exciting artist?

7 E: link between 'Each one' at the start of E and 'the sketches' that Kieron is doing.

8 G: link between the fact that Kieron correcting the writer about the use of certain terminology is not typical of seven-year-old boys and the fact that Kieron is not an 'average' boy; link between his 'precocious articulacy' (knowledge of and ability with words that would be expected of someone much older) in G and the fact he gives an adult a lesson in terminology (before the gap); link between 'Kieron actually can and does' after the gap and 'my seven-year-old could do better than that' at the end of G.

9 B: link between 'Standard seven-year-old boy stuff there' and Kieron's references to going to school and playing football, which are typical of seven-year-old boys.

10 D: link between the 'melee' (noisy mass of people and activity) in D and the scene described before the gap (a room containing a film crew making a film, family members and pets).

11 F: link between 'This' at the start of F and Kieron creating sketches based on those in the Seago book; link between 'it' in 'takes it back off me' and the 'sketchbook' he hands to the writer before the gap.

12 C: link between 'this' in 'aware of this' and the reaction if Kieron is still 'doing similar work when he's 28'; link between 'having none of it' (not accepting it) and the idea that he may stop doing art and take up other interests.

Part 3: The new management gurus

13 C: When *Smart Swarm*'s author wrote an article on the same subject as his book some years ago, 30 million people read it and the writer predicts that it will 'become the most talked about in management circles'.

14 A: 'Miller believes his book is the first time anyone has laid out (demonstrated) the science behind a management theory.'

15 C: The writer draws a parallel between bees who have to make a decision – 'and fast' – and managers who 'need to be able to make the right decisions under huge amounts of pressure'.

16 C: They need to 'encourage debate' among a group of people and get them to vote on 'which idea is best'; they need to involve a variety of people in their team and get them to take part in the decision-making process.

17 D: Ants do what they think is required in the circumstances, and 'the right number' of ants do each different task. This system works well and it can show managers that their own system of hierarchy and bureaucracy is stopping employees from being as effective as ants are ('is getting in the way of getting the work done').

18 C: they decided to keep their system of 'letting customers choose where they sit' because they discovered from studying ants that 'assigned seating would only be faster by a few minutes'.

19 B: The book is aimed at managers who are 'concerned' (worried) 'about surviving the next business cycle' and who want to make sure that their company can respond to 'challenges that you can't anticipate' (difficult situations in the future that can't be predicted).

Part 4: The unstoppable spirit of inquiry

20 B: 'though it (the World Wide Web) impacts us all, scientists have benefited especially'

21 D: 'Whether it is the work of our Science Policy Centre, our journals, our discussion meetings, our work in education or our public

events, we must be at the heart of helping policy makers and citizens make informed decisions.'

22 C: 'Within a day, 20,000 people had downloaded the work, which was the topic of hastily convened discussions in many centres of mathematical research around the world.'

23 C: 'The latter cries out for' (the blogosphere urgently requires) 'an informal system of quality control.'

24/25 D: 'The way science is applied is a matter not just for scientists. All citizens need to address these questions. Public decisions should be made, after the widest possible discussion.'

F: 'to ensure that wherever science impacts on people's lives, it is openly debated. Citizen scientists, with views spanning the entire political and philosophical spectrum, should engage more willingly with the media and political forums.'

26 A: 'Those who want to celebrate this glorious history' (of scientific research and discovery) 'should visit the Royal Society's archives via our 'Trailblazing' website.'

27 E: 'Scientists often bemoan' (complain about) 'the public's weak grasp of science – without some 'feel' for the issues, public debate can't get beyond sloganising' (lack of understanding of the issues causes public debate on them to be too simple).

28/29 B: 'After 350 years, our horizons have expanded, but the same engagement' (as when the Society was founded) 'is imperative in the 21st century.'

F: 'We should aspire, like our founders, to "see further" into Nature and Nature's laws, but also to emulate their broad engagement with society and public affairs.'

30 A: 'The Society's journals pioneered what is still the accepted procedure whereby scientific ideas are subject to peer review.'

31 E: 'But science isn't dogma. Its assertions are sometimes tentative.'

32 C: 'in the old days, astronomical research was stored on delicate photographic plates; these were not easily accessible.'

33 E: 'there are other issues where public debate is, to an equally disquieting degree, inhibited by ignorance' (the public do not only lack knowledge of science; they lack knowledge of other things too).

34 D: 'we can be sure of one thing: the widening gulf between what science enables us to do and what it's prudent or ethical actually to do.'

Test 5, Paper 2, Writing (Page 120)

Part 1

Question 1 (proposal)
Style: Proposal format, and formal language. Your paragraphs must be clearly divided and you can use headings, numbering or bullet points, but remember to use a range of structures and formal language.
Content: Include the following points from the notes, but don't repeat the actual words from the survey or email as they are too informal for a proposal. You should:
- outline the results of the survey.
- provide some background information about the current facilities.
- discuss the possible options for the future.
- recommend what should happen, with reasons (some can be based on the result of the survey).

Part 2

Question 2 (review)
Style: Semi-formal moving towards informal. In this review you need to narrate, explain and recommend.
Content: You need to include:
- a description of the film.
- an explanation of why it made such a lasting impression on you.
- reasons why it should be included in the series.

Question 3 (report)
Style: Formal or semi-formal as this report is for a magazine. You should present facts clearly. You can either use paragraphs (one for each point) with or without headings, or bullet points. Don't make bullet points too simple and don't use them in every paragraph because you need to show a range of language. As this is for a magazine it needs to be presented in an interesting way.

Content: You should:
- describe the shopping habits of young people in your country.
- evaluate whether shopping habits are changing.
- consider what affects what young people buy.

Question 4 (competition entry)

Style: Semi-formal, but with colourful language to interest the reader and persuade the magazine editor that you should win the competition. Use clear paragraphs, and include a conclusion giving reasons why your entry should win.

Content: You should:
- identify and describe your favourite place to live.
- identify some of the things you can do there.
- explain what makes it such a good place to live.
- justify why it should win the prize.

Question 5a) (report)

Style: Semi-formal to informal as the report is for an in-flight magazine, and it needs to be interesting. Your paragraphs must be clearly divided. You can use headings, numbering or bullet points, but in this context it may be better to use block text. Remember to use a range of structures.

Content: Include:
- a brief description of the plot.
- a description of any absorbing scenes or characters.
- general recommendation for the book.
- an explanation of why it is good for long journeys.

Question 5b) (essay)

Style: Formal or semi-formal, and objective as you are presenting a point of view, with reasons and/or evidence. Use clear paragraphs, one for each character, and include an introduction that leads in to the topic and a conclusion that rounds off the essay, giving your overall point of view about the statement given in the task.

Content: You should:
- identify and briefly outline the book.
- describe one or two funny or colourful characters from the book.
- outline some scenes in which they behave in a funny or colourful way.
- explain why you find them funny or colourful.
- conclude by giving your point of view about whether there are any colourful or funny characters in modern fiction.

Test 5, Paper 3, Use of English (Page 122)

Part 1: Book review – Galapagos

1 D: Only the right answer creates the fixed expression with 'at'.
2 A: The other words are not correct in this context.
3 C: Only the right answer fits grammatically in this sentence.
4 B: The other words don't collocate with 'job'.
5 A: Only the right answer completes the fixed expression.
6 B: The other words don't create the fixed expression in context.
7 B: Only the right answer collocates with 'point'.
8 B: The other words cannot be followed by the preposition 'in'.
9 C: Only the right answer completes the compound noun with 'life'.
10 A: The other words cannot be followed by the preposition 'with'.
11 C: The other words don't express the idea of 'just' in this context.
12 D: Only the right answer collocates with 'inspiration'.

Part 2: A history of table tennis

13 along/together (conjunction) part of 'along with' or 'together with'
14 such (determiner) part of 'such as'
15 which/that (relative pronoun) introduces defining relative clause
16 made (verb) passive form
17 became (verb)
18 being (verb) present participle
19 By (preposition) time marker
20 (al)though (linker) introduces a concessive clause
21 rather (preposition) part of 'rather than'
22 against (preposition) collocates with 'warn'
23 on (preposition) part of phrasal verb
24 into (preposition) follows 'developed'

25 who (relative pronoun) used to indicate people
26 Despite/Whilst (linker) Introduces concessive clause
27 Since (adverb) time marker

Part 3: Dancing is good for you

28 participating (verb to present participle)
29 historians (noun to plural noun)
30 behaviour (verb to noun)
31 significant (verb to adjective)
32 ridiculous (verb to adjective)
33 innumerable/numerous (noun to adjective)
34 effective (noun to adjective)
35 depression (verb to noun)
36 relationships (noun to plural noun)
37 enabling (adjective to verb)

Part 4

38 passage: specific meanings
39 run: collocation, specific meaning, phrasal verb
40 lies: specific meanings
41 safe: specific meanings
42 easily: collocations

Part 5

43 has taken over the management: passive to active + phrasal verb
44 no account must this door ever: negative head inversion
45 on the recommendation of: verb to noun phrase
46 occurred to us that: fixed phrase
47 it made no difference to Kevin: fixed phrase
48 I would/might be able to make: conditional sentence
49 should have been informed of/about: passive form of conditional
50 talked into entering: passive form + phrasal verb

Test 5, Paper 1, Listening (Page 129)

Part 1

1 C: 'I wasn't prepared for something written in the form of two first-person blogs.'
2 B: 'That was really quite a wake-up call for me, because I think I may have been guilty of doing that.'
3 A: 'I'd say the thing that sets it apart is its multi-functionality.'
4 B: 'It'd be a shame if she lost that edge. You know, if the commercial imperative began to dictate the flow of creativity. We've seen that so many times before with designers.'
5 A: 'Perhaps a CEO shouldn't be interfering in that stuff, but this company's my baby, so I guess it's inevitable.'
6 B: 'The real challenge is trusting yourself to pick the moment to go for it.'

Part 2: Ecocamp holiday

7 miserable
8 branches
9 (the) wind
10 privacy
11 (efficient) showers
12 boardwalk
13 medium
14 iceberg

Part 3

15 D: 'I look back and think: "Why wasn't I training? I just played games!" But that's how it was!'
16 A: 'After ice-hockey, I ran cross-country with moderate success, and guys I met there put me onto rowing.'
17 B: 'It was just bad luck really; so near and yet so far.'
18 C: 'after about six months of arm-twisting, decided to make the leap.'
19 B: 'to put up with what I call the "full-on suffer".'
20 C: 'You don't have a lot of protection if you come off and hit the ground. So I run and row as cross-training as much as I can.'

Part 4

21 C: 'looking at two drawings that were given to me as gifts.'
22 D: 'I can warm up with them, and they've taught me loads of stretches and things … really makes you more supple and able to cope.'
23 F: 'I'll usually pop into dressing rooms putting little notes or candy on people's tables.'
24 H: 'I still find myself walking up to have a look (at the props) prior to curtain going up.'
25 A: 'I go in the courtyard where I can just catch the breeze.'
26 A: 'On my last one, I came down with a sore throat.'
27 H: 'so I came out with a line I was supposed to say later.'
28 C: 'the press … what they wrote initially wasn't that complimentary.'
29 E: 'I missed a step and stumbled on the way down.'
30 F: 'The actor looked around and saw a pigeon standing right behind him.'

Test 6, Paper 1, Reading (Page 135)

Part 1

1 C: The writer contrasts people who are frightened by UFOs (they feel 'creeping unease', think UFOs are 'sinister' and feel 'fear' of them, all in the first paragraph) with Ufologists, who are enthusiasts and 'true believers' and who feel great excitement about UFOs (second paragraph).
2 D: 'for many years, UFOs were a much bigger deal than we suspected'; 'RAF jets were scrambled to investigate UFO reports no fewer than 200 times a year' ('no fewer than' = a surprisingly high number of).
3 C: The plane 'jogs on the spot' (bounces up and down without moving forwards) first of all before it starts to move across the bay.
4 A: It no longer delivers mail, another company has the contract to do that; it delivers 'people instead of parcels' – it takes passengers, not mail.
5 A: She is 'having another go'; she is doing 'precisely the same challenge' that she did once before; she is 'revisiting an attempt that almost killed her last time'; she is 'about to try to finish the job' that she did not finish the first time.
6 B: 'In some ways you could say it's insecurity. I have always wanted to excel at something.' (A possible reason for doing it is that she has feelings of insecurity and wants to achieve something big so that she won't continue to lack confidence in herself.)

Part 2: The birth of *Coronation Street*

7 F: link between 'At that stage' at the beginning of F and when the writer was 21, mentioned at the beginning of the article; link between the work described in F and the work described before the gap.
8 D: link between 'the genius who created the show' before the gap and 'that person' in D.
9 A: link between 'this' at the beginning of A and the idea that the creation of the programme would be a good subject for a television drama, mentioned before the gap – the writer wasn't the only person who thought this was a good idea because someone commissioned him to write the drama.
10 G: link between the fact that there had never been a show about ordinary people and their lives and the fact that there had also never been an original show featuring regional actors – link between two things that had not happened before but which were both true of *Coronation Street*; link between the question 'so what was the point?' in G and 'It was that …' after the gap.
11 E: link between the statement that 'It' (the idea of *Coronation Street*) should have ended there after the gap and the fact that the idea was rejected, as described in E; link between 'written and discarded' after the gap and the events described in E – Warren writing the script and the TV management rejecting it firmly ('in no uncertain terms').
12 C: link between 'that inauspicious beginning' in C and the problems just before the first episode was broadcast, described before the gap; 'inauspicious' = suggesting that something will go badly and not be successful; link between 'that event' in C and the broadcasting of the first episode, described before the gap.

Part 3: Cooking shouldn't be child's play

13 C: The writer says that if you 'take the fun out of cooking', your child might become 'a chef with a great future' – if cooking isn't simply fun for children when they are learning it, it's possible that they might develop into successful chefs.
14 B: Her mother noticed that she was very interested in cooking and gave her 'challenging tasks' to do; she gives an example of advice her mother gave her while she was doing a task to help her do it better.
15 A: The writer says that there is a belief that parents should praise their children all the time, telling them 'how clever and talented' they are, but there is evidence that this approach 'demotivates children' – it has the opposite effect from the one intended.
16 D: There are adult men who think that a piece of fish should be in the shape of a creature, in the same way that the food they ate when they were children was put into the shapes of certain things to amuse them. This is an example of the idea that all food is 'nothing but fun, fun and more fun'.
17 C: A 'chore' is a task that requires effort and is not fun; the writer says that because her mother made cooking a chore for her, she has eaten a lot less convenience food than she would have eaten if her mother had made cooking fun. Her point is that taking cooking seriously has an influence on the kind of food you eat.
18 B: Nigella thinks the way she was taught to cook in her family as a child was 'normal' but the writer thinks the 'culinary regime' (the cooking system) in her family was not 'ordinary' – it wasn't typical of most families. Nigella thinks it was fine but the writer thinks it should have involved more fun.
19 B: The writer concludes that learning to cook for children should be both serious and fun, but more serious than fun. Having talked about her and Nigella learning to cook as children and discussed the idea of food being fun, she talks about a book that she believes has the right combination of seriousness and fun.

Part 4: Activities for visitors to Norway

20 A: All riders are 'given a comprehensive safety briefing' (a talk about safety).
21 D: It 'is suitable for novices, though you should be reasonably fit' (it's appropriate for beginners but only appropriate for people who are reasonably fit).
22 E: 'it might be imagined that bathing in the frigid waters would be at best masochistic and at worst suicidal'.
23 E: 'the North Atlantic Drift keeps it ice-free through the year' – because of the North Atlantic Drift, the Barents Sea is not covered with ice at any time of the year, making swimming in it possible.
24 A: The snowmobile is 'nothing less than a lifeline for those in more remote areas' – it is the everyday means of transport for people living in those areas and they depend on it. This is said to be true in the present (dog sledding was 'vital' in the past).
25 D: 'When the signal is given to depart, you may well be surprised at the speed that they can reach.'
26 B: Some people from warmer countries 'think it is something that exists only in old footage' (film) 'of Eskimo living, but this isn't the case at all'.
27 D: 'whenever they realise an outing is imminent, they become as keyed up as domestic pets about to be taken for walkies – howling, leaping in the air and straining at their leashes' – this is how the dogs behave just before 'the signal to depart' and the activity begins.
28 D: 'Half- or full-day sled safaris are most popular, although overnight and longer tours are also available.'
29 C: 'Snowmobiling has high-octane attractions, but to appreciate fully the stillness and peace of the mountains, it's best to use your own feet to get around' – the contrast is between the energy and excitement of snowmobiling and the quiet and relaxation of skiing or snowshoeing.
30 B: 'you'll find out how the experts use the auger to drill through the ice, a skimming loop to keep the water from freezing over again and a familiar rod to catch the fish'.
31 C: 'gliding around the snowy terrain is not just a great way of getting close to nature, but also fantastic aerobic exercise'.
32 A: 'The only controls to worry about are a thumb-operated throttle and motorcycle-style brakes.'
33 A: 'It's a thrill indeed to roar in convoy' (in a group together) 'through a landscape of wooded trails'.

34 E: 'You'll first need to be sealed into a bright orange survival suit, which leaves only the face exposed and lends bathers a rather peculiar appearance.'

Test 6, Paper 2, Writing (Page 144)

Part 1

Question 1 (report)
Style: Report format and formal language. Paragraphs must be clearly divided; you can use headings, numbering or bullet points, but remember to use a range of structures and language.
Content: Include the following points from the given information and your notes, but don't 'lift' the actual words and add details of your own:
- what you did during your work experience.
- how you felt about it.
- how useful it was for making decisions about your future.
- whether you recommend it to other students.

Even if you have not done work experience yourself you can use the information given to write the report, and can add other details that you think might be relevant.

Part 2

Question 2 (essay)
Style: Formal or semi-formal, and objective as you are presenting a point of view, with reasons and/or evidence. Use clear paragraphs, and include an introduction that leads in to the topic and a conclusion that rounds off the argument and states your point of view.
Content: You should:
- consider the benefits and advantages of foreign travel, with detail to support your ideas.
- compare actual travelling with watching travel programmes on television.
- evaluate whether the statement is true or not.

Remember to state your opinion in the conclusion. You can agree or disagree with the statement.

Question 3 (article)
Style: Semi-formal as you are trying to interest and inform the magazine readers. Use persuasive language and features such as rhetorical questions to engage the readers and persuade them of your opinion. Use paragraphs, and give your article a title.
Content: You should:
- consider the kind of people who make the best role-models.
- evaluate any responsibilities celebrities have in their lifestyle and behaviour.
- discuss the place of role-models in general in today's society.

Question 4 (proposal)
Style: Formal or semi-formal as this is for the organisers of a music festival. You should present facts clearly. You can either use paragraphs (one for each point) with or without headings, or bullet points. Don't make bullet points too simple and don't use them in every paragraph because you need to show a range of language.
Content: You should:
- suggest what might make the festival a success.
- outline ways of staging the event.
- recommend any extra facilities the town might need to provide, including transport and accommodation.

Question 5a) (article)
Style: Either semi-formal or informal, but as you are trying to interest and entertain the magazine readers you should use colourful language and features such as rhetorical questions to capture the reader's interest. Use paragraphs, and give your article a title.
Content: You should:
- give brief details about the book and the film.
- explain how the book is different from the film.
- explain what was good about either the book or the film and which one you preferred.
- recommend which people should do first – read the book or see the film, with reasons.

Question 5b) (review)
Style: Semi-formal moving towards informal as this is a review for a book club. The purpose of the review is to tell people about the book, explain why you think the ending of the book was dramatic or surprising and whether you would recommend the book to members of the club or not. You will need to use the language of description or narration, and evaluation. Use clear paragraphs – introduction, description, evaluation and conclusion with recommendations.
Content: Remember to:
- briefly narrate the story.
- describe the main characters.
- explain why the ending was surprising or dramatic.
- explain whether you recommend the book or not (you don't have to recommend it – you may not have enjoyed it!).

Test 6, Paper 3, Use of English (Page 146)

Part 1: Mr Espresso

1 C: Only the right answer collocates with 'universally'.
2 A: The other linking words do not create meaning in this context.
3 B: Only the right answer collocates with 'credit'.
4 D: The other words do not mean 'in other places'.
5 A: Only the right answer collocates with 'leading'.
6 B: The other words all need a preposition.
7 D: Only the right answer can be used for a country.
8 B: The other words do not collocate with 'seeds'.
9 B: Only the right answer can be followed by 'as'.
10 A: The other words do not collocate with 'sector'.
11 D: The other words do not indicate two things joined together.
12 B: Only the right answer collocates with 'sure'.

Part 2: Drift Diving

13 who/that (relative pronoun) used for people
14 from (preposition) follows 'a change'
15 so (pronoun) refers back to the content of the previous sentence
16 makes (verb) collocates with 'use'
17 on (preposition) follows 'depend'
18 which/that (relative pronoun) introduces non-defining relative clause
19 or (conjunction) combines with 'either' to make a contrast
20 to (preposition) follows 'equivalent'
21 (al)though/but (linker) introduces concessive clause
22 no/little (determiner) to indicate absence in 'no need'
23 as (conjunction) part of 'as if'
24 more (adverb) part of the linking phrase 'what's more'
25 a (article)
26 gets (verb) part of fixed expression
27 up (preposition) phrasal verb

Part 3: The Limits of Technology

28 impression (verb to noun)
29 awesome (noun to adjective)
30 settlement (verb to noun)
31 breakthroughs (verb to plural compound noun)
32 isolation (verb to noun)
33 unexpected (verb to negative adjective)
34 disapproval (noun to negative noun)
35 annoying (verb to adjective)
36 regardless (noun to preposition)
37 unwelcome (adjective to negative adjective)

Part 4

38 missed: phrasal verb, collocation, specific meaning
39 cool: collocation, collocation, specific meaning
40 lift: collocation, collocation, phrasal verb
41 sharp: collocation, collocation, collocation
42 broke: collocation, phrasal verb, collocation

Part 5

43 remains to be seen (fixed phrase)
44 Patrick if he could borrow his (reported speech and verb change)
45 has every intention of writing (verb to noun + gerund)
46 unless there are/anyone has any (negative linker + verb + noun)
47 met with the disapproval (verb + noun)
48 to his/Philip's surprise he got (inversion)
49 to be thought of as (passive form)
50 took it for granted (fixed phrase)

Test 6, Paper 4, Listening (Page 153)

Part 1

1 A: 'I went with high hopes of seeing something really spectacular from the headline band, and it just didn't happen.'
2 A: 'I think they should've been presenting us with something a bit more exciting.'
3 B: 'I sense that there may actually be little substance to stories that his job's on the line.'
4 C: 'If a top flight football team isn't getting points, then something's got to change and that comes back to the manager because that's his responsibility – getting the results.'
5 C: 'But it really makes you think, you know, about more than just the art – about aspects of life itself.'
6 A: F: 'I'd have been happy to have seen some of his other stuff actually.' M: 'Yeah, more of a range.'

Part 2: Learning the sport of surfing

7   national park
8   (the/a) period
9   tight
10 arm(s)
11 gloves
12 plastic
13 (their/the) knees
14 hair(-)dryer

Part 3

15 B: 'The upside was that I'd established that I was able to write.'
16 C: 'I wrote it as a kind of one-off book,'
17 A: 'It was a chancy thing to do.'
18 B: 'I've had some hairy experiences.'
19 B: 'The sense of place in a crime novel is as crucial as the characters themselves.'
20 D: 'Whereas at the time I never even considered the police, I'd have more of an open mind now.'

Part 4

21 D: 'The thing I'd really recommend, is trying all the stuff that's grown in the region.'
22 F: 'Rolling up your clothes to put in your bag can be your saving grace.'
23 B: 'You can often actually get much better deals elsewhere.'
24 H: 'My general rule is to take half the stuff I think I'll need, and twice the money.'
25 C: 'We got really into the local music … I'd recommend doing something like that.'
26 F: 'On the coach to the airport still trying to fit various clothes and papers into my luggage.'
27 E: 'I saw this locally-made rug I just knew would look fabulous at home. Sadly, no one pointed out that it wouldn't be easily transportable.'
28 G: 'I remember not joining a two-day trek with friends in South America for that reason.'
29 A: 'When I finally bothered to look, I found my ticket was actually for the previous day.'
30 C: 'I hadn't bothered researching the lie of the land.'

Test 7, Paper 1, Reading (Page 159)

Part 1

1   B: The writer says it is 'an invaluable tool', that it contains 'all the wonderful and clever, and ugly aspects of being human' and describes 'everything we can see or sense around us'. We 'eat and breathe' it – it is extremely important to us, it affects everyone's lives.
2   C: People wondered whether elements were 'inherently chaotic' (by nature not in any order, not capable of being organised), 'a jumble of substances that could be arranged equally well by any old trait' (a disorganised mixture that could be arranged according to any characteristic chosen because there was no obvious way of organising them).
3   A: By 'low-hanging fruit' the writer means, in this context, knowledge that can be reached, knowledge that people can get easily. He compares this with knowledge that humans are not able to get through science and therefore knowledge that humans don't have. People can't get knowledge of these 'uncharted areas of science' because they are 'so complex'.
4   C: He thinks that scientists will apply existing knowledge in new ways and therefore make new breakthroughs but that soon they will have got all the knowledge they can get about 'fundamental laws of nature and the constituents of the world'. Scientists will soon reach their limit – they will have found out 'everything that's open to understand' but not 'everything about the world'.
5   D: They are given for research that people consider ridiculous but these things must also 'then make them think' – the results of the research are worth thinking about, they are interesting and not just silly.
6   B: The Italian research suggested that companies should not have a hierarchical system in which people climbed up the hierarchy in a fixed and organised way. They should abandon this system and instead promote people up the hierarchy 'randomly' – by chance, with no system for choosing.

Part 2: The sky's the limit for cloudwatchers

7   E: link between 'here' at the beginning of E and the Cloud Bar, where the writer is before the gap; link between 'this place' after the gap and 'here' in E.
8   G: link between 'Other beachgoers aren't as convinced' and the comments made by the person before the gap – other people don't think the place is 'fantastic' and 'inspiring' and don't think Britain has been 'crying out for' (really wanting) a place like this to be created; ('the society' mentioned in B has not been previously mentioned in the text at this point; B does not fit here because we would not know which society is being referred to).
9   B: link between 'Absolutely' at the start of B and the opinions expressed in the sentence before the gap; link between Ian Loxley's travels, the fact that his favourite place is local in B, and his view that 'you don't really need to travel at all to see interesting clouds' after the gap.
10 A: link between 'why this is' and the statement before the gap that for cloudwatchers, the most important factor is 'your philosophical disposition'; the way that clouds move and develop, mentioned in A, are the reasons why someone's philosophical disposition is the most important factor in watching clouds (their slowness suits people who want to think philosophically); link between 'That said' after the gap and what he says in A, to introduce a contrast between the two views of cloud watching (slow and exciting).
11 F: link between 'all such places' at the start of F and 'wilderness' just before the gap; the writer's point is that humans want to explore all wildernesses – 'them' in the first sentence of A = 'clouds' before the gap; link between 'similar experiences' after the gap and the experience described by the pilot in F.
12 C: link between 'such encounters' in C and the encounters with clouds described by Gavin Pretor-Pinney before the gap.

Part 3

13 C: She had 'stacks of cassette recordings of herself reading the news in a cool, assured voice' and later she became a presenter on CNN television, so at this time she was practising for the career that she later had.

14 D: Lomba didn't know the answer and she gave him not only the answer but also 'a lecture' about the capital of Iceland (more information he didn't know).

15 A: He replied 'in the negative' (that he didn't know the answer) and her response to this was to jump up 'gleefully' (in a very happy way) and get her sketchbook – she was glad that he didn't know the answer because she wanted to show him what the jacket looked like.

16 D: At first he thought that the father's 'taciturnity' (he was quiet, he didn't speak much) was because of 'moodiness' (that he was often in a bad mood, often feeling angry) but then he realised that he had 'laughter kinks behind the eyes' (his eyes showed that he was amused), and that his lips were often moving, ready to open because he wanted to smile or laugh.

17 B: When she called him 'dear' and 'honey', he thought she was talking to someone else, one of her children, not to him, because he wasn't used to someone using those words for him.

18 A: She told Lomba that she wanted him to take care of Bola, because Bola was 'impulsive' and 'headstrong' (he acted without thinking, he did unwise things without considering the consequences) and Lomba was 'quiet' and 'level-headed' (sensible). In this way she wanted to follow the tradition of finding a friend of 'opposite temperament' for her child because that friend would be a good influence on the child.

19 C: The whole extract is about what Lomba thought of each family member and the powerful impressions each member made on him; each person is described in turn and the effect each one had on him is described. They are not compared, he doesn't say he developed close relationships with each one quickly and the extract is mainly about Lomba interacting with each family member, not about how they interacted with each other.

Part 4: What lies beneath

20 C: 'It is easy to be captivated by intelligent, seemingly friendly sea creatures such as dolphins, or even by the hunting prowess of the more sinister sharks.'

21 D: 'The Mediterranean has the largest number of invasive species – most of them having migrated through the Suez Canal from the Red Sea.'

22 B: 'a myriad range of creatures that could have slithered out of the pages of science fiction'.

23 D: 'As Mediterranean turtles lose their nesting sites to beach developments, or die in fishing nets, and the vanishing population of other large predators such as bluefish tuna are fished out, their prey is doing what nature does best; filling a void. Smaller, more numerous species like jellyfish are flourishing and plugging the gap left by animals higher up the food chain.' Predators are disappearing and being replaced by creatures they used to eat.

24 A: 'In total, the Census now estimates that there are more than 230,000 known marine species, but that this is probably less than a quarter of what lives in the sea.'

25 D: 'Hidden within the Marine Census results is a dark message. Maps showing the density of large fish populations in tropical waters reveal that numbers of many of the biggest open ocean species have declined.'

26 C: algae that look like 'a pair of pink stockings' and octopuses that look like 'ornaments' of a certain kind.

27 D: 'it is unwise to talk as if the jellyfish have some kind of plan'.

28 A: 'The truth is that at present much of what passes for scientific 'facts' about the sea and what lives in it are still based on guesswork.'

29 A: The Census contains the numbers of 'individual forms of life that can be scientifically classified as species'.

30 B: It is the creepy-crawlies that are out there in really big numbers. Almost 40 percent of identified marine species are crustaceans and molluscs' – 'creepy-crawlies' is used as an informal term for crustaceans and molluscs.

31 C: 'how would we begin to start naming the 20,000 types of bacteria found in just one litre of seawater trawled from around a Pacific seamount?'

32 A: The scientists involved in the Census 'hope that by creating the first catalogue of the world's oceans, we can begin to understand the great ecological questions about habitat loss, pollution, over fishing and all the other man-made plagues that are being visited upon the sea.'

33 D: 'we need to start loving jellyfish, because in the not too distant future, they may be the most plentiful marine species around'.

34 B: 'Chiasmodon niger – 'The Great Swallower' – with its cadaverous skull, metallic pink flesh and needlelike teeth, accompanied by an enormous ballooning stomach that allows it to swallow animals bigger than itself' – its stomach gets bigger so that it can eat an animal bigger than itself.

Test 7, Paper 2, Writing (Page 168)

Part 1

Question 1 (article)
Style: Semi-formal; remember that you are writing for your school magazine, so try to make it interesting and include interesting details and examples.
Content: Use information from your notes and the programme for the school visit. You should include information about:
- your experiences with the host family.
- attending school.
- evening activities.
- excursions.
- your overall reaction to the trip as a whole.

This question is compulsory, so even if you have not done an exchange visit yourself you can still answer the question by using the given information.

Part 2

Question 2 (letter)
Style: Informal, but not too colloquial. Use letter layout with clear paragraphs.
Content: You should:
- identify the advantages and disadvantages of going to university compared to work, with reasons and examples.
- advise your friend on what they should do.

This information should be the main part of the letter but don't forget to include a friendly beginning and ending following the usual conventions of informal letters. 'Dear … All the best / Best wishes …'

Question 3 (contribution to a longer piece)
Style: Semi-formal, as this is a contribution to a book. Use clear paragraphs, and present your points clearly.
Content: You must:
- describe any problems your town has with pollution.
- outline any initiatives your town has implemented, and evaluate their success.
- recommend what people should do as individuals to help with the problems associated with pollution.

You should include a conclusion rounding off your contribution.

Question 4 (report)
Style: Formal or semi-formal as this is for an international travel magazine. You should present facts clearly. You can either use paragraphs (one for each point) with or without headings, or bullet points. Don't make the language you use with bullet points too simple because you need to show a range of language. As this is for a magazine it needs to be presented in an interesting way.
Content: You should:
- describe facilities at a bus or train station you know.
- evaluate what is good or bad about these facilities.
- outline any problems you have experienced using the facilities.
- suggest ways in which the bus or train station could be improved.

Question 5a) (review)
Style: Semi-formal moving towards informal as this is a review in a college magazine. The purpose of the review is to tell people about the book, explain why it is your favourite and why you read it many times. You will need to use the language of description or narration, and evaluation. Use clear paragraphs – introduction, description, evaluation and conclusion with recommendations.

Content: Remember to:
- identify the book and briefly narrate the story.
- describe some of the main characters.
- explain why you like to read it many times.

Conclude by giving reasons why you would recommend it to others.

Question 5b) (essay)

Style: Formal or semi-formal, and objective as you are presenting a point of view, with reasons and/or evidence. Use clear paragraphs, one for each part of the task, and include an introduction that leads in to the topic and a conclusion that rounds off the essay, giving your overall point of view.

Content: You should:
- identify and briefly outline the book, explaining why you chose it.
- explain what its theme is and why it is relevant to society today.
- suggest what we can learn from the book.
- conclude by giving your point of view about the overall value of reading this particular book.

Test 7, Paper 3, Use of English (Page 170)

Part 1: Renewable energy comes of age

1   C: Only the right answer is 'used to describe' something
2   B: The other words cannot be followed by the infinitive + 'as'
3   D: Only the correct word creates the idea of 'mirrors'
4   A: Only the correct answer completes the set phrase 'far from being'
5   A: Only the correct answer creates a phrasal verb that has meaning in context
6   C: The other words do not collocate with 'behind'
7   B: Only the correct word refers back successfully to the change mentioned in the previous paragraph
8   D: The other words do not collocate with 'rise'
9   A: The correct answer is the correct term in this context
10 A: Only the correct answer can be followed by 'as' in this sentence
11 D: The correct answer collocates with 'public'
12 C: The other words would need a preposition

Part 2: The demise of the motor car

13 so (quantifier) part of 'so much that'
14 other (preposition) part of 'anything other than'
15 came (verb) part of 'along came'
16 in (preposition) follows 'low'
17 one (pronoun) refers to 'car' earlier in the sentence
18 by (preposition) indicates the agent
19 gave (verb) part of phrasal verb
20 up (preposition) part of phrasal verb
21 more (determiner) part of 'what's more'
22 For (preposition) part of set phrase
23 do (pronoun) refers to previous verb
24 others (pronoun) refers to people
25 would/might (modal verb)
26 such (intensifier) intensifies the adjective
27 what (determiner)

Part 3: Do green products make us better people?

28 according (noun to preposition)
29 definitely (adjective to adverb)
30 supposedly (verb to adjective)
31 criminals (noun to plural noun)
32 behaviour (verb to noun)
33 satisfaction (verb to noun)
34 charming (adjective to noun)
35 complexity (adjective to noun)
36 undoubtedly / doubtlessly (noun to negative adjective)
37 invariably (adjective to adverb)

Part 4

38 fallen: phrasal verb, collocation, collocation
39 due: specific meanings
40 strong: collocation, collocation, specific meaning

41 favour: specific meaning, collocation, set phrase
42 mind: specific meaning, phrasal verb, specific meaning

Part 5

43 completely lived up to Caroline's (intensifier + collocation)
44 in case it broke down/should break down ('in case' + past verb)
45 (should) happen to bump (set phrase + phrasal verb)
46 despite / in spite of her refusal (linker + noun phrase)
47 having had an argument (regret + '-ing' + noun)
48 has been a sharp increase in (collocation + preposition)
49 is due to be launched ('due to' + passive)
50 is no saying whether (or not) (fixed phrase + 'whether')

Test 7, Paper 4, Listening (Page 177)

Part 1

1   A: M: 'But actually I've come round to thinking it's the real strength of the course, don't you agree?' F: 'Undoubtedly. I mean, that's why I went for it in the first place.'
2   B: 'sophisticated software … I still think it's a shame we can't come in and use it out of class time.'
3   A: 'I'm still looking for the ideal rucksack or carry-on actually.'
4   B: 'I mean, without that – and a lot of people you meet don't have that – would I ever have had the courage to do half the things I've done?'
5   A: 'We got all these irate bloggers going overboard.'
6   C: 'We were misquoted in the first piece written about it. It said that I wanted to kill album artwork, which is just so far off the mark.'

Part 2: The swift

7   without feet
8   scream
9   new moon
10 (a) cliff/cliffs
11 paper
12 (a) thunderstorm/thunderstorms
13 silent
14 youngest/younger sons

Part 3

15 A: 'But what really appeals to me about kayaking is that it calls for several different skills to be used simultaneously.'
16 C: 'But most importantly, when you first start kayaking, just have fun.'
17 D: 'there aren't many competitions coming up, but (all the training's) worth it in the summer when the big ones come around.'
18 C: 'I'd weigh up the risks and only have a go once I felt up to the challenge.'
19 B: 'but it's tough doing the research yourself. As a beginner, I'd say get some insider tips from someone in the know.'
20 A: 'My most valued are those where I'm on a great trip, getting to know new rivers and their surroundings with people I know and like.'

Part 4

21 F: 'But what made it perfect was all the ancient ruins in the area.'
22 A: 'I was about to take it up professionally but then injured my leg quite badly and had to drop the idea.'
23 D: 'It was my big chance as it would get me exactly where I'd always wanted to go.'
24 H: 'I'd lived in the city all my life and had plenty of friends there but we were all rushing around frantically as city-dwellers do.'
25 B: 'if I wanted to top up my qualifications, meant going abroad.'
26 F: 'Once there, I felt really driven to do well – there was just this new sense of optimism.'
27 D: 'Their recommendations opened a number of doors for me once my studies had finished.'
28 C: 'I'd never really seen myself as a movie buff before.'
29 H: 'We could go anywhere where I could set up by myself. It was exactly what we all needed.'
30 A: 'made me feel I really belonged in the place.'